Facts and Fallacies (1988) Reader's Digest:

"In a series of books published between 1946 and 1949, British journalist William Comyns Beaumont astonished the world with the following extraordinary revelations: Jesus of Nazareth had been crucified just outside Edinburgh, Scotland - the site of the ancient city of Jerusalem. Satan was a comet that collided with the earth and caused Noah's Flood. The ancient Egyptians were in fact Irishmen. Hell is to be found in western Scotland. The Greek hero Achilles spent his childhood on the Isle of Skye. Galilee, birthplace of Jesus, was Wales. Ancient Athens was in reality Bath, England... Comyns Beaumont started his radical revision of history with the belief, innocuous enough, that the lost island of Atlantis might be Britain."

INTRODUCTION

Most who have looked into catastrophism are now familiar with Comyns Beaumont's pioneering research and startling conclusions. Not so many are familiar with the actual man and his life. Here then is his own life story, told in his own words, formed into his own, famously often paragraph-long, sentences.

We discover how he was at the centre of things in diplomatic and press circles for most of his life, which gave him the insight into the machinations of powerful institutions that inspired his later works. He was a rebel before he got anywhere near Fleet Street, and did not mellow with age.

Only now are his ideas becoming acceptable, though still not accepted, in mainstream thought. Dr Benny Peiser, currently heading the Global Warming Policy Foundation, has long been an advocate of Comyns Beaumont's ideas on the influence of NEO's on the weather, albeit he is sceptical, to say the least, about Comyns Beaumont's more radical ideas on revised history and geography! Benny's work was the inspiration for bringing these titles back into print.

Dr. Peiser:

WILLIAM COMYNS BEAUMONT (1873 - 1956)
BRITAIN'S MOST ECCENTRIC AND LEAST KNOWN
COSMIC HERETIC

It is generally believed that the American scholar and founding father of meteoritic studies, H.H. Ninninger, was the first 20th century scientist to have associated mass extinctions with cosmic impact catastrophes. In his paper "**Cataclysm and Evolution**" (*Popular Astronomy 50/1942, pp. 270-272*), Ninninger reviewed the new research on Apollo asteroids and the handful of the known (and relatively small) meteorite craters. He added one and one together and hypothesises that:

"Violent climatic changes would have resulted, locally at least, from the heat of the impacts and from changes in the content of the atmosphere. Many general changes might have resulted from a possible shifting of the poles, in the cases of the largest impacts. These changes would have necessitated faunal and floral readjustments. Species would have disappeared and new ones would have developed to take their places. Changes in geographical range would have brought about new adaptations, and we should expect, in general, just those breaks in the series that are actually found in the rocks."

That was back in 1942. It took almost 40 years, when, in 1980, Luis Alvarez and his colleagues arrived on the stage of mankind's global debating club, before the scientific community was ready to engage in a general discussion about Ninninger's original suggestion. Harvey Ninninger, however, was not the first 20th century catastrophist to speculate about impact triggered mass extinctions. As early as 1925, one of Britain's leading scientific publishing houses (*Chapman & Hall*) released a rather inconspicuous book (**The Riddle of the Earth**) by William Comyns Beaumont, an English super-eccentric, in which he anticipated most of the current neo-catastrophist paradigm.

John Michell describes Comyns Beaumont's move to Newcastle upon Tyne in the 1900's:

"There he met the daughter of an old Catholic family from nearby County Durham, and proposed marriage. Her family objected, not because of religion - Beaumont had earlier converted to Catholicism - but on account of his poverty. So the couple married in secret, and immediately parted, the bridegroom going off on a mission abroad while the bride returned innocently to her family. It was three years before they met again, by which time Beaumont had obtained a good position in London, on the **Daily Mail**. The marriage was successful, and so was his career.

Ida Beaumont's family was in fact from Northumberland, and for a short while the couple lived near Hexham where the family Law firm, Gibson & Co., still operates today.

The Gibsons were an influential Catholic family, their ancestors having established Ushaw College, a magnificent recently restored building - formerly a priests' training establishment close to the editor's home - and Comyns Beaumont reportedly adopted Catholicism when he met Ida, somewhat surprisingly in light of the subject of his researches.

Michell continues:

"To the public eye Comyns Beaumont was handsome, talented, worldly, well-connected and the last sort of person one would normally suspect of heresy. Yet in his mind strange ideas were brewing. Some are hinted at in his autobiography, **A Rebel in Fleet Street**, which is mostly an account of his professional career, but also includes warnings about a Zionist plot to subvert the British Empire and a brief outline of his unusual opinions on earthquakes and volcanoes.

The **London Daily News** (13 November 1950) published Beaumont's offer to conduct any qualified archaeologist round Britain and prove to him 'that this island and not Palestine is the Holy Land of the Bible'."

Michell, J, Eccentric Lives and Peculiar Notions, London, 1984

I was unable to locate any such article in archives of the **London Daily News**, but I did find the following piece in The **Courier-Journal** (Louisville, Kentucky, Nov 13, 1950):

Writer Says British Isle Is 'Holy Land'

London, Nov. 12 (U.R)

Comyns Beaumont offered today to take any qualified archaeologist around Britain and prove on the spot that this island and not Palestine is the Holy Land of the Bible. Beaumont, a sprightly 71 with a long career in writing and publishing, has spent 40 years developing the theory that the Garden of Eden actually was in Somerset County and that civilization sprang into being in what are now the desolate areas of northernmost Scotland. Now he has assembled what he regards as final proof, and is completing the manuscript of a book, complete with maps, in which the familiar sites of Palestine are superimposed on Britain. "It's a tremendous theme," he exulted in his country home. "I believe there's no question about my facts. I've been an editor and writer too long to be misled, and I am convinced I can prove that Edinburgh was the original Jerusalem and, for example, that York was the original Babylon."

Heartfelt thanks, then, to Dr Benny Peiser of GWPF; to Prof. Mike Baillie of QUB; to Hexham historian Yvonne Purdy and Newcastle journalist Tony Henderson for local knowledge; to Edinburgh researcher Andrew Hennessey; to John Michell; to Jim Naples for proof-reading, and especially to Du Maurier expert Collin Langley, for his invaluable textual contribution without which this book would not have reappeared. But of course my deepest gratitude goes to CB's wonderful grandson, without whom none of this would have been possible.

Happy Birthday, Christopher Toyne.

Jan Mendez (Ed.), October 24th., 2016

The Author

A Rebel in Fleet Street

COMYNS BEAUMONT

THE COMYNS BEAUMONT ARCHIVE
RESONANCE BookWorks
www.resonancebookworks.com

First published 1944 by Hutchinson, London.
This edition published by RESONANCE BookWorks 2016

ISBN 978-1-326-79282-4

CONTENTS

CHAPTER I

START OF THE LOCUST YEARS

"The history of a people, like the history of Macbeth or Hamlet, is simply the unrolling under the pressure of times and circumstances of their hidden qualities. A vigorous and capable stock turns situations to its purposes and necessity to its profit."

W. MACNEILE DIXON, in *The Englishman*.

FOR OVER FORTY YEARS I have watched passing events from the viewpoint of a journalist mainly in the vicinity of Fleet Street and its purlieus. In the course of my life I have met a good many men and women, some of great fame and other lesser lights in what Philip Gibbs terms the *Street of adventure*. I have been on the staff of "Dailies", edited several "Weeklies" and created a few, reconstructed others, indulged in propaganda and publicity work, mostly of a political nature, and have in fact led a busy and active life. I do so at this minute and hope to continue for many more years in the land of live activity; as a journalist one does at least live.

The years embrace the two most momentous, terrible and expensive wars, have entailed prodigious sacrifices and ghastly losses heroically borne, and prove, if proof were needed in view of Britain's illustrious history, that while our nation is usually unready for war, it stands indomitable and undefeatable in the end - a fact which those arch-gangsters Hitler and Tojo by this time more than dimly comprehend. Mussolini, as I pen this, has already bitten the dust.

The forty-odd years of the present century have witnessed many and great changes in the world but whether they have all been conducive to greater human happiness is possibly disputable. Life at the beginning of the century was certainly less disturbed, more leisurely, and in a sense more spacious than to-day, where there is scarce a square mile of territory over the habitable globe that can be said to exist without someone coveting or exploiting it in the name of

Progress. The romantic Pacific isles of our youth, for instance, are today scenes of slaughter and destruction. Perhaps only the upper reaches of the Amazon can yet boast of a pristine Utopia, but probably they have sophisticated vices of their own special type.

In a word, what with two great world wars, inspired by a restless, arrogant, ambitious, and prehistorically-minded Germany - with apologies to the primitive peoples - and the marvellous development of flying and the radio, our sphere has been so completely harnessed to science that the world can be flown round in a few days and the spoken word can be transmitted from one end of the earth to the other in a matter of a few moments. The world has advanced materially with giant strides which recall the words of the Book of Genesis but whether it has advanced spiritually is another question. Many consider that it has retrograded.

In this same era the British people have seen many and great changes, except that the slums remained always with us often cheek by jowl with the rich in their mansions, poor relations if you like, but proud and independent and often more than a little scornful of the moneyed but frequently less happy class. The nation has suffered many vicissitudes, and while applied science progressed the well-being of the wage-earners failed to keep pace with it, despite the fact that we have been blessed with three political Parties vying with one another for their suffrages, making prolific promises before elections and promptly forgetting them afterwards.

At the beginning of the century Great Britain and Ireland - then an integral part of the British Isles - was unquestionably the leading Great Power. Its Royal Navy maintained the two-power standard. Its military machine, if occasionally rusty, as shown in the Boer War, was well-trained, disciplined, and formidable. Financially it was the wealthiest country in the world and the money centre of the universe, for the United States could scarcely be said yet to have emerged into the hurly-burly of world politics and regarded the old world as practically outside its vortex, being content to stand by the Monroe Doctrine which it could not have sustained by force of arms.

Hence its main interest lay in the attractions of Paris, Vienna, and Rome so far as Europe was concerned.

With the opening years of the century Britain began to lose her grip on world affairs and her prestige waned while our politicians strengthened the Party machines. Queen Victoria, who kept Ministers in their place, had passed away and was soon followed by Lord Salisbury, who had maintained Britain's prestige against all comers. The United States, Germany, Austria, Italy, Japan, and France were busy erecting high and growing tariff walls, and Britain's manufacturers were being steadily squeezed out of the world markets as she stood for free trade and was made the dumping ground for the surplus wares of foreign Powers building up their industries, frequently subsidising their exports, and producing at a price which a far lower scale of living permitted. Gradually Britain found her oversea markets being lost, unemployment increase, while international bankers and financiers waxed rich.

Joseph Chamberlain, after the Boer War, was the first English statesman to grasp the nettle of tariff reform, put his finger on the right spot, resigned from the Government in order to be free to preach the gospel of Colonial Preference in order to cement the Empire, and filled with missionary fervour to stump the country. In a wise world his proposals should have been weighed scientifically and coldly, the benefit or otherwise to the nation being the only determinate factor. Arthur Balfour (later Lord), Salisbury's nephew and successor as Prime Minister, sat uncomfortably on the fence watching to see which way the cat jumped. He was a master of philosophic doubt.

No English politician ever enjoyed such foul abuse as did Mr. Chamberlain. He was attacked by the Liberals with a vituperation rarely found in our annals. Behind the scenes the Liberal Party was awaiting the moment to pluck the ripe fruit of Patronage and Power from the hands of the discredited Tory Party, which was tired and whose muddles over the Boer War had lost it the confidence of the electorate. The thought that "wily Joe" might yet snatch the prize from them and dish the Whigs with his proposals of Colonial Preference was gall and wormwood to these gentry, and as a matter of fact tariffs only came into operation in 1915, oddly enough introduced by the Liberals themselves by necessity in the second year of the first German war. Unfortunately by that time the rival industrial nations, with their strongly erected tariff walls, import restrictions, and with the aid of a free British market, had prospered greatly and Britain had become correspondingly the poorer, although still wealthy with the assets she had built up in the past century.

In the period between the last war and the massacre war of the present time - writing in the year of Our Lord 1943 - Britain's wealth, already largely hypothecated, continued to shrink for a variety of reasons into which I will not enter here. It will suffice to observe that as I have watched the sinister game of Party politics played at home and abroad, in which international finance took a leading hand, the British people were little more than pawns in the sport. Tens of millions of taxpayers' money - for which they have to foot the bill - were lent and loans guaranteed to inimical States, practically all of them today being bad debts if not actually repudiated. Of course some people made a handsome profit out of these generous contributions.

The trusted Political leaders did not put Britain first in their policy, for their main allegiance was to the Party, and scrambled into office and power, meaning the division of the swag and the distribution of honours which in many cases were sold to the highest bidders regardless of merit or even honesty.

For many years now the British people, as I see the political game, despite their boast of freedom, have been actually in the grip of a potent political machine which has been oiled by the contributions of interested parties, as to which I might have nothing to say against were it directed for the benefit of the nation as a whole instead of for a class. It is an ill-growth of democratic government and it can only be defeated by the vigilance of the Press but unfortunately there have been ways and means of tampering with the Press - not by direct bribery as was practised on so large a scale in Europe - but by the giving of honours, a most pernicious system, not to editors or the men who make papers, but to the financial magnates who direct them. Frankly I am in favour of limiting political honours very drastically.

A highly organised political machine has too often duped the electors to support a Party at the polls by lavish promises which are conveniently forgotten immediately afterwards. When this war is over and men return to civil life perhaps the politicians will find it not so easy to throw dust into the eyes of the public. I have enough faith to believe it will be so, but the great free Press of this country needs to be adamant and to show no hesitation in throwing the limelight wherever subterranean intrigues are at work. Patronage Secretaries should be exterminated by an Act of Parliament!

Political corruption has played a great part in lowering the standards of public life in the last forty years and is the diagnosis I suggest of the disease which led to our unpreparedness for the two awful world wars that have scourged the world in what have been aptly termed the locust years. I do not deny that political corruption did not exist long before as it did certainly in the days of rotten boroughs, but with the uprise of industry and the era of big money interests Mammon was permitted to capture strong points and the little man became exploited.

The political education of the nation is the cure. Travel is the eye-opener, and the millions of men who have seen service overseas have imbibed a new idea I fancy of what Great Britain's power and strength mean to the world. and hence to themselves and their children. Here, indeed, is a chance for the Press, the organs of publicity, whose editors need to overcome their timidity to speak out with directness and boldness, assured of the fact that the great mass of the nation will applaud their patriotism. In short the Press is in need of reform but my criticisms do not include working journalists in any way. I may be a Fleet Street rebel and I have suffered from the ignorance and flabbiness of newspaper directors but my criticisms relate to them alone.

Perhaps I was fortunate that soon after leaving school I was sent out to India where I had some influential relations and so started to travel early. I had the opportunity of seeing that great dependency over a wide scale and it broadened my outlook. Unfortunately I contracted malaria in Guzerat and so was sent home, long before I had intended.

I have visited the United States, studied the antiquities of Egypt, am familiar with most of the Mediterranean, know Germany, France, and Switzerland from within, have tip-toed into Spain, and spent some little time in Florence and Rome. Shortly after I had returned from India. I became tutor to two young Italian nobles closely related to the famous houses of Borghese and Salviati, a family allied to the Papacy as contra-distinguished from the House of Savoy. I loved Italy and respected the *contadini*, an honest peasantry, but found Italian society decadent and rotten to the core. Through my Italian friends I met, while staying at Lucerne, the American Minister to Switzerland, whose private secretary I became and learned a good deal about German espionage years before the first German war.

The U.S. Envoy Extraordinary and Minister Plenipotentiary in question was John G. A. Leishman, a pleasant and kindly little man in his early forties, with no particular pretensions to learning but what was far more important to a man in his position, a multi-millionaire. From the humblest beginnings he had risen to be President of the great Carnegie Steel Company at Pittsburg, Pa, and, influenced by a socially ambitious and beautiful wife, he was persuaded to retire from business and embark on a career of diplomacy, Switzerland being his first post, but he later became U.S. Ambassador in Turkey and finally in Germany. He had two attractive daughters, the elder, Martha, marrying later a Spanish nobleman, and the younger, Nancy, the Prince of Croy. I fell on my feet in this my first real job, for he paid me well and life was easy and set in pleasant ways.

Although only his private secretary I became his constant companion and interpreter - for my French was reasonably good - and in effect his Secretary of Legation for the position was not filled from Washington. I had to dance attendance on him, be present on all official occasions such as calling upon the President of the Swiss Confederation on New Year's Day, write official letters, attend him at social functions and when he invited guests arrange the table and place them in their proper order of precedence, a very tricky task, for woe betide anyone placing an envoy junior to a diplomatic colleague if he were his senior. In short I had to make myself generally useful and never err.

Among other tasks was to leave my chief's cards on various diplomatic or Ministerial personages. All who called on the Minister, and they were legion, had to receive his cards in return. There were a few compensations, for I became acquainted with the wives of diplomats on less formal terms than with their husbands, and the ladies often were far less discreet. One of these was the Baroness von Bülow, wife of the German Minister, himself a younger brother of the Prince von Bülow, then Kaiser Wilhelm's Chancellor and Principal Minister. I wondered why the brother of the most important functionary in Germany should not hold a higher post than Berne. I did not know then that it was a key position for espionage.

The Baroness was a blonde, well past her first youth, who strove desperately to fight a growing tendency to obesity. She tight-laced, and the effect was to distribute her *embonpoint* to other parts. It seeped down in rolls of fat below her ankles and wrists. Her arms became immense, likewise her legs but these were happily concealed under the long dresses then worn. My chief was lavish with flowers for distribution to wives of the diplomatic circle. His monthly account with the florist was really prodigious. Hence, when I was received by the blonde Baroness, paid my chief's respects, paid her some lavish compliment, and begged her to accept the bouquet I brought, it was usually orchids or some expensive exotic flowers.

Ready for a mild flirtation with the millionaire Minister's secretary, bored as everybody was in beautiful but dull Berne, and greatly interested in the Leishman *ménage* - she always suspected that Mrs. Leishman, who led a gay life in Paris, was pursued by admirers - the Baroness would beg me to be seated and offer me an *apéritif*. She was enraptured by the bouquet and was all smiles.

21

"How *gentil* is excellence Leishman, Monsieur. Pray convey to him my cordial thanks, *n'est-ce-pas?* Ah, how charming a man, and he is here so little. But why should he be? *Mais vous, mon cher! Encore en vacances - toujours en vacances, hein?* How do I know? *Un petit oiseau, monsieur! Oui, il me dit que le Ministre est allé a Monte Carlo - et vous aussi, n'est-ce-pas? - chez M. Zaharoff et sa charmante Duchesse de Marchena. . . ."*

"That was some little time ago, Madame," I reply. "Since then Mr. Leishman has been in Paris."

"And you, too?" She sighs with an expansive bust. "Monte Carlo! Paris! Ah, if only *mon mari* had occasion to visit these places and take me! Paris! Tell me, does it still exist? It is ten years since the Baron took me to Paris with its gay life, its opera, theatres, boulevards, restaurants, its divine shops! Here I am just a cabbage! And how did you find the ravishing Madame Leishman, with her Titian hair, lovely figure, and beautiful gowns? Has she still the same apartment in the Champs Elysées? And many admirers? - though there is no need to ask!"

I discreetly give Madame the news and end up by saying that Mrs. Leishman had remarked recently that Berne did not agree with her and that she never wanted to live anywhere except in Paris.

"Of course. Why would you? But I am sorry for the dear Minister. If he desires to caress his beautiful wife he must go to Paris, *hein?*" She shakes her head knowingly and laughs coquettishly. "Who can blame her? No one not tied down would suffer this tedious town they call a capital."

"But a very important diplomatic centre, Madame, I fancy."

I remember the Baroness giving me a queer, half-quizzical glance.

"Why do you think that?" she asked.

"Because otherwise would so important a diplomatist as His Excellence the Baron von Bülow be placed here, Madame?"

A friend of mine in the Dutch Legation had lately hinted that Berne was the centre of German espionage and secret service, and he had added significantly that the English first and the Americans secondly should be on the *qui vive,* for we were Germany's secret enemies. Hence I chanced my arm with the question.

"You are right, *mon ami,*" flashed back the Baroness suddenly. "My husband is the pivot of - " she paused. "He has the brains of his family, not his brother the Chancellor. He is the eyes of the Kaiser himself, and his work never ends. Day and night, night and day, cables come and go. Persons come across the oceans to interview, him. Never has he a moment free for gaiety and that is why he cannot leave his post and take me to Paris or London or Washington. . . ."

My Dutch friend was not far wrong.

She regretted her outburst as soon as she had given utterance to it, and begged me to remember that what she had said was in strict confidence. I gained some insight into the network of intrigue issuing from so innocent-looking a capital as Berne with the ulterior object of overthrowing the power of Britain and establishing a German hegemony in her place.

At this time as the result of the Boer War relations between England and Germany were considerably strained. Nor were Anglo-French relations over-cordial, for the French in their hearts have always been jealous of *La perfide Albion* whatever their outward manifestations of friendship might be. We were *les cochons Anglais* as always in their eyes and the French Press, confident in their Franco-Russian Alliance, did not hesitate to disguise their sympathy for the Boers, much as they detested the Germans. The Tsar Nicholas profoundly distrusted the Kaiser, despite his German Tsarina, but he was certainly no Anglophile.

Life with "*Excellence* Leishman" was not, however, all a bower of roses. At the time the British and American Governments were engaged in a tiresome dispute with Portugal, the Delagoa Bay Arbitration, and the Swiss Government had been invited to act as the arbitrator, the case being heard by the High Court judges at Lausanne. The circumstances were simple enough. The Delagoa Bay Railway was a British-owned concern, capitalised with British and some American money, and had possessed a concession from the Portuguese Government. This railway had been seized illegally by the Mozambique authorities together with all its assets, and this high-handed action was no less than a *casus belli*. The Boer War was in full swing and the aid deliberately given to the Boers by the Portuguese had aroused intense anger at home, so much so that a considerable demand arose for a declaration of war on Portugal.

The Government, however, in London, had no desire to widen the war and especially to attack little Portugal reprehensible though her conduct was. After strong diplomatic protests arbitration was agreed upon since Portugal refused to restore the railway to its owners, and the issue at Lausanne turned upon the assessment of damages. Money, however, was not the sole issue. Delagoa Bay and its railway was the only means whereby war equipment and munitions could be sent direct to the Boers, and thus the seizure was an important strategic move. Germany was active in sending munitions nominally to Portugal as a neutral, but really for the army of President Kruger. In fact Germany was the real instigator of the entire business, and for many years plotted to seize the whole of Portuguese East Africa where up to the present time she has big financial interests.

There was no disguise as to German hostility. The Kaiser had shown his hand from the moment of the Jameson Raid when he sent his notorious telegram of sympathy and congratulation to President Kruger. Whilst the High Court judges at Lausanne were examining documents of the claim in leisurely fashion the German Minister was busily engaged among his other activities in engineering ways and means to defeat the Anglo-American demands and so score a diplomatic triumph for what Germany was pleased to term the "rights of an oppressed small nation." The German Press, officially inspired, shrieked out scurrilous abuse, and with the vituperation always so handy to the Teuton mind, lampooned John Bull as a fat-bellied lout, clutching his money-bags and stamping on poor little

Portugal. In short, the same stale old acrimonious stock-in-trade she has used with few original variations for half a century at least.

In addition to this propaganda the Kaiser, having done his worst to inflame Europe to almost combustion point, took direct steps to induce France and Russia to combine with Germany and force Britain under threat of war to make peace with the Boers. Fortunately for the peace of the world at that time neither France nor Russia were prepared to enter into a cabal to gratify the spleen and ambitions of Wilhelm II. All this time, moreover, Germany was selling arms to the Boers and we gave her free access to our markets with all the facilities of our bankers and financiers in the city of London only too anxious to give her shippers and importers every accommodation.

Switzerland was a neutral country, but Swiss nationals were for the most part overwhelmingly anti-British and many of my countrymen and countrywomen who had lived for years in Lausanne, Montreux, Geneva, etc., in disgust quitted the country. I escaped being spat upon because I was thought to be an American and the Swiss had no desire to alienate American sentiments. I was sent to Lausanne a good deal during the leisurely hearing of the claim, and the big hotels at Ouchy, nestling at the foot of the hill on which Lausanne stands, at the edge of the lovely lake of Geneva, were packed out with interested parties, including international lawyers, who pocketed huge fees for little work.

Among those present, ubiquitous but modest of demeanour, was a special envoy of Portugal, the old Marquis de S., sent by Lisbon solely to safeguard its defence, and, so to speak, rig the market behind the scenes. A courtly old gentleman of benevolent appearance, ancient lineage, and bearing a distinguished name, he had rented a handsome villa in convenient proximity to the law-courts, and brought with him two invaluable assets in the shape of a perfect chef and a cellar stocked with the choicest vintage wines of France, Spain, and Portugal. His *déjeuners* and dinners and his hospitality were the talk of the town, but needless to say neither my chief nor the British Minister, Sir Frederick St. John, were among are *invités*.

Strange enough - or was it? - his most favoured guests were High Court judges and certain German diplomats and officials. What exactly transpired in the way of talk round his hospitable board I can only retail from hearsay, but it is certain that he never missed a chance to enlarge on his theme of "my poor country," while others contrasted it with the wealth of "plutocratic England." As their glasses were filled with delicate wines of rare bouquet, followed by precious old cognac, coffee, and cigars, no doubt the conversation drifted towards the fabulous wealth of England now demanding millions from the impoverished little State represented by the Marquis. How tyrannical it would be to expect Portugal to pay immense sums for having taken over a railroad concession whose future value was at best problematical!

The British Foreign Office trusted to the equity of international law to obtain just compensation for the sheer robbery of a British undertaking which the Portuguese were unable to excuse or palliate. Against this the wily old Marquis, by the judicious expenditure of a few thousands, an excellent cook and a choice cellar, added to blandishments and flattery, hoped to nullify or at least whittle down the British claim for compensation to some nominal figure. Meantime Germany was banking on a diplomatic trump .

Sir Frederick St. John - to whom I had been loaned to assist in the pressure of work - and my chief saw clearly enough what the game was, but they were powerless to intervene. They expected, as did everyone behind the scenes, that Portugal would get off cheaply, but few realised how cheaply, an award so trivial that it was almost ludicrous. "Utterly indecent!" exclaimed Sir Frederick indignantly. "Not worth collecting!" laughed Leishman. "But what else could we expect?" The British newspapers, little aware of the intrigue that had proceeded behind the scenes, had swarmed to Lausanne to report the Court's findings, but I got a scoop, for I was allowed to see a copy of the judgement before it was released to the Press and cabled it to the Paris edition of the **New York Herald**. of which I had shortly before been made correspondent by James Gordon Bennett, and got ahead of all others. Paris sent it by its private cable to New York and altogether I scored over the others by some hours.

The Continental papers, and especially the German, whooped with delight that "plutocratic England" had been signally defeated in trying to "plunder" Portugal. It was an unpleasant diplomatic set-back at an awkward moment and it certainly did not redound to the prestige of Lord Lansdowne, our Foreign Minister, whose leanings towards Germany were always suspect. That we were swindled out of millions was bad enough, although it has always appeared that our Foreign Office has shown itself supremely indifferent to the losses of British subjects at the hands of foreign governments. It is, indeed, only within recent years that a Commercial Attaché has been included in the personnel of Chancelleries and the Consul Service has hitherto been the Ishmael of the Foreign office although, as every importer or exporter is aware, it has to look after the interests of British subjects. My chief used periodically to call all his Consular officials to a conference and discuss business of a hush-hush nature.

That the British Foreign Office should be the perquisite of political hucksters has commonly been Britain's undoing and will be until it is lifted clean out of the maelstrom of Party politics. "Foreign affairs," says Lord Vansittart, "should be recognised for what they are - the key business. They govern - unfortunately - all other trades. If a country is unhappy in its handling of foreign relations, the most perfect conduct of its internal affairs will be vain." His Lordship should know, seeing that he was Permanent Under Secretary from 1930 to 1938, and Diplomatic Advisor to the Foreign Secretary until 1941, to say nothing of his earlier experiences in foreign diplomatic missions. They govern - unfortunately - all other trades, says he, and these trades control the national prosperity or otherwise. Yes, we want a really big forthright man, one who has travelled a great deal, a man of the world, a good mixer, a man with a business brain and not too much appeasement as our Foreign Minister. We could do with a Lord Palmerston.

"In less than a generation," adds Lord Vansittart, "Germany has twice tried to plunge the world into night without a quiver of compunction, a flicker of shame, a shadow of remorse." How well did the Foreign Office anticipate these ghastly forays with Britain as the destined victim of Teutonic ultramontanism? Why is it that one after another since Salisbury's day our Foreign Ministers shut their eyes to German intrigues and plans for war and attempted to tame the savage beast by appeasement? If no worse it is proof of misguided psychology and has added thousands of millions to the National Debt.

A little before the time I speak of, cables from America began to shower on my chief from various sources. One day he was rung up by a man whose name was then strange to me, Mr. Basil Zaharoff. He hung up the receiver and turned smilingly to me.

"Ever heard of Zaharoff, Beau?"

"No, sir."

"The great arms capitalist of Yurrup! Your ignorance is shocking. Wal, he invites me to Monte Carlo for a few days; and, incidentally, he owns that burg. I guess you had better come along, too, in case I want you. Will you tell Christian" - his courier-valet - "to book two reservations on the sleeper to-morrow night for Monte and report arrangements to me?"

CHAPTER II

ARMAMENTS FINANCE

ZAHAROFF, THE COSMOPOLITAN - he was yet to be knighted by King George V - had engaged a royal suite for my chief at the *Hotel Metropole*, which overlooked the beautiful exotic gardens of the Casino on one side and the restful, blue Mediterranean on the other. With his Duchess he resided at the famous *Hotel de Paris* on the opposite side of the Casino Gardens.

Slightly above the medium height, slim, with an imperial which gave him some resemblance to portraits of Napoleon the Third, Basil Zaharoff greeted us soon after our arrival and led my chief on to the balcony where he entered into a long and confidential conversation. Archie de Bear, the theatrical producer, journalist, and at one time Zaharoff's secretary, has said that whenever he entertained a guest there was a motive behind it and sooner or later business was discussed. I guess that on this occasion it began sooner rather than later.

During our visit over several days we were entertained to *déjeuner* and dinner throughout at the Paris, I being fortunate enough to be included in the party of four which embraced, of course, the beautiful Duchesse de Marchena. Scarcely more than thirty at this time, some twenty years younger than our host, the Duchesse was slight, very elegant, an attractive brunette, talented and wholly amiable. She spoke English with the slightest accent, and she possessed the most exquisite hands with dainty tapering fingers. These repasts were merry lively with *badinage* and repartee, mostly conducted by the Duchesse and Leishman, for Zaharoff was usually quiet, although he possessed a dry wit on occasions. In the afternoons they generally took us for a drive and in the evenings they occasionally accompanied us for a short time to the Casino where my chief, who loved dearly to gamble, enjoyed himself thoroughly. He patronised the *trente-et-quarante* table in the Sporting Club, lost gaily, and one night broke the bank with 100,000 francs in his pocket. He was mightily pleased and so was I, for he gave me a thousand-franc note as a gift - and that was in the days when 23 francs equalled a golden sovereign.

The association between Basil Zaharoff and the Duchesse was strange, for their disparity in rank was notable, and the more so in view of the stricter etiquette prevailing at the end of the last century. The Duchesse de Villa-franca de los Caballeros in her own right, one of Spain's greatest patrician families, she had been given in marriage when only seventeen to Don Francesco de Bourbon, Duke of Marchena, of the Blood Royal of Spain, and cousin of King Alfonso. The origin of the famous arms financier, on the other hand, was mysterious and humble. After his death a Levantine tobacco-blender who made a claim as a relative to part of his estate swore that he was an Armenian, born in Aleppo, and that his real name was Chacaty. Very intelligent as a child, this claimant declared that he was stowed away on a ship bound for Istanbul where a wealthy Greek adopted him. Other accounts said that as a boy he hung round the docks at the Piraeus and ran errands for a living, and a Hollywood film depicted him as a guttersnipe of the Levant who rose to be a millionaire. Zaharoff himself vaguely mentioned that he was born and reared in Bedfordshire, and so was a British subject, but later naturalised himself as a Frenchman. Whatever his origin he had all the finesse and manners of a *grand seigneur*, and looked an aristocrat all over.

For an account of their first meeting I am indebted to Archie de Bear. Some eleven years before I met them, Zaharoff, who had already become a figure in the arms industry, was among a throng of distinguished guests at a formal reception given at the Escorial in Madrid by King Alfonso and Queen Victoria - our English princess Ena, daughter of Princess Beatrice. As he descended the stairs about to leave he observed a slender and lovely girl accompanied by a man in uniform just in front of him. "I did not know who she was, he said, describing the occasion, "but she had the loveliest face I had ever seen. The man was ablaze with orders and I noticed that guests stood aside to let them pass, when suddenly the man took the girl's arm and brutally crushed it." She gave a little cry . . . and before he knew what he was doing, Zaharoff hit him across the face. At once a fearful commotion arose in the Palace.

"It was Don Francesco de Bourbon, Duke of Marchena," continued Zaharoff, "and the girl was his nineteen-year old wife. I had struck a Prince of the blood, cousin of the King of Spain, merely because he had been rough with his own wife!"

The outraged Duke at once challenged Zaharoff to a duel, swords were drawn, and honour was avenged, for the arms magnate was taken to hospital somewhat badly wounded. A few days later the Duchesse herself, heavily veiled, visited him in hospital to inquire as to his condition and to thank him for his chivalrous conduct. She also mentioned that she was about to leave Madrid. Zaharoff ascertained where and when she was leaving and insisted on leaving hospital, although in no fit state to travel, ordered masses of flowers to be taken to her railway saloon and duly met her again. She was induced to accept his advances, and the two thenceforth were never separated until the day when she died in his arms.

Such was the romance between the highly-placed royal princess, member of the proudest and most exclusive Court in the world, and the arms manufacturer. It had a pathetic ending. She could not marry Zaharoff while her husband lived, for there is, of course, no divorce in the Catholic Church, and Don Francesco lingered on, under constant medical supervision, it was said suffering from insanity, until 1924, when Zaharoff was seventy-five years old, and less than two years later the princess died, leaving him a grief-stricken old man.

De Bear says that Zaharoff experienced many ups and downs before he "struck lucky." His first chance came when he got the job as agent of the Anglo-Nordenfeldt Gun Company in the Balkans. He happened to be in Vienna, trying vainly to obtain an order, when one day he heard by chance some newspaper men say that an American named Maxim was going to demonstrate a new machine-gun. Zaharoff thought quickly:

"A great performance for the Nordenfeldt gun," he said. "There is nothing to compete with it."

"Nordenfeldt?" repeated one of the Pressmen present. "Isn't the inventor Hiram Maxim?"

"Oh, no," was the calm reply. "That is the Nordenfeldt gun, the finest weapon in the world."

Next day the world's Press had marvellous stories about the performance of the Nordenfeldt gun demonstrated by Hiram Maxim. It made the famous inventor of the Maxim gun furious, but Zaharoff managed to pacify him and what is more from his trick there emerged the new armaments firm of Maxim and Nordenfeldt. Friction later developed between the two inventors and Zaharoff decided to throw in his lot with Maxim, and in conjunction with Albert Vickers there arose the great arms combine of Vickers-Maxim.

It set Zaharoff on the high road to fame and fortune. He frankly admitted to de Bear that he peddled arms to all. "I sold armaments to anyone who would buy them," he confessed; "I was a Russian in Russia, a Greek in Greece, a Frenchman in Paris, and all the time I bought shares in the firm for which I was working. I was rich, but I worked for my wealth," he said, with a chuckle. "I sold a submarine to the Turks, and then I went to the Greeks and sold them a couple."

Lord Balfour was reputed to have said that he engineered the last war, and whilst this may be a gross exaggeration, assuming it were said, there is no doubt that he was the world's arch-pedlar of arms. Whether the fact that a man who sells arms is the creator of wars may be highly debatable, for wars have been generated by rulers who seek territory, loot, or markets, greed generally, and whilst the desire for war cannot be gratified without arms it would rather seem to be putting the cart before the horse to suggest that arms inspire nations to go out in search of conquest and that without a Zaharoff the last war would not have happened.

At all events, Sir Basil Zaharoff, as he became, performed notable service to the Allied cause in the war of 1914-18. His Paris residence, 30 Avenue Hoche, where I visited him on several occasions subsequently, became in effect the Headquarters for the output of munitions to the Allies, and he was virtually the supreme controller. British Ministers of highest rank stayed there, including Mr. Lloyd

George, the Prime Minister, and when Zaharoff crossed the Channel he was often taken in a British destroyer. A fine linguist, disguised as a Bulgarian doctor, he volunteered to pay a visit to Germany to discover certain matters of great moment which Lloyd George and Clemenceau ardently desired to know. He took his life in his hands and obtained the information. He was in the train making for the frontier when to his horror he noticed a German officer sitting opposite him who hardly ever took his eyes off him. For three solid hours he remained there in suspense and certain incriminating papers in the lining of his coat began to burn a hole in his chest. At last he could stand it no longer and when the frontier was at hand he leant over and asked the officer why he was so interested in his appearance.

"*Herr Doktor,*" replied the German, twisting his moustache, "pardon me if I annoy you, but you are exactly like my sister's husband who is reported missing."

As a result of the information he took to Allied Headquarters he was given the G.C.B. by Lloyd George. His information was regarded as of major importance in the winning of the war.

Zaharoff backed Venizélos against King George of Greece. "Kings are out of date" he said. "I believe in the dictatorship of brains and ability, not of chance."

Monarchs and rulers sought help from him. Among them was Queen Marie of Rumania, mother of Carol, the vivid and brilliant English-born granddaughter of Queen Victoria, who visited him in the Avenue Hoche to try to raise a loan to build up her country's defences.

"She had lovely hands," ruminated Zaharoff, "but my wife's were even more beautiful. Queen Marie sat in that chair with her veil thrown back looking like a nun who had eaten an apple off the Tree of Knowledge."

He made some curious confessions to that ubiquitous traveller, writer, and interviewer, Rosita Forbes. He told his secret of finding purchasers for his arms. It was the usual method - *cherchez la femme*!

"Flattering the wife or mistress of the Minister in power," he owned. "As a very young man I realised that there is always a woman behind the public personage. I got introduced to her, sent her flowers or jewels, courted her and eventually sold what I wanted to her husband or lover."

A cynical avowal of the weakness of human nature or the frailty of man. Let us hope it doesn't apply to our country!

His absorbing ideal was to see Greece become a great Power. During the Peace Conference, Lloyd George called to see him, and while standing in the hall waiting for his hat, he said casually:

"So it's your birthday to-day, is it? Well, go along and tell your friend Venizélos that I make you a present of Asia Minor."

That birthday gift cost Greece 100,000 lives, and failed to succeed although the Prime Minister attempted to induce Britain to support Greece in the field. It also cost Zaharoff between three and four millions sterling.

The fortune he left behind him was another mystery of this prince of mystery men. He was reputed to have amassed a fortune of at least ten million pounds but he left estate in England worth under £200,000, and in France it was estimated not to exceed one million. So passed away the great Arms dealer, the International Financier, the humbly-born lover of a most beautiful, sweet-natured, and, in fact, virtuous royal princess, who died with the name of Greece on his lips and his adored mistress engraved on his heart. A strange stroller-by in this world of ours, something of a sorcerer, who in his latter days grew smaller, looked bored and unhappy, and some-times sat in the sun at Monte Carlo wrapped in a long black cloak, or wearily slouching along looking like a medieval wizard. . . .

I often wondered how much Basil Zaharoff cleaned up as a result of his invitation to Leishman to Monte Carlo, but I should imagine it was considerable, and that he got in on the ground floor in a huge arms deal then secretly hatching and of which he must have obtained prior knowledge through his secret service. To be fêted and honoured for nearly a week by a hostess so beautiful and charming, heroine of the greatest love romance of the age and a royal princess of the House of Bourbon to boot could be expected to have had an exhilarating effect on any man and decidedly on an American, who always adores such a *rencontre*. *"Excellence* Leishman," moreover, had an eye for feminine charms, and was not above flattery.

I can lift a corner of the secret. There was a big merger in the air between the United States Corporation and Carnegie's and those in the inner ring were playing the market for big fortunes. Accomplished host as he was, it is scarcely rash to suggest that Sir Basil Zaharoff had an ulterior motive and that he also was enabled to add a few dollars to his majestic fortune.

If I should have given too much space to Sir Basil's career, it is because he was an outstanding figure of the cosmopolitan world in a day now long since gone. Behind the scenes he exercised a powerful political influence not to create war but to check the insatiable ambition of Germany whose peril to peace until such time as she was literally ground to dust he clearly foresaw. I suppose in the Brave New World we are promised and where independence and initiative will be at a discount there will be no room for other Zaharoffs. It may be advantageous although he was a colourful figure in a colourless world but it will be too optimistic to suppose that somehow the International Financier will not edge his way through the stage door and fascinate the Stars of High and Low politics.

Less colourful, but inordinately rich, were a bunch of steel magnates I met some little time later in America, for my chief, accompanied by his entourage, namely the courier Christian - who always dressed in brown, which resembled his outlook - and his secretary, sailed for New York on one of the luxury American liners of the day. I gathered that big financial negotiations were in the near offing, and sure enough they were.

We had no sooner checked in at the old Waldorf - now the Waldorf-Astoria - when various household names in America appeared on the scene, Leishman's steel trade cronies, including Henry Clay Frick, the great steel magnate, and Charles M. Schwab, then President of the Carnegie Company. At once four of them sat down to stern business. The Merger? It makes me smile! *Poker.* On the boat my chief had spent most of his time in the smoking-room indulging in the same diversion, and for the best part of several days he and his friends seemed to dispense with sleep except for a few minutes here and there. Occasionally they took their clothes off and indulged in a bath and shave. Meals were served in the salon, almost it might be thought between deals. Mind you, when I said it was stern business, indeed it was, for they went to it hammer and tongs, sitting there in their shirt sleeves always with a cigar in their mouths and a drink by their side, usually rye whisky. They insulted one another with amusing Yankee quip and repartee, and all enjoying themselves thoroughly.

How they would have laughed had they known that at the tail end of 1942, with England stuffed with Americans who all play the national game, a solemn magistrate of London should discover that poker is a pure game of chance and impose a stiff fine on an unfortunate wight guilty of playing it! Such a judgment is almost enough to break the oft-boosted friendship and fraternity between the U.S.A. and ourselves which our public orators are so fond of declaiming! When every American knows only too well that it needs all the qualities of consummate bluff, of sizing up one's opponents, of knowing exactly when to draw and when not, and the great technique of staking. Poker is the very epitome of American business technique; the science of benefiting from the weaknesses of human nature!

Let it not be thought that the financial magnates who had assembled in New York to do honour to their comrade the Envoy Extraordinary to Switzerland were nit wits and unmindful of the real business in hand Their poker was a sort of rite with them, a variety of freemasonry, the means of frank intercourse. In between bluffing one another with their hands, winning or losing considerable sums to lesser men, now and again side-lights on the merger came into view

Seemingly casual remarks which all present understood cemented. tacit agreements and the result was the birth of the great Steel Trust of America and the amassing of further fortunes by men who were already multi-millionaires.

Of these cronies I liked best Henry Clay Frick Although largely self-educated he was a lover of art, and his collection of Old Masters and his Armoury collection, on both of which he had lavished immense sums, were unequalled in the New World and scarcely rivalled in the Old. He was kind enough to show these to me at his New York mansion and it pleased him that I was delighted. He died in 1919, having bequeathed these priceless collections to the City of New York, and, in addition, his residuary estate valued at over fifty million dollars was left to charitable institutions.

I am correct in stating that he was the real genius who made Carnegie's vast steel business what it was, for old Andrew Carnegie, another great philanthropist, had for long been little more than a figure-head. Carnegie's works were at Pittsburg, tenth largest city of the United States, with a population of over half a million, and as Pittsburg was the key city in the State of Pennsylvania the political pull of the Carnegie bosses was very considerable. It was the support it gave to the election of President McKinley, the Republican candidate, which enabled Leishman to ask in return a diplomatic appointment as a *quid pro quo*. Yet Carnegie's was a democratic organisation for all that. My own chief, Frick, and Schwab had all worked their way to eminence from small beginnings to become multi-millionaires and none of them, except it were Frick, knew how to spend their money to gain happiness.

Whilst the unending game of poker proceeded, infiltrated with high finance, my chief gave me *carte blanche* to amuse myself in New York. He put my name down for honorary membership of two or three big clubs, including the Manhattan, handed me a roll of dollar bills and told me to have a good time. As I had met many amusing New Yorkers on the liner, who had offered me the spontaneous hospitality which New York, and come to that, as all America so generously hands out, I did not find time lag on my hands. In fact I seemed scarcely to have slept at all, but since New York's night life was kept up without intermission and there seemed to be more people in the hotel lounges and the restaurant at about 4 a.m. than at other times it was difficult to feel that there was a bedtime.

Among other cities I visited on my first American trip were Pittsburg, Chicago, Philadelphia, Washington, Baltimore, and Harrisburg, to which latter city we were taken in the President of the Railroad's own private saloon where drinks were served without ceasing and my chief never rose from the poker table and won a good amount from the Railroad President, his host. At Washington we entered the respectable zone and "Jahn" became the Hon. John Leishman, Minister for Switzerland, who was closeted with the U.S. Secretary of State, then Col. Hay, while his two pretty daughters took me in hand and showed me the sights of the capital.

Pittsurg was my chief's home town and here we stayed for three weeks in a swanky hotel whose name I fancy was the Shelburne. Here His Excellency had big and serious business on hand and I was left to kick my heels around. However, with his accustomed generosity he put me up for the best club, the Pittsburg Club, and here again I was touched by the extraordinary hospitality offered me, merely an unsophisticated English boy, by everyone, who insisted on taking me to their homes and introducing me to their families and who stared at me as though an Englishman were a *rara avis*. I suppose I enjoyed prestige as the secretary of their esteemed citizen who was a Minister and Envoy and who, in their imaginations, rubbed shoulders with all the kings and aristocracy of Europe. Pittsburg was wealthy, busy, smoky with half a million chimney stacks, and parochial in outlook.

I have always found Americans homely and friendly and quite easy to understand if you recollect that they are not a nation as we are but really a conglomeration of many varying races and creeds, loosely cemented together by catchwords and slogans and that beneath their apparent sophistication - leaving aside such cities as Washington, New York, Philadelphia, Boston and a few more - they are not really so sure of themselves as they would like to pretend to strangers. They know that they are new and raw, and that few among them can point to pedigrees or claim any history for a length of time. Hence, to keep their end up they love to beat the big drum and wave the Stars and Stripes and to perform other antics which those from old European countries think vulgar and boastful. But we should recognise that they possess illimitable wealth and energy and a population which could make them the dominating nation of the world, whether we like it or not, for in addition they enjoy an exhilarating climate and a constitution which makes them really free men and women.

They are rather too fond of sneering at our "effete" institutions and customs, and they are not far wrong too in those matters, although many are laudable and might be imitated by them with profit, such as chivalry, good manners; and politeness. They are apt to preen themselves upon their vastly superior enterprise but Britain's efforts in this war owe little apology to the United States. They forget that they have been able to expand in the last century because of natural advantages we do not possess, having vast agricultural areas and immense mineral resources to say nothing of their great oil reservoirs for which they should bless the Almighty. They started unhampered by age-old vested interests and the expense of maintaining an army and navy. In short they might show more recognition of the fact that their Anglo-Saxon ancestors first blazed the trail for them and not scold us because we happen to have had a foolish German monarch who quarrelled with them.

Let me not seem to disparage them. They are a great and virile people even though they have their idiosyncrasies. They are generous by nature, far less trammelled by outworn tradition, and they have the inestimable virtue of being sympathetic to new ideas and refuse to be bound by convention. In Europe and most certainly in Britain if you have a new outlook which crosses the path of accepted tradition you are regarded as a crank or a Philistine. In America you are received open-armed and are given all attention and a fair hearing. Appeasement, sludge, gush and flattery leave them cold. They respect realism in every phase and form, and if we were to drop our false modesty, puff out our chests, and tell Uncle Sam occasionally that we are as good a man as he is and even better he would respect us and probably like us all the more for straight talking.

In Switzerland, although Berne was the seat of the Legation, a good deal more of our time was spent at the Château de Hapsburg, situated on a branch of the Lake of Lucerne about a couple of miles from the town of Lucerne by road. A picturesque chalet rather than a Château, yet preserving its ancient tower, it has historic connections with the royal Hapsburgs and its green lawns led down to the lake opposite the towering bulk of the Rigi-Kulm. The chalet with its wide covered balcony overlooking the lake, provided an ideal place in which to entertain visitors or to admire the chameleon like changes of colour in the mountains and the limpid waters.

Leishman instructed me one morning to take his electric launch, glittering white and gold with an enormous Stars and Stripes fluttering in the stern, on to the *Hotel National* in Lucerne, and, presenting his compliments to the celebrated newspaper proprietor James Gordon Bennett, escort him back to the Château for luncheon. I landed at the National stage and picked my way through the usual concourse of visitors sitting idly at small tables, shaded from the hot sun by large coloured umbrellas, and entered the lounge. Although in his sixtieth year, with silvered hair, Gordon Bennett scarcely looked his age. He was tall and upright, bronzed, slim, and sprucely attired in white duck trousers - in which few men can look smart - a pea-jacket with gold buttons, a carnation in his button-hole, and carrying a peaked white and gold yachting cap in his hand.

Always an intriguing personality he was totally indifferent to the scandals associated with him and the alleged orgies supposed to happen on his yacht which at the time lay at Cannes. His well-preserved appearance, his power and influence, and his considerable wealth caused many a woman to set her cap at this eligible bachelor, but none had succeeded.

Although his father James Gordon Bennett the First had established the New York Herald as the most enterprising and well informed newspaper in America, his son James the Second was its great inspiration. He was the first newspaper proprietor to create spectacular ideas which set the whole world agog, such, for instance, as when he commissioned Sir Henry Stanley to discover the lost Livingstone in then "darkest" Africa who, when he found him in the wide open spaces thousands of miles from white man's civilisation perpetrated the unconscious immortal joke by greeting him with the question, "Dr. Livingstone, I presume?"

From the equator Gordon Bennett's eyes roved to the other extremity of the earth, the North Pole, and so he financed the Jeannette expedition, fore-runner of several successors. Probably, however, his greatest claim to popular celebrity was the inauguration of the Gordon-Bennett Trophy, to encourage motoring when automobilism was in its infancy, an international competition for teams of three which for many years held pride of place in Motoring circles throughout the world.

Apart from the **Herald**, now the **Herald-Tribune**, he founded the **New York Evening Telegram**, and ran for some time a daily edition of the *Herald* in England, including a Sunday edition. The daily proved a failure, but the Sunday edition, with its huge budget of magazine and coloured sections, obtained a large sale. His Paris edition, which ante-dated the **Paris Daily Mail** by many years, was widely read throughout the Continent before the Was, and was more cosmopolitan in outlook than its English rival. **The Paris Herald** was an especial pet of his and he indulged in many eccentric experiments. Some may remember even yet the inquisitive and never satisfied Old Philadelphia Lady, who wrote persistently to ask to have explained to her the difference between Fahrenheit and Centigrade. It was one of Gordon Bennett's little jests.

As the electric launch cut lightly through the water on its way to the Château, he remarked in a slow drawl, "You're English, I guess? The manager of the hotel told me you are Jahn Leishman's secretary." He grinned. "Sort o' puzzles me how Jahn came to pick on an Englishman for a kind of confidential job. He's gettin' Europeanised rapidly, I guess."

41

"I don't quite understand what you are getting at, Mr. Bennett," I said.

He laughed. "No? Wal, you see, Jahn in his business days in Amurrica used to call every Englishman a god-darned son-of-a-bitch. Seems to have shifted his viewpoint a bit since then."

"He is rather inclined to do so now when he's annoyed. I always hope that he doesn't include me in that category, but I must admit it's fairly comprehensive."

He laughed again, seemingly tickled by my remark. "Jahn don't mean it. If you ask me he's all out for pomp and glory. I reckon he'll marry those two kids of his to princes or counts before he's through. Diplomacy is a ticklish profession. Wants much tact, good manners, bowing and scraping. Jahn's wise to employ an Englishman. Suppose you're a linguist as well, eh?"

"I'm afraid I can't make a claim to that, sir. I am at home with French, have picked up some Italian and a smattering of German - just enough to ask my way about."

He stared about him at the changing scene, for we were just rounding the bluff to the arm of the lake where a glimpse could be caught of the Château. Then he remarked:

"It looks like an ideal life in these surroundings. Yet I guess a secretary-ship like this is a dead-end job. Maybe Jahn will settle you in business when he's through with this. Would you like that idea?"

"I am afraid I am not cut out for commerce, Mr. Bennett," I replied with a smile. "It wants special qualities I fear I don't possess."

"What sort of a line do you want to follow?"

This gave me my chance. "I should love to get into journalism. As a foreign correspondent, or foreign editor, starting maybe as a reporter. Foreign Affairs always fascinate me. I've found out some things since

I have worked with Mr. Leishman. Even when I was a boy at school I gloated over the foreign intelligence more than anything else."

"Is that so? Wal, we must have another talk, I guess . . . . Hi! There's the Minister! Hello, Jahn!"

Awaiting the launch on his private landing-stage was my chief and the two men, old friends, walked off together after friendly insulting remarks. Later that day I was sent for and Leishman asked me if l would like to become Mr. Gordon Bennett's correspondent in Eastern Switzerland. Seeing my crestfallen expression he explained that the idea was an extra free-time occupation, and would not interfere with my position with him. He thought it might be a good plan. It would keep me busy and out of mischief.

"Thank you, your Excellency," I cried almost overwhelmed. "And thank, you, Mr. Bennett. But, as you know, I have had no experience and I don't know what I would be expected to do."

"Listen here," interposed Bennett, "I want to place Lucerne on the *Herald's* list of gay resorts, and I want a breezy, chatty series of topical notes on the goings-on. Understand me? You have only to look at the paper to see the kind of stuff we want. It's a seasonal job, of course, for the place is dead after September until June. A couple of columns a week, racy, full of meat about the celebrities and you've always got your own Minister to write about as a start and Mrs. Leishman when she's here. Mention the hotels because that means advertisements. Anything in the way of news out of the ordinary and you can wire it to the News Editor. You got me?"

"Anything he writes about me," said my chief, chuckling, "will have to pass my blue pencil first!"

Thus did I make my first start in journalism. Subsequently I was offered a post on the **Paris Herald**, but I decided to refuse for various reasons, mainly because I was anxious to return to England and, if possible, get on the staff of a London newspaper.

CHAPTER III

A RUNG ON THE LADDER

In every ordered state wealth is a sacred thing: in Democracies it is the only sacred thing.

ANATOLE FRANCE

IN LONDON MY CASTLES IN THE AIR were rudely dispelled. I failed to obtain a job on any London newspaper when a chance took me to Newcastle upon Tyne where before long I was directing a magazine and an advertising agency. Whether I learnt much or little I experienced the vicissitudes of the business and learnt to set up type at the printers.

The magazine had possibilities if it could be capitalised and so in agreement with my co-director I trained to Town to see if I could discover any altruist who might be induced to put up a few thousands. At this time my family dwelt in Chelsea and my father was not too pleased with me. He was a bit of a Victorian tyrant who expected his offspring to quail under his frown and had long been certain that I was a rolling stone unable to settle down in a gentleman's profession. He approved of my secretarial post with an American diplomat, but could not forgive me for throwing in my hand when Leishman went to Constantinople, where circumstances were very different from easy going Berne and where I could only have held my job if I adopted American nationality, and this I refused to do.

Perhaps I should say a few words about my family at this point to any who may be in the least interested. My grandfather was a small squire or gentleman farmer who was killed in the hunting field, leaving a strong minded widow and three young sons, my father being the second. They were brought up in the family home at Waddon, Cambridgeshire, a delightful old house surrounded by a moat, and learnt to ride as soon as they could walk. Eventually the estate was sold, and with this and certain legacies each of the sons inherited about twenty thousand pounds and all of them managed somehow to dissipate their resources. The eldest became a priest, the youngest died childless, and I am the only surviving son. My father, greatly against his will, for he wanted to go into the Army, was made a lawyer.

Our branch of the Beaumont family is descended from a divine and poet of the seventeenth century, the Rev. Joseph Beaumont, D D, who became Master of Peterhouse, Cambridge, where his remains lie in the College Chapel. He married the niece of Sir Christopher Wren and was accounted no mean poet in his day. Two other poets were among my forebears, one being Francis Beaumont, the Elizabethan dramatist in conjunction with Fletcher and Thomas Gray, whose relics my grandmother presented to the Fitzwilliam Museum, Cambridge. The said Joseph was lineally descended from the Leicestershire Beaumonts, of whom the present head is Sir George Howland Beaumont, of Cole Orton Abbey.

These Beaumonts trace their descent in turn to Louis, the second son of Charles Capet, youngest son of King Louis VIII, who was crowned king of Jerusalem and Sicily in the crusades. King Louis died in 1226, and his grandson and namesake Louis married the heiress of Beaumont in Normandy, she being Great-grand-daughter of Waleran de Beaumont, Count of Meulan and Beaumont, also Earl of Worcester. His fourth son Henry, came to England with Edward I in 1502, was granted large estates in Leicestershire and made king of the Isle of Man for life. He married the daughter of Alexander Comyn, Earl of Buchan, and succeeded him as Constable of Scotland, also claiming the title of Earl of Buchan on the death of his brother-in-law John Comyn. He was summoned to the English parliament as Baron Beaumont. This family was related to the Plantagenets and John second Baron, was termed "consanguineous" by Edward II and Isabella of France, his Queen. The family produced many well-known statesmen, judges, and lawyers.

But this heiress of Beaumont in Normandy relates the family as direct descendants of earlier Beaumonts. Roger de Beaumont, of Beaumont, Meulan, and other castles in Normandy, was William the Conqueror's principal supporter, originally of Norwegian descent and closely related to the House of Normandy. His two sons Roger and Henry crossed to England with William, while their father remained behind as Chief of the Council. Robert the elder, married Ysobel, daughter of Hugh the Great, and a niece of King Philip of France, took a leading part in the Battle of Hastings, and received large grants in Warwickshire. Warwick Castle, built by the Conqueror, was entrusted to the care of his brother Henry. When, on the death of William, Robert, Duke of Normandy, made claim to the English throne, Robert de Beaumont supported William Rufus, admitted him to his Castle of Meulan, and opened the road to Paris.

This knight was the principal adviser and most powerful vassal of Rufus both in England and Normandy, and later, when Henry I succeeded, and most of the Norman Barons espoused the cause of Robert of Normandy, he was Henry's principal supporter and defeated them. In 1101, Ivo de Grantmesnil, one of the leading barons, was sentenced to death, but Robert induced the King to permit Ivo to embark on a pilgrimage to the Holy Land, the Comte de Beaumont and Meulan lending him the funds he required on the security of his Leicestershire estates, and as Ivo did not redeem the loan they became the English seat of the family, Henry created him Earl of Leicester and in 1103 he commanded the second line in the critical Battle of Tenchbrai, at which Robert of Normandy was utterly defeated and taken prisoner.

So it went on. Robert's twin sons, Robert and Waleran, were very prominent. Robert, second Earl, became Chief Justice, and Waleran principal adviser to King Stephen, who acted as Vice-Regent from 1158-1163 built abbeys and owned Worcester Castle, but he supported the Empress Matilda, daughter of Henry I, who married Geoffrey Plantagenet, and on her defeat and withdrawal he found it convenient to Withdraw to his Castle de Meulan, 34 miles from Paris. He married a daughter of the Count de Montfort, and his descendant was the Beaumont heiress who married Louis Capet, grandson of Louis

VIII. With Robert, the fourth Earl, the older Branch became extinct except for his two sisters, and the great inheritance of the de Beaumonts passed to them, who married into the two noble houses of de Montford and de Quency. The famous Simon de Montfort, fifth Earl of Leicester, called the "Father of Parliament," leader of the Barons, acquired his inheritance as the son of Amicia, the elder daughter of Robert, third Earl. Hence both branches of the de Beaumonts came together in Leicestershire, now represented by the present young Baronet.

These ancestors who were outstanding during the Norman kings and up to the sixteenth century, produced statesmen, warriors, administrators, judges and prelates, like Waleran's great-grandson Louis, Bishop of Durham, a haughty and turbulent priest who played no small part in the history of his time, and poets as well. The remains of their castles exist today more or less at Leicester Warwick, and Worcester, many in Normandy, and the remains of many abbeys and churches they endowed to perpetuate their fame, although their names, like their deeds, are to-day almost forgotten. Such is the ephemeral fate of many families who helped to weld the strong character of the British nation.

I don't know whether my father inherited his qualities from swash-bucklers of the past, but he was certainly dictatorial, haughty and proud. He was pretty good at invective when he got going, and the thought that I had buried myself in a northern city, engaged in running a bankrupt magazine and advertising conveyed the notion to his mind that I was daft. He did not know, and I did not tell him, that there was an attraction in the shape of a fair damsel whose people lived near Hexham, and who married me many years ago.

He was convinced that I was there for no good purpose and he was certain that my sister Muriel was destined to tread the road to ruin because she had the temerity to go on the stage, and to his mind the stage and immorality were synonymous terms. As a matter of fact, Muriel was a member of a pattern company that of Cyril Maude and Winifred Emery, and played small parts in a succession of successes at the Haymarket Theatre, such plays as *The Little Minister*, *The*

Manoeuvres of Jane, and *The Second in Command*, all of which played to full houses for over a year. She acted with Arthur Bourchier and Violet Vanbrugh that most charming an accomplished actress whose death has recently occurred - in *The Walls of Jericho* and subsequently with H B Irving in Barrie's *Admirable Crichton*, in which Gerald Du Maurier was in the cast and played opposite her. She married him shortly afterwards.

Bourchier called Muriel "my mascot," and it is curious that every play for which she was cast in her brief stage career proved a winner. One of the daintiest and prettiest of young actresses of the time, with a charming voice, she should have had a big stage career before her, but soon after her marriage she elected to adorn the domestic hearth although yet in her early twenties, she is to-day a remarkably young-looking woman, without a grey hair on her head, and forms a sisterly quartet with her three talented daughters, Angela, the eldest, and Daphne, both well-known novelists, and Jeanne, the youngest, an artist

When Muriel heard of my needs, being a girl of resource, she at once found a remedy. I must go and see a friend of hers who owned a weekly called **The Car Illustrated**, a great motorist and sportsman, a friend of King Edward, and a Member of Parliament. She arranged an appointment with him and I was invited to call.

The offices of this society-cum-motoring weekly were round the corner in Shaftesbury Avenue, and they overlooked Piccadilly Circus, that oft-dubbed hub of the British Empire, the rollicking centre of gaiety and bustle by day and night, for London kept far later hours than our rulers now permit, war conditions aside, for pubs kept open until 12.30 a.m. and strangely enough nothing terrible happened The roar of traffic was never-ending, though mostly horse-drawn, with the bustling hansom, but cars were making a growing if demure appearance on the streets.

In due course I was ushered into the Editor's room. He was out, but it did not seem to matter, for there were a number of persons sitting on divans or strolling about with cups of tea in their hands, while one tall man, who afterwards transpired to be Archibald Marshall, the novelist, was offering the assembled party bonbons, cakes, and fruit. There was a handsome, smartly dressed woman to whom I was introduced named Lady Troubridge, whose husband was Admiral Troubridge, and heaps of others all talking loudly and amusingly, several of whom appeared to possess titles also. The room, with several windows adorned with flowers looking across Piccadilly Circus, with its easy chairs and divans, its masses of flowers, and thick with cigarette smoke, gave me a first impression of being rather a social club than the Editor's sanctum.

Nobody took any notice of me until a tall and strikingly pretty girl with red hair took me in hand, gave me a cup of tea, and explained that Mr. Montagu was detained in the House of Commons, but she expected him at any minute. She transpired to be Miss Thornton, Montagu's personal secretary, and really the brains of the business, She was devoted to John Scott-Montagu, son and heir of Lord Montagu of Beaulieu, M.P., and lost her life in the last war when she accompanied him to India on the P. & O. liner *Egypt*, where he had been appointed Adviser in Mechanical Transport to the Government of India. It was one of those diabolical deeds which the Boche loves to perpetrate, for the crowded ship was unarmed and so they torpedoed her in a rough sea and left passengers and crew to drown. Few were saved, but Montagu was held up by a Guive vest.

Eventually the great man arrived. A little above medium height, strongly built, of athletic figure, he had a round merry face with wide-apart laughing blue eyes, curly brown hair and a slight light moustache. Democratic, unassuming, friendly, he was equally at home with the aristocracy or the working classes. Aged about thirty-five or six at this time, he was famous as a racing motorist, a first-class shot, a yachtsman, fisherman, cricketer, golfer, trained engineer, Member of Parliament and a J.P. for Hampshire, editor and journalist - for he often wrote articles on transport for the Press - and with all this contrived to manage the property at Beaulieu in the New Forest to which he was heir. His greatest interest lay in motoring, of which he was one of the earliest pioneers, and he did more to popularise it perhaps than any man with the exception of Lord Northcliffe. He had established his paper **The Car** about two years earlier.

Busy as he was, he listened to my plea patiently, advised me to cut my losses and return to London. Finally he offered me a job on his paper and remarked that he was thinking of establishing a monthly to be called **The Car Magazine** and that I would be useful on it.

It accepted his offer then and there, thanking him profusely, for he had certainly taken a weight off my mind. His terms were not over lavish, two pounds ten shillings a week, extra for any articles I might contribute. My job was sub-editing under C. L. Freeston, a sardonic person with a short aggressive beard and untidy hair, a man of great Fleet Street experience, an expert on motor journalism, and nursing a hearty contempt for the paper's "amateur" contributors.

Nevertheless **The Car**, printed by Eyre and Spottiswoode on the finest art paper, was an attractive journal of its genre, with beautiful pictures of ducal homes and the like, and of society lovelies and theatrical stars photographed in their latest de luxe, car - or one lent for the occasion by the manufacturers - although in justice be it said the paper had its technical side directed by a man named Pedley, a handsome young engineer always perfectly dressed by Savile Row. Fashions were in the capable hands of Lady Troubridge, Archibald Marshall reviewed the latest books, and Scott-Montagu himself wrote the leading article.

Life was pleasant and agreeable. Sometimes I was taken for a jaunt in a new type of car which Pedley was trying out. I first represented the journal when the old London General Omnibus Company took a Press-load on its initial full upper-decker motor-driven bus which climbed up Richmond Hill and we were entertained to luncheon by the Company at the Star and Garter Hotel. People in the streets stood and gaped as they saw the successor to the horse-drawn bus passing by. What was the world coming to? Yes, forty years have witnessed considerable changes.

If Scott-Montagu did not pay me a handsome salary he made it up in other directions. He always reserved a table for luncheon at Oddenino's Restaurant and often invited me to join his party, And I must say that his staff showed no hesitation in plain speaking. "Freeky," otherwise Freeston, a die-hard liberal with an undisguised contempt for the Tories and all their works, of which our employer was a supporter as M.P. for the New Forest Division, used to press home attacks on the Government and found amiable assistance from Marshall, whose Liberalism was somewhat of the idealistic character of the age before it took up with Socialism. Archie had a pretty house on the Montague Estate overlooking the Beaulieu river, where he wrote novels - **The House of Merrilees** and others which brought him some fame - and indulged in gardening, usually making his week-ends spin out from Friday to Tuesday. He was a close friend of Scott-Montagu and in conjunction with Lady Troubridge wrote his biography.

I was invited occasionally to spend the week-end with the Scott-Montagus at Beaulieu my hostess being his first wife Lady Cecil, a daughter of the Marquess of Lothian, who died many years ago. My host possessed several cars, high-powered for those days, including a big, red, four-cylindered Mercedes, the leading car of the time, and a week-end with him meant driving to the New Forest and back at break-neck speed. Motor cars, and especially powerful ones, were yet much of a novelty. Horses commonly shied at sight of them and it was usual for the motorist to stop as a terrified horse tried to charge a hedge, run into a ditch, or bolt. Motorists were necessarily detested by owners of horse-flesh and there was a legitimate reason for it because the highways were as yet innocent of tarring and a car moving at speed either raised a whirlwind of dust or hurled banks of mud and water on passers-by.

There was a speed limit of 20 m.p.h. but it was generally ignored. Scott-Montagu was an accomplished driver and engineer, so observe us racing along the main London-Southampton road at high speed in his big red Mercedes, wearing goggles - for a windscreen was not yet adopted - in an open touring car, he striving to reach Southampton before the London express which left Waterloo not long after us, and full of professional joy when he beat it, though we reached our destination covered in dust and grime. How he escaped the police, for there were police traps even then, I cannot say. It was believed that his popularity with the police forces of Surrey and Hampshire was such that when they heard the deep boom of his engine they conveniently looked the other way.

Anything with pulsating power behind it infatuated him. He was a director of the South-Western Railway but he was assuredly more interested in its transport and big engines than in its other business. The story is told that in the General Strike of 1926, Lord Montagu (as he was then), took over the driving of a main-line passenger express, and on arrival at Waterloo as he stood leaning on the plate-board, in overalls and a greasy cap, an old lady came up to him beaming.

"Well done, young man," she said, handing him sixpence, "I am so glad you are defying your Union."

To please her no doubt he accepted the tip and probably touched his cap in response. He was like that.

Another story about him also relating to a nimble sixpence, is worth telling. He was a favourite of King Edward, whom he first interested in motoring and taught to drive at Windsor. One day, near the Solent, a car rapidly approached a toll-bridge, when the keeper hurriedly shut the gate and forced the driver to a standstill.

"You don't sneak through wi'out payin' anyhow," he said, looking suspiciously at the two men in the car. "Two o' your sort slipped past me this mornin' and you don't catch me nappin' agen!"

The younger of the two men laughingly tendered the toll fee of sixpence and said that they had no intention to bilk him.

"Maybe not," grumbled the toll-keeper, "But now you just wait there till I've let that donkey-cart through."

Needless to add that the driver of the car was John Scott-Montague and his passenger King Edward.

His father the first Lord Montagu of Beaulieu was the third son of the fifth Duke of Buccleugh, and in one way or another John was related to the Marquesses of Bute, Lothian, and Bath, and the Earl of Wharncliffe. He succeeded to the title in 1929, with his seat at Palace House, once the great Gatehouse of the famous Cistercian Abbey built by King John in 1204, one of the many centres of the ancient Church seized by Henry VIII at the dissolution of the Monasteries, inspired, of course, by religious fervour and not with any desire to break the Tenth Commandment. They made good wine and strong beer did those Cistercians.

John Scott-Montagu's only weakness was that he tried to bite off more than he could chew. He was in demand by so many people and for so many important occasions that, if his time-table was thrown out in one place all the others followed. This recalls an amusing experience.

One Friday afternoon I found Miss Thornton bordering on distraction. She was desperate and almost in tears.

"I have tried to track him down everywhere," she cried, as she replaced the telephone receiver. "There is scarcely twenty minutes before the train leaves King's Cross and if he misses it everything will be ruined."

"Where has he to go?"

"To Welbeck Abbey for a week-end shoot with the Portlands. You know how fussy they are about their parties!"

Actually I knew nothing about it but held my peace. It seemed to be one of those unwritten social laws which everyone except an oaf was expected to know. I suggested that perhaps he might catch the next train.

"Nonsense! It's the only train to get him there in time for dinner. They are sending to meet him. . . . Oh, dear . . at last!"

In walked the boss, smiling and unconcerned. He carried an untidy brown-paper parcel whose contents threatened to disperse at any moment.

"What have you there?" demanded Miss Thornton.

"I was held up," explained Scott-Montagu, "and I forgot to order my man to pack my clothes and I couldn't find - "

"Are you proposing to go to Welbeck Abbey with that disgraceful parcel?" she exclaimed, snatching it from him, "I don't see how you can catch the train - "

"I don't either, if I waste any more time here," cried John, grabbing the parcel from her. "Where is my gun-case?"

"Here." She handed it to him. "Please see him off at King's Cross."

As luck would have it a hansom cab was just passing the door and Scott-Montagu caught the train just as it was beginning to pull out of the station, minus ticket, dropping articles out of the parcel on the platform. However, he had caught it, and if he reached the ducal mansion with a deficient brown-paper parcel, the Portlands' butler, no doubt, was equal to the occasion.

I met several well-known men when I was working on **The Car**. mainly under the *ægis* of Archie Marshall, a deer, genial, and wholly delightful companion. There was E. C. Bentley, then a leader-writer on the *Daily News*, to-day still in harness on the **Daily Telegraph**. Contemporary and friend at Oxford of "F.E." (later Lord Birkenhead), and Hilaire Belloc, versatile and witty, with a quiet dry sense of the ridiculous, Bentley, besides being an essayist and writer of detective novels, is the inventor of the "Clerihew," a new art form of satire.

Another man rather similar to Bentley was Ian Colvin, for many years the delightfully ironical leader-writer on the *Morning Post*, who at the time of the first Great War Wrote a revealing book called *The Germans in England*, in which he exposed Prussian machinations from early times as the Hanseatic League in the Middle Ages, and the way they murdered, robbed, committed acts of piracy, practised "frightfulness," and bribed kings of England - in short showing them in their true character through the ages. Colvin wrote the life of General Dyer, broken in India by the British Government because he did his duty and saved a massacre, the life also of Lord Carson among others he too, was no mean poet I met him last a short time before Lady Houston died, when with Warner Allen, another versatile litérateur and journalist, we motored down to Sandgate to luncheon with that redoutable lady. He, alas, is also no longer among us.

With Archie I first met the Falstaffian Gilbert Chesterton, essayist, poet, philosopher, master of paradox, then in his most sparkling period and inseparable from Hilaire Belloc. He was the great paradox himself, for he combined the simplicity of a child with the depth of a profound philosopher. He worked for me when I was later editing *The Bystander*, and we sometimes adjourned for a pint or so of beer to one or other of the hostelries in Fleet Street. He was always short of ready money, although he earned a considerable income by his pen, and I discovered that his wife deliberately kept him on an allowance, because if he had any large sum on him he would spend it immediately on some white elephant. In fact, like a child, he could not be entrusted with money.

Mrs. Gilbert Chesterton used to collect her husband's earnings and bank them. On the first occasion when she called on me and asked for his cheque. I remarked innocently that I supposed he was too busy to drop in himself.

"Shall I tell you what Gilbert was doing as I left home?" she inquired.

"Please do."

"He was playing a game with his toys."

Perhaps most famous of the young men of those days whom I met with Archie was Philip Kerr, later Marquess of Lothian, whose premature death at the end of 1940, when our Ambassador in Washington, came as a heavy blow to Americans as well as to ourselves. His succession to the title was scarcely dreamed of in the first years of the century. His father, Major-General Lord Ralph Kerr was the third son of the seventh Marquess and no fewer than three other holders of the title died before he succeeded his cousin in 1930 as the eleventh holder of the Marquessate and about a dozen lesser titles. He was a cousin of Lady Cecil Scott-Montagu.

In those days Phil Kerr dwelt in an old-fashioned house with a long refectory like dining room in Old Scotland Yard, where his friends turned up for "pot-luck" luncheons when he was down from Oxford. Conversation was invariably on political questions, and generally speaking most of the educated young men were ardent Liberals when English Liberalism was a living force and its ideals, if often mistaken, were sincere.

He first made his mark as one of Lord Milner's young men, who took a prominent part in the resettlement of South Africa after the Boer War, when Milner, as High Commissioner, with Kitchener signed the Treaty of Vereeniging, granting such generous terms that it exacerbated public opinion at home, but it was far-seeing and sowed the seeds of conciliation whose fruits ripened in the last great war as in the present. Milner, though a Liberal Imperialist, next to Joseph Chamberlain became the *bête noir* of the Liberals, and both, I might remark, were great Englishmen.

The Boer War was in a way a mild replica on a small scale of the present war. We were compelled to go to war with the Boer Republics because they denied our citizens their legal rights in South Africa, just as we were compelled to go to war with Germany in 1939 because they destroyed the freedom of Poland and Czechoslovakia. European public opinion, whose idea of legality profoundly differs from ours, only chose to see the moral right of the Boer Republics to do as they liked with their own, just as certain Axis sympathisers held the same views in regard to Germany and her neighbours. We began the Boer War disastrously, with a succession of serious defeats, because we were unprepared and sent out an inadequate force, as in this war. We treated the defeated Boers generously and they responded - with some exceptions - and by the Atlantic Charter we appear to be intending the same policy with the Axis when defeated. I trust second thoughts will prevail, for here the analogy ends. Generosity to international gangsters and thugs is quite another matter. It is a pity that Anglo-American statesmen fail to appreciate the foulness of mass German psychology.

When I first met Philip Kerr he was a slim and extremely good-looking boy, with wide apart eyes, his dark hair untidy, possessing a most infectious enthusiasm for his somewhat sentimental ideals. He could arouse enthusiasm among us, too, and he certainly performed the like wizardry with Mr. Lloyd George, whose principal private secretary and close confidante he was in the critical years from 1917 to 1921, in which latter period he played a considerable part behind the scenes at the Versailles Conference. In that Treaty, whether we took a leaf out of Milner's book or not, Germany was let off far too lightly and the fruit of this deed was Prussianism again rearing its hydra head with the physiognomy of Hitler.

Round Philip Kerr's table we argued frankly and fiercely the while we quaffed good beer out of tankards. In those halcyon days it cost fourpence a pint and was the real stuff at that, while whisky was 3s. 6d. a bottle and not 30 under proof either. In this damp climate it is difficult to arouse enthusiasm for any cause, good, bad, or indifferent, on soft drinks or next door to it, as our beer is nowadays with wines and spirits almost unprocurable, and I live in hopes that when this war is ended the people will insist upon being treated as adults and not as drink addicts by the authorities. We must put an end to the cranks and faddists who have so long kept us in chains.

All this time I was picking up a good deal about newspaper production, and Scott-Montagu, at the suggestion of Lord Northcliffe, who often dropped in to see him, decided to start his new monthly motor review which was called **The Car Magazine**, and he entrusted its joint-editorship to Archie Marshall and me.

A primary mistake was made with it. Scott-Montagu. proposed to price it at one shilling and I endeavoured in vain to persuade him to sell it for sixpence, for I felt sure that there was an abyss in newspaper psychology between sixpence and a shilling, more so than to-day when money purchases so little. Northcliffe threw out my proposal with the remark that motorists were a moneyed public and would as soon pay a shilling as sixpence, a strange argument from him since he was the arch-priest of cheaply-priced newspapers, on which he had amassed a great fortune.

Northcliffe for once was wrong. The magazine did not prove a financial success because the publisher reported that it was too expensive. People did not mind putting down a "tanner," but thought twice about a "bob." However, I wrote articles for it and was congratulated by both Northcliffe and Scott-Montagu on a "special" advocating the building of big trunk roads with connecting viaducts, the cost to be collected partly by tolls, a system later adopted in the U.S.A., Germany, and Italy.

I found myself becoming restless. It was a pleasant existence, but I was ambitious to get close to the heart of newspaper life. *The Car*, with its "high-life" appeal, left me cold. I kept my eyes on the political situation in which I saw Britain sitting in what was termed "splendid isolation," with not a friend in Europe, Germany looming steadily more dangerous on the horizon, and the Tory Government tottering to defeat. Besides that I was twenty-four and drifting. I began to keep my eye on the advertising columns of the *Times*.

One day I saw that an "old-established and high-class" firm of newspaper proprietors required an editor for a new illustrated light weekly. He had to be well-educated, a public school man, with ideas and originality, some knowledge of production, and young. Replies had to be sent to a box number. I wrote a somewhat perky application criticising the existing light Weeklies and throwing in a few ideas of my own.

The next day I received a wire: "Kindly call immediately at **Graphic** Office, Tallis Street, and ask for Carmichael Thomas." I had never heard of Mr. Thomas, but **The Graphic** was a household name since my birth. I picked up my hat and went straight away for the interview.

CHAPTER IV

MY FIRST JOURNALISTIC "CHILD"

"We who have lived through so many wars and rumours of wars are apt to imagine that the years before 1914 were days of over-confident tranquillity. No such feeling animated the British Foreign Office at the beginning of the century. At the end of the Boer War England was isolated and very much afraid of her isolation."

DOUGLAS JERROLD

THE PROSPEROUS-LOOKING offices of **The Graphic**, including **The Daily Graphic** and one or two odd journals, were only separated by the breadth of the street which then housed the **Daily Mail** and **Evening News**. It lay in the heart of the newspaper world.

As I walked up a wide oaken staircase to the first floor, the panelled wall on one side hung with original paintings and sketches signed by renowned artists of the time, including many Royal Academicians, it gave me a glow of satisfaction. It would be fine to work in this atmosphere. Before long I found myself ushered into a large room with several windows, some looking out on the Guildhall School of Music, others on the play-ground of the City of London School.

Seated behind a very large desk in a corner, surrounded with pictures and bound volumes, having a thick Turkey carpet and comfortable saddle-back chairs, was a benign little man with snow-white hair, a pink complexion, and rotund figure. He bestowed a fatherly smile on me, shook hands, and in a a high-pitched, squeaky voice, which descended in an amazing octave until it became lost in is boots, when he started again from a top note, waved me into a chair. He was Carmichael Thomas, Managing Director and Editor of **The Graphic**. Everyone called him Mr. Car.

It appeared that my application had arrived very late. The advertisement had been appearing for several days and I had only replied at the very end. Over five hundred applications had been received and the Directors had practically decided on the appointment, but certain remarks in my letter had interested "Mr. Car" so that he thought he would like to meet me. I murmured my acknowledgments. He then asked me all about myself and what I was doing, which seemed to meet with his satisfaction, after which he waxed enthusiastic about the new sixpenny weekly his directors had decided to put on the market.

It had to be very high class as became a daughter of *The Graphic*, concerning, itself with the lighter side of life, Society, travel, sport, art, theatres, books, and so on, and it would be printed on fine art paper and include colour supplements. There was, of course, an army of well-known artists whose work could be used. It was to be of handy size. He folded a copy of **The Graphic** in two and showed it to me.

"A handy size, you see," he crooned enthusiastically. "You can carry it in your pocket, such a convenience when travelling. Do you agree?"

"If that is the idea I agree," I replied. "But do people purchase six-penny Weeklies to put them in their pockets?"

He owned up that it was not the true reason. The object was purely utilitarian. The company printed **The Graphic** on their own machines and for nearly half the week they remained idle and yet they had to pay their printers full-time wages. The new weekly should fully occupy their machines. I congratulated him on his perspicacity.

"We have decided," he squeaked, "on the title. Ashby Sterry contributes a weekly gossipy article in **The Graphic** under the heading of '*The Bystander*.' This is to be the paper's name. Do you like it?"

I said that it did not appeal to me very much. Mr. Car gave me a glance of surprise and re-lighted his pipe, which was always going out.

"Surely it covers all we want?" he objected.

"You asked my opinion, didn't you? To my mind a bystander lacks personality. It doesn't mean a thing. It's too - static. I imagine your new paper will compete with **The Sketch** or **The Tatler**. both of which suggest gaiety. Still, after all, a rose by any other name - you know, and if your new weekly is gay and audacious the name will catch on. But such a name as '**Life**' would appeal more to me."

"I am sure," said Carmichael firmly, "that my brothers would not consent to alter the name."

Anyhow, I got the job.

The first issue of **The Bystander** was published in December 1903. The bookstalls were plastered with copies having a full-colour cover by Reginald Cleaver, who vied with Frank Craig in drawing the most beautiful and elegant young ladies of the period. Cleaver depicted a demure girl. in a pink dress seated on a divan with a copy of the new paper on her lap, placed in an Edwardian drawing-room, with a vase of flowers and other adornments. Frankly, it was of the chocolate-box type, but it gave an impression of refinement though certainly not of audacity. The Directors had decided on the cover as they had on the name and it continued for some months until I was sick to death of our inappropriate shop window. Fortunately the time arrived: when the advertisement manager came to my rescue by selling space and Cleaver's young lady had to go, much to the joy of the staff.

Crippled in this way, looking small for its price - journals were then very much cheaper than now - **The Bystander** dragged for some time. However, the staff working with me were young, inclined to ribaldry, and the journal tilted at many windmills, especially the snobbery and hypocrisy of the period, mixing a little seriousness with good-humoured fun. The best known humorous artists of the day found ready space on its pages, granted the jokes were amusing as well as well drawn but to present ideas very circumspect.

Chance threw across my path a brilliant young social contributor, Olive Viner, known as '*Blanche of The Bystander*' and subsequently as '*Eve of The Tatler,*' the sister of Richard Viner, well known in Fleet

Street, who was reported missing in Java when the Japs seized that island in 1942, he being a Flight Lieutenant in the R.A.F. Olive began by submitting paragraphs about celebrities, wittily written and revealing inside knowledge until she joined the staff and took over all the social pages. She knew a good many people and possessed an uncanny instinct for delicious sallies. It should be realised that at the beginning of the century Society - with a capital "S" - was essentially dominated by the aristocracy who revolved round the Throne. The landed nobility and gentry had not yet been ruined by death duties and paralysing taxation. Agriculture still remained the principal occupation of the nation. The era of the great industrialists was dawning, but had not socially arrived. Mere wealth and no pedigree did not admit into the inner ring and when King Edward became friendly with parvenu millionaires it shocked the nation. True, Trade was knocking hard on the door and *The Bystander* managed to get a good deal of fun out of its manoeuvres.

The youthful **Bystander** treated certain matters with due reverence, such as sport, racing and games It was to the fore in racing, having a winning tipster, and in the hunting season its records and pictures were the best in the country. Games like Rugby football, rackets, lawn tennis - it was the first illustrated to feature tournaments and give prises - Varsity sports, were all fully dealt with. Our photographers were everywhere. Country homes were presented in beautiful pictures.

Eric Clement Scott was our dramatic critic; Archibald Marshall reviewed books; Sir John Hammerton, so widely known as "J. A. H." gossiped about authors and forthcoming volumes , Alfred Hunter— later a director - was our first motor correspondent; and art, including *objets d'art*, was in the capable hands of Egan Mew, who composed a little jingle to cover the activities of the paper which was for years printed above the first editorial articles.

> *From London Town to Babylon,*
> *The pageant of the world goes by,*
> *For you, for you, I pause and con-*
> *A Stander-By.*

It was scarcely a classic, but we embellished it with a sketch of a he-man "conning" the said pageant of all sorts and conditions, from coronets to slaves. Altogether we gave the public a well up-to-date show for their nimble sixpence.

Yet for some time it languished. The reason was that so common among newspaper managements - Directors would not risk spending much money to popularise it. It came out as demurely as the girl on the cover instead of being thrust on the public. Weeklies were then inclined to be rather mealy-mouthed and subservient to convention and the Established Order of All Things, and the only way out, one I have practised several times always with success so far as the public are concerned if not with the proprietors, is to be audacious. We caricatured celebrities of the day and light-heartedly pilloried them. Thus the journal gradually got to be known and talked about.

Holt Thomas was my severest critic. He was the second son of the defunct founder of **The Graphic**, Carmichael being the eldest of some six sons who pretty well all contrived to fall out with one another. Holt was the Business Manager who controlled revenue and expenditure, printing, and so on. Except that he possessed an even funnier squeak than his brother he was otherwise totally unlike him. He was lanky, with inordinately long legs, dressed in latest style, foppishly in fact, had a small head, an immensely long nose and no chin, which gave him an undeniably parrot-like appearance. In reality he was no fool and no weakling, was ambitious, had married a wealthy woman, and led a cabal against Carmichael with the object of supplanting him, in which he was supported by most of the Thomas clan.

Failing in this overture, and as a result getting kicked out himself, he became one of the first pioneers of flying in England and was instrumental in bringing over Henri Farman, who gave a display at Sandown Park Racecourse, the first flight demonstration in this country where, before a thrilled and excited crowd, Farman limped round the course in a dangerous-looking contraption at a very low height, myself being one of the spectators. Holt was very much Old

School Tie and objected to our irreverent sallies at the expense of politicians and Society. However, as our circulation began to move upward his doubts evaporated.

Marie Corelli, more than anyone else, really sent **The Bystander** on the upgrade. That extraordinary flamboyant little creature was possessed with a conviction that she was destined by the Almighty to reform the morals of mankind in general and those of Britain in particular. In her **Sorrows of Satan** and in other novels she flagellated the sins of Society with a certain amount of truth and a good deal of cheap rhetoric, and the more she lashed out the better her books sold. There was some excuse for her enormous self-esteem, for she was far and away the biggest seller of the day. Hall Caine was a poor second.

She was all the rage in the Highest Circles. Queen Victoria had been one of her fans and Edward VII expressly invited her to his coronation. Even Gladstone, who may have been a sentimentalist but was certainly an intellectual, was said to have lingered for two hours drinking in her words while Mrs. Gladstone was left to wait outside her door in her brougham. T. P. O'Connor, then the most popular literary critic, raved over her work and other admirers included Swinburne, Ellen Terry, and Dean Stanley of Westminster Abbey, who in an Easter Sunday sermon in the Abbey quoted at length and with evident relish from **The Sorrows of Satan**, which same novel the erudite littérateur Andrew Lang described as "a gory nightmare."

It was not all luck that enabled me to acquire a series of articles from her pen, for it appeared that she was a reader of **The Bystander** and thought it would be a good medium for the launching of her shafts against Society, so she instructed her agent to give me the first offer. It is true that her price was stiff, but I persuaded my "Mr. Car" to give his authority. Her very first article, entitled *"Pagan London,"* hit the bull's-eye, a typical Corelli-like lashing of the Church with words stinging like scorpions. The London and provincial Press quoted largely from it and the clergy charged into the fray as she scourged the "sham Christianity" of the time. From a material standpoint the issue sold out immediately and subsequent numbers followed suit, although the printing order was largely increased, after which the journal never looked back. It became a "property" and in later years when William Harrison purchased **The Graphic** and **The Bystander** from their then owners, Iliffe's, he paid £250,000 for my journalistic offspring and only £200,000 for the parent journal. As they say, "money talks."

Marie Corelli was tiresome to manage. Not a word or comma of her copy must be altered or deleted. She besieged me with correspondence, using lavender-scented notepaper embossed with the name "Marie" in golden facsimile, together with her Stratford-on-Avon address. She affected violet ink and her handwriting was big but scratchy and she had the habit of rubber-stamping every page with the words 'not for Publication.'

This squat, plump little woman with faded, fuzzy, once-golden hair, called unexpectedly on me one day. "Are your the Editor?" she questioned, with the stress on "you." "You look a mere boy!" Then she asked abruptly, "Are you pleased with my articles?"

"More than pleased, Miss Corelli," I answered gravely, "I am delighted. They have created quite a furore."

"Everything I write always does," she said. "It is my object to make people think." She proceeded to explain that she was saving the country from becoming decadent and after implying that her name would be immortal she departed after inviting me to pay her a visit at her home in Shakespeare's stronghold. Here she drove about in a phaeton drawn by a pair of Shetland ponies, or exhibited herself to the townsfolk as she was slowly rowed up and down a stretch of the beautiful Avon, reclining on purple velvet cushions in her Venetian gondola with her swarthy gondolier complete in Venetian costume. She boasted of a noble Italian ancestry but it was said that she was born of British parents in the East End of London and had a scrappy education. If so, that she could become a force in the world of that time, redounded the more to her credit. Her weaknesses were her profound vanity and her lack of a sense of proportion.

Vanity is not generally a vice of authors, who are a singularly modest and retiring class of the community and who as a whole shrink from publicity. Phillips Oppenheim, whom I have known well for many years, is a case in point for he is singularly coy in respect of his work although he has over a hundred novels to his credit, but the same could not be said of his former rival in the field of romance where crooks and spies hob-nobbed with heroes and heroines in an international setting. I refer to William Le Queux, a big seller in his time using the same sort of technique as Phillips Oppenheim and Edgar Wallace. He was a journalist first and a novelist second, and as a rule journalists have the conceit knocked out of them. But he was as vain as a peacock.

I recollect walking with him in the Strand just opposite the old offices of **The Globe**, that venerable, pink-faced evening newspaper which was read by everyone. London was then far better served with evening papers than since the advent of newspaper trusts for besides the existing trio, **The Evening Standard, Evening News and Star**, there were **The Globe** as aforesaid, **The St. James Gazette, The Pall Mall Gazette** - all three Tory journals - **The Westminster Gazette**, printed on green news-print, and **The Sun**, a halfpenny like **The Evening News and Star**, whose outlook was independent. Competition between them all was throat-cutting and the public got the benefit of it, but it is noteworthy that they had scarcely invaded the domain of woman, social gossip was not in vogue, and they had not as yet published photographs.

This takes me to another point. The first picture daily was the **Daily Mirror**, which antedated **The Bystander** by a few weeks. Northcliffe founded it as a woman's paper and called it **The Woman's Mirror** but as such it proved an utter failure, and with his genius for improvisation he changed it over rapidly to a picture daily, using a very coarse screen, and its success was immediate. Actually the **Daily Graphic** was an illustrated daily and preceded **The Mirror** by several years but it relied mostly on line drawings in addition to which it was old-fashioned in display and its news material and editing were not imposing. Northcliffe, who had visited the United States many times, was acutely alive to the value of first-class news service and its adequate display which our conservative newspapers had failed to develop.

As I was saying, I was passing the *Globe* offices in the Strand with le Queux, whose site is now occupied in part by the Strand Palace Hotel. When that little bantam cock of a man - for he was scarcely over five feet of height - stopped dead, pointed his walking-stick at the great clock with a man of the world on its dial and exclaimed, "Look at it, my boy! Look at it! For years I was that paper's Parliamentary Reporter and then became it's foreign editor. That's where I learned my business. Many of the best plots of my novels were worked out within those four walls."

He stared moodily towards Burleigh Street where the red dog-carts then in use were waiting for an edition to come of the machines, and clutched my arm. "The day will come, Comyns," he said, "when papers like **The Globe** will be swallowed up by great newspaper trusts like Harmsworth is building up. Mark my words! It will be a bad day when public opinion is spoon-fed and controlled by powerful men who are commercialising the Press."

As a matter of fact **The Globe** was not swallowed up by a newspaper trust. It was to all intents and purposes sabotaged by the Government of Mr. Asquith in 1915. Our Army was being badly mauled in Flanders and on 15 November 1915, after Lord Northcliffe in the *Daily Mail* had exposed the chaos and had directly accused Kitchener as responsible for the shortage of high-explosive shells, **The Globe** reported that the Chief of the General Staff had offered his resignation because he could no longer tolerate the intrigues of his colleagues. The Press Bureau - the equivalent of the Ministry of Information - sent out a disclaimer that Lord Kitchener had resigned, which was not quite the same thing, for resignation would imply acceptance of it.

Next day **The Globe** insisted that Kitchener was going, and that same evening Major-General Sir "Frankie" Lloyd, in command of the London area, a dapper little Guardsman who was popularly reported to wear corsets, sent a pantechnicon to the offices, seized the last edition, and removed vital parts of the presses. This high-handed procedure aroused a perfect hullabaloo in Parliament, where Mr. Asquith denied the resignation and dismissed the *Globe* story as a "malignant and wicked lie," but it was later shown to have been well founded. "Jimmy" Hogge, the irrepressible Member for East Edinburgh, tried hard but in vain to extract some reply to his question why the Government had vented its spleen on *The Globe*, which had not been the only newspaper to spread the report.

The unfortunate **Globe** was suppressed for a fortnight, after which time Sir John (now Lord) Simon, as Home Secretary, who had issued the order, accepted an abject apology from the Managing Director who declared that there were no grounds for believing any dissension existed between Lord Kitchener and the Cabinet. However, in the second week of December the Chief of Staff tendered his resignation exactly as mentioned by *The Globe*, and it transpired that it had been the Ministerial intention to force his resignation earlier. Hence Asquith's "malignant lie" was what Winston Churchill would have termed a "terminological inexactitude." Its editor, the late Charles Palmer, flatly refused to associate himself with the apologia, and in a brief letter to *The Times* announced his own resignation. He was immediately invited by Mr. J. S, Elias, of *Odhams*, (now Lord Southwood), to become Assistant Editor of **John Bull**, where he succeeded Horatio Bottomley, entered Parliament, and was among the first initiators of the Federation of British Industries. I knew him quite well, an amusing companion, a hustler, and also a well-known dramatic critic.

This high-handed act of the Government greatly injured **The Globe** and before long there was one fewer evening paper in London. If the Press had stood solidly together on this matter by regarding it as an attempt to suborn the Press, and had contended, as it well might, that if a newspaper published something which the Government considered detrimental to the war effort its proper remedy was to prosecute the editor and publisher as in fact happened to **The Bystander** in 1916, Whose editor published a cartoon to which official exception was taken, and he was fined £100 and costs. If the Press combine to oppose some injustice no Government can stand up against it, but whether it is due to jealousy, or timidity in presenting a united front to the Government - who, all said and done, are our paid servants - it is rarely or never done.

I have however, gone too fast ahead in discussing the shortcomings of the Asquith Government. It was not until January 1906 that the Liberals, led by Sir Henry Campbell-Bannerman, in the General Election made a shambles of the Tories who had been in office for nearly ten years and had blotted their copy-book by muddles and unpreparedness in the Boer War.

Admittedly there are many operative reasons and many side-issues which cause electors to switch from one political Party to another, but it has been my experience that the most powerful influence among the rank and file is loss of confidence in their Ministers and never more is this evident than when they feel the effect by heavy losses in men and materials in a war where mistakes and carelessness or red tape lead to defeat as was the case in the first part of the Boer War. The British public may be peaceful but it does not mean that they are unwarlike when war is deemed necessary and when the nation is fighting they are adamant when excuses are made for humiliations for they expect Britain to prove victorious. When an election occurs they take swift revenge upon the offenders.

In 1906 there were additional reasons. The Radical wing of the Liberal Party made a huge song about Chinese labour which Lord Milner had permitted to be introduced into the diamond fields and frightened British labour by contending that the Trade Unions might be faced with the same competition at home. Doubtless it earned them many votes.

Perhaps more than all else was the violent contest between Free Trade and Protection, where the nigger in the woodpile was Joseph Chamberlain, far and away the most outstanding statesman of his age, and who, more than any man, had the merit of attracting either the most devoted followers or the most furious opponents. Having visited South Africa immediately after peace was made, and with the laudable idea of conciliating the late enemy, he was imbued with the necessity of developing trade with the Colonies and hence his scheme of Colonial Preference. He resigned office in 1902, so as to be free to preach his gospel while a preferential tariff was excluded from the Conservative Party programme. Despite the violent opposition of the

71

Free Traders in the Tory and Liberal Parties his policy made considerable headway and after the defeat of Balfour it was incorporated in the Conservative programme.

Instead of examining the proposals on their merits the Liberals endeavoured to cover him with scorn and contumely. They taunted him with having drawn a red herring across the path to lure the people away from the realisation of the Tories misdeeds, and with having twice wrecked his Party, in the first place the Gladstonian Radicals on the question of Home Rule for Ireland, and now the Unionist Party on the question of Imperial Preference. Frank Gould, the able cartoonist on the **Westminster Gazette,** the Low of the age, cleverly ridiculed "Joe" day after day, always representing him as a political twister, a sly fox, who was campaigning with his tongue in his cheek. Yet in my lifetime he stands out as the most honest sincere, and single-minded public man of all. He was so singularly frank that he disdained any subterfuge and never disguised from the people that if they gave a preference to the Colonies it must be a tax on food, which the Liberals seized on and plastered the country with posters saying "Your food will cost you more."

"Joe" addressing enormous audiences up and down the country, always smartly attired in a frock coat, the essential garment of formality of the time, with a tall hat, and an orchid in his buttonhole, slightly built, youthful-looking spoke bluntly. "Your agriculture is practically destroyed, he said sugar has gone, silk has gone, iron is threatened, wool is threatened, cotton will go." He explained that "the Colonies, in return for a very moderate preference will give us a substantial advantage in their markets." They turned a deaf ear to his logic. They believed that there was a trick in it. He addressed the bankers and financiers in the City of London, who gave him its Freedom engrossed in a golden casket, on which auspicious occasion he adjured the money-lenders in his famous phrase to "think Imperially." His last public speech in Birmingham, in July 1906, contained these words, "The Union of the Empire must be preceded and accompanied by a better sympathy." They might well be recalled to-day and to-morrow too, for the future of Britain is irrevocably bound up in the prosperity and development of the overseas Empire.

Big business was divided on the question. Manufacturers wanting export trade, from which they were being squeezed by the tariff barriers erected by all foreign nations, naturally supported Chamberlain. Bankers and financiers, bill-discounters and the like hated his very name, for they had waxed wealthy by giving accommodation to foreign importers who dumped their produce on our market while closing their own. Many of them transferred their subscriptions from the Unionist Party Chest to the Liberal. Thus with one thing and another the Liberals romped into office and power which they held by rapidly decreasing majorities until they collapsed under the weight of their incompetence in the year 1916.

It was the hey-day of the Little Englander and the Conscientious Objector. It was the era in which our national wealth was rapidly being dissipated. It was because the Liberals stuck to Free Trade and living was cheap. It was the day which saw the uprise of Germany in the economic sphere as in the military because our international financiers gave her merchants and manufacturers untold credit which brought many of them to ruin when war was declared in August 1914. The Bank of England had to go to their rescue to prevent a financial panic in the City.

For some of these years I edited **The Bystander**, and was promoted to **The Graphic**, joined Northcliffe and bitterly regretted it. I came to realise the vulgarity of Party politics, their inherent insincerity and huckster methods of duplicity. They knew enough during an election to beat the big drum of patriotism and afterwards to hide it away and play the wretched game of Party politics. There was not much I could do but I did what I could and never failed to support the policy of Colonial Preference as an essential step towards the prosperity of Britain and her Empire overseas. I began to feel that I had had enough of editing a journal whose *métier* was to philander with the more frivolous side of life.

Just then fate played apparently into my hands. The Thomas clan fell out, and a concerted move was made to get rid of Carmichael. In the result a committee of inquiry was set up and the clan were utterly defeated. A new board was elected and the three members of the investigating committee were on it with Carmichael as Chairman but shorn of some of his powers. The three men in question were typical of business. One was Alan Lupton, a Yorkshire woollen manufacturer of aristocratic bearing and Liberal leanings, Israel Davis, a wealthy barrister of the Middle Temple, and Alfred Hunter, a stockbroker, who with his brothers was the founder of the great process and photogravure firm, the Sun Engraving Co., of Milford Lane and Watford. Alfred, a friend of mine, was well known in lawn tennis circles.

The result of these changes soon became apparent. Carmichael retired from the Art Editorship of **The Graphic**, and became Managing Director solely. I was offered the full editorship - not the art side alone - and was told that the Directors proposed to give me full control and a free hand, with power to make any changes I thought necessary. It was a flattering offer to a young man still in his twenties.

To the present generation the name of **The Graphic** conveys little, but In the first decade of this century it held an almost unique position in illustrated journalism. Royalty patronised it, the Arts and Sciences swore by it, and almost every artist of note reproduced his work in its pages. Founded in 1869 by Mr. W. L. Thomas, who had been chief engraver on **The Illustrated London News** under Sir William Ingram, it quickly sprang into the front rank, rivalling the parent journal, its admirable treatment of the Franco-Prussian War of 1870 and the Siege of Paris having been very ably handled. Looking back to the years before I was connected with it **The Graphic** appealed to me as bolder and brighter in its presentation of subjects than the famous *I.L.N.*, for its artists used more "wash" and crayon and pencil, and it was to the fore with half-tone reproduction as opposed to line and wood engravings still often employed. Its artistic staff included such well-known names as Sir Luke Fildes, R.A., Professor Herkomer, R.A., R. Caton Woodville, the war correspondent, Paul Renouard, Frank Craig, E. J. Sullivan, Reginald and Ralph Cleaver, Bror Kronstrand, portrait-painter to the King of Sweden, Frederick Whiting, with a genius for drawing horses, Fred May, the humorist of *Punch*, and many others. In its representation of big events boldly treated it is safe to say that no illustrated journal on the earth could surpass *The Graphic*. On the literary side it was not so good. It usually dished up the same menu with little variety and its articles were set in such small type as to be uninspiring. Carmichael had dominated the picture side at the total expense of the reading side, yet to be effective there must be complete co-operation between the two.

When "Mr. Car," with a considerable gesture, told me what had been decided by the board his eyes nearly popped out of his head when to his astonishment I did not immediately jump at the offer, for to his mind the editorship of **The Graphic** was almost equal to that of *The Times*. I mumbled something to the effect that if I made a change my tastes lay more in the direction of becoming foreign editor of a daily.

"Are you serious?" he chirruped. "My dear young man, you have the chance of a lifetime! **The Graphic** is the most important property of the firm, for the **Daily Graphic** has never been financially successful and **The Bystander** is only now beginning to yield profits for the capital expended on it. There is another side also. **The Graphic.** is famed throughout the world and its editor enjoys a prominent position in the journalistic world. The Board are paying you the greatest compliment in their power and you would be foolish indeed to reject it."

He was right, of course. When I said that I was afraid that I might find myself hampered if I wanted to make any drastic changes he assured me that I was to be given a free hand. He said frankly that the Directors had agreed that the paper wanted some new blood and that maybe he - Carmichael - had become somewhat in a groove in the many years he had edited it. He told me that he should not interfere with any innovations I might propose, but that he was always at my disposal, especially in regard to the art side of the paper an offer I gratefully accepted and of which I frequently availed myself. To have surrendered his position must have been a considerable blow to him, but he never showed it, helped me generously over many stiles, supported me against a critical Board, and was a sincere friend. He passed away only a few months ago at the age of eighty-four, sprightly and kindly to the end.

In other respects I was treated generously. I remained as responsible editor of **The Bystander** for some months with the right to return there if I wished, leaving my assistant-editor, subsequently editor, Vivian Carter, in charge. My salary was placed on the four-figure mark and a new order established on **The Graphic.**

Thus less than five years since I first entered the portals of Tallis Street, with its panelled walls, I became tenant of the big, heavily-carpeted room where I was first interviewed, and into which the staff entered with some veneration.

CHAPTER V

THE INSULAR OUTLOOK

"It is a strange truth that no force has been so disruptive and iconoclastic, has torn up so many ancient roots, and pulled down so many holy places, as contentment with the world."

GILBERT K. CHESTERTON.

DULY INSTALLED in my new office I began to effect improvement in the appearance of the type or semi-type pages by using larger type and accordingly somewhat shorter articles, which I found could stand reduction, and in stronger headings. It had seemed to me that it was a fallacy to suppose that the editorial side of a pictorial newspaper should be made too subservient to the purely illustrated portion. I also varied the text and published articles by well-known writers whenever opportunity offered itself.

The greater problem, however, was whether to accord more space to photographs and less to drawings. I found that the Directors were inclined to larger photographic display. They considered that drawings of events were getting out of date except in special circumstances, and argued that **The Illustrated London News** and **The Sphere** - especially the latter - were using more photographs and fewer drawings. They also urged the question of saving money, for photographs were immeasurably cheaper than the work of artists.

My view, on the other hand, was that it depended on circumstances and I argued, that photographs gave on the whole a far less satisfactory representation of an actual event than an effective drawing. A race meeting, for example, could never adequately depict the main object itself, namely the race, as it appeared to the human eye, like the Derby that year to which I had sent Gilbert Holliday, who was brilliant in presenting horses, being a great horse-lover, and at the same time equally capable of figure subjects. Gilbert had swiftly sketched the finish, had included the Royal Family, King Edward, Queen Alexandra, the Duke of York, afterwards George V, the Duchess, later Queen Mary, and others in the Royal box, with the excited crowd along the rails. In a word, he got the atmosphere, and hurriedly completing his double-page drawing in the office it was rushed to the process and appeared in the paper that same week.

There was another aspect as well to be considered. Photographs were becoming more and more a feature of the daily Press and a weekly using the same photographs or something similar was in danger of giving its readers a stale dish. Drawings had been the distinctive feature of **The Graphic** from the beginning and to subordinate them to photographs would probably prove false economy. We wanted to give the public representations of events, such, for instance, as a Royal Drawing-room at Buckingham Palace - delightfully covered by Frank Craig - well away from the rest of the Press, always excepting **The Illustrated London News**, which we could only excel by sheer merit in representation.

In this argument I was successful. Carmichael Thomas was wholly with me, the more so since he had suspected that I might have leaned more towards the modern idea. Alan Lupton, who drove a coach-and-four, and tooled it down to Ascot during that delightful meeting, supported my viewpoint. The only discordant voice was that of Israel Davis, an elderly man without any *joie de vivre*, who looked on the question of economy alone and thought that ten or twelve guineas for a page drawing and sometimes much more was out of proportion to its value as against photographs which cost but a tithe. Sometimes, he complained, leading artists like Sir Luke Fildes were paid a hundred guineas or more for a plate. I foresaw that Israel Davis was going to be a thorn in the flesh.[1]

As a matter of fact the expense of drawings was good business, for the extra cost even if it amounted to a hundred pounds a week was a flea-bite compared with the total cost of production and the ever-

1 Mr Israel Davis, who died in March, 1943, made a great fortune by building cinema theatres.

headache to the publisher of returns of unsold copies. Far more accumulated in consequence in extra sales and more especially in advertising, for publicists were always on the alert and when they realised that **The Graphic** was going ahead increased advertising support followed.

Northcliffe realised the truth of this axiom absolutely. He never stinted expenditure if it brought results and he knew that in journalism penny wise is pound foolish. The proof of the economy policy was seen with my successor, J. M. Bulloch, formerly of **The Sphere**, who largely eliminated drawings made photographs his mainstay, and gradually whittled away the personality of **The Graphic**. Its popularity steadily waned, especially, too, since it lacked punch in its treatment of events until in the end it was impossible to resuscitate it. Strangely enough, it fell to my task to make the effort to restore it, but too late.

Very soon after I had taken over an opportunity arose with the Armenian Massacres at Adana in 1908, a series of savage and cruel attempts by the Young Turks to exterminate the National Armenian Party, whose aim was to establish an autonomous Christian province, whereas the Young Turk Party, which had seized power by a *coup d'état*, although affecting to be a constitutional régime and really aimed at restoring the Turkish Moslem Empire, showed its true face. The massacres were directed by Talaat Pasha - originally a telegraph clerk at Salonika - and the streets of Adana ran with blood. Public opinion in Britain was greatly stirred, the more so since to begin with the Young Turks, who had compelled the old Sultan Abdul Hamid to restore the Constitution of 1876 and call a Parliament, had been the pets of the Liberals, who now began to realise that it was only a blind to bid for British support.

War correspondents were sent out by the dailies and news agencies, but pictures of events were practically unprocurable. I decided that steps must be taken and found a young black-and-white artist named Booth, who had worked for **The Bystander** as a free-lance humorous artist, was ready to undertake a commission. He was packed off

79

quickly and, having made all the necessary arrangements, I saw him off to Paris where our office people met him and put him on the Constantinople express.

Booth reached the scene of events rapidly and sent home a number of valuable sketches of actual events by way of Syria and Greece. Some of his pencil sketches were published as received and others formed the basis of big drawings by Gilbert Holliday and de Hainen, a quick and reliable French artist on the staff. The result was gratifying, for *The Graphic* benefited considerably by this scoop both in sales and publicity. Here an enterprise, although necessarily expensive, left the photographers stone cold, and put the paper ahead of all its rivals. The new directors were very pleased with the result.

In the meantime I had not forgotten the lesson I had learned in Switzerland and I kept my eyes religiously on Germany's intrigues.

The year before the Young Turk Revolution, Sir Edward Grey, who succeeded Lord Lansdowne at the Foreign Office, had effected the Anglo-Russian Treaty, a very long-sighted move, and destined to have enormous repercussions. It is strange how the rippling waves of an important international pact may surge and envelop in due time individuals of no importance whatsoever and play a leading part in their careers. This was so in my case, for indirectly **The Graphic's** treatment of Russia led eventually to my resignation from that estimable journal and striking out in other directions altogether. Directly it led to an invitation to get in touch with the Foreign Office. It appeared that Sir Edward Grey was pleased with the display made by **The Graphic**, whence I was invited by his Private Secretary, then Mr. William Tyrrell, to call on him. It became a weekly arrangement and over a cup of tea I obtained a good deal of insight into the Foreign Office outlook. Tyrrell became later Under-Secretary of State for the Foreign Office, and subsequently Lord Tyrrell, our Ambassador in Paris from 1928 to 1934, a man of great charm and sagacity, to-day President of the British Board of Film Censors.

Grey's Anglo-Russian Treaty of 1907, except for the Balkans, completed in effect the encirclement of Germany. It actually removed causes of dispute in zones of interest in the Middle East, and Sir Edward was strongly attacked in Parliament by his own followers and on the Tory side especially by Nathaniel (later Lord) Curzon for making unnecessary concessions. That was strictly correct, but Grey set a sprat to catch a whale, for he removed long existing Russian suspicions of our good faith and evoked a new friendship, which continued without intermission until the Lenin Revolution. It was not popular among the millions in England, but its tremendous importance was seen when the last Great War opened up, for there was complete confidence between the Allies.

It was this same Treaty, however, which precipitated the Young Turk uprising, for previous to it Great Britain had supported Abdul Hamid against the Tsar. The Young Turks ascribed the turnover to Liberal dislike of the Sultan's despotic rule and hence they disguised their real aspirations behind a facade of a democratic movement, and it is probable that Germany, whose ideas about England have always been a thousand miles wide of the mark, put Enver and others of their leaders up to it all. There is no doubt but that the German secret service were working up trouble in the Balkans as an off-set to the Anglo-Russian Treaty, and as we discovered before the last war Enver, Talaat, Djavid, and others of the Young Turks were mere puppets in German hands, and were forced into the war against ourselves, ancient allies, to their immense loss.

While the Turks were in the throes of revolution, Germany in 1908 staged her next show-down. For in October Austria pounced on Bosnia Herzegovina and annexed it, although it was a flagrant breach of the Treaty of Berlin of 1878, which had for thirty years given peace to the stricken Balkan peoples. These provinces were under mandate to Austria-Hungary, but were a suzerain state of Turkey, like Bulgaria, whose monarch, the crafty Ferdinand, at once repudiated her dependence on the Porte.

The active role in this grab of Bosnia-Herzegovina was performed by Count Aerenthal, the Austro-Hungarian Foreign Minister, who was quick to recognise that Germany would support his action. Russia, realising at once that a disturbance of the Balkan *status quo* must lead to war, and as protector of the Slav people, protested. But Russia was weak. She was still licking her wounds after her great defeat by the Japanese in 1905, and was unprepared for a major war. Berlin intimated to St. Petersburg that refusal to accept the new situation meant war and actually delivered a quite uncalled for ultimatum which enabled the vainglorious Kaiser to turn the limelight on himself when he boasted in one of his orations that Germany has proved her loyalty to her Austrian ally by appearing on the scene in "shining armour." The world outside Russia tittered. The Muscovites said little, but they did not forget.

With Europe in this shaky condition it seemed to me that it might be a good plan if I could find an independent correspondent - independent in the sense of away from ordinary newspaper correspondents who found it difficult to get behind the news or, if they were to do so, be able to communicate it owing to close German espionage - who might keep me posted of what was going on behind the scenes. My thought turned to Ronald Squire, today widely known as a leading actor.

He was then a very young man, whom I had first met on one of my jaunts abroad, when I happened to visit Freiburg in the Black Forest, where his family lived, his father, Colonel Squirl (the real name, originally Norman d'Esquerel) having been in command of the Black Watch and now retired. I had accompanied most of the family to Switzerland, playing in a series of tennis tournaments at *Montreux*, *Chateau d'Oex*, and *Les Avants*. Ronnie was a fine player, held challenge cups, and played a very pretty game and whenever he played drew the gallery not only because of his strokes but because of his wonderful command of colloquial German. His vocabulary of German expletives was exhaustive and when he let them out in gallery asides it caused great amusement to those who could understand them.

Ronnie was at this time at a loose end. He had been fortunate enough to win a thousand pounds in a German State lottery, much to the disgust of the Frieburgers who regarded it as next door to highway robbery that a damned Englander should take their money. It was on the strength of this that he had treated his mother, brother, and sister to the Swiss visit, and as he was extravagant by nature I calculated that he had spent most of it. In addition, his father had written to me to beg me to discourage his son from going on the stage as he was threatening to do. But most of all I hit on him for my purpose because he not only spoke German like a native but he understood their mentality, having been largely brought up among them.

"Have you got through all that thousand pounds yet?"

"Nearly," he admitted.

"Would you like a job - an easy one?"

"What sort of a job?" He eyed me suspiciously.

"I want a representative in Berlin, Ronnie. You speak the *argot*. Probably you have some acquaintances there. What about it?"

He burst into laughter. "My dear chap, I couldn't possibly. I can't write for a paper. I should let you down absolutely."

"I don't want you to write for the paper. All you will have to do is to write me personally every week, telling me anything interesting you see or hear round you. Drop in at the Bier-Hallen, make yourself agreeable to any Germans who might know what is on the *tapis*. In other words, try to get behind the news and tell me. We can arrange a code in case letters are opened."

We two had discussed Germany quite a lot and both believed that she was preparing for war sooner rather than later. I hoped he would jump at the opportunity. I offered him a weekly allowance which would keep him in comfort and payment of expenses for entertainment, all for the price of a weekly letter, and suggested that a job should be found for him in the firm afterwards. He was by no means enthusiastic.

"I want to go on the stage," he admitted. "I would rather you would introduce me to Gerald du Maurier."

However, I obtained his acceptance and his father, delighted with the idea, promised him an additional allowance. He reported at Berlin and wrote his weekly letter, often giving me tit-bits of value, including one warning me to be careful about the foreign correspondent of **The Graphic**.

One day, to my surprise, he walked into my office and said he had thrown in his hand. He said he was miserable in Berlin and could stand the job no longer. After some questioning I elicited that he was still stage-struck and that through the influence of two friends of his on **The Bystander**, one being Douglas Miller, the other Basil Macdonald Hastings - a well-known wit, essayist and playwright, who died in 1926 at the early age of forty-five - he had obtained a theatrical job. It was useless to reproach him. I shrugged my shoulders and asked what sort of a theatrical job. He murmured something about "Harry Tate," and left me. Later I had a word with "Doug" Miller, a queer Fleet Street character, who wrote on motoring for **The Bystander** and other journals. I asked him what was this job with Harry Tate.

"Huh, Beau," replied "Doug" - as everyone called him - who spoke in short, clipped sentences which proceeded from deep down in his shoes. "Quite all right . . . Harry fixed him up . . . started last night . . . went round in Harry's big car. . . . All as merry as crickets. . . .".

"I shouldn't wonder," I said ironically, "that he's the chap in Harry's sketch '*Motoring*' who walks past the car and strikes a match on the panel work to light his cigarette. One of those thoughtful, silent parts!"

"You're right, Beau . . . first shot . . . Ronnie has his foot on the first rung of the ladder to fame."

So that was it. Ah, well, *chacun à son gout*! Yet Doug was right, for Ronald Squire had set his foot on the first rung of the ladder to fame, He got his first real chance after all with du Maurier, playing in many of his productions, and has often been compared with the late Charles Hawtrey. It was disappointing for his father no doubt, but Ronnie was like thousands of individualists who prefer to choose their own path to one selected by parents, in his case the Army.

Douglas Miller was a well-known Fleet Street character, a man of considerable knowledge, an M.A. of Cambridge, who had hunted a lot and was said to have ridden in the Grand National. He earned quite a good income writing on motoring and sport, but he was usually in an impecunious condition and yet always a cheerful optimist. A small and slight man of nondescript age, anything between the late thirties and fifties, with soft brown hair, a wrinkled skin, and a big strawberry nose, he was no Adonis. He lived in dingy lodgings in Bloomsbury, which he could not quit since he was ever in debt to his landlady, and spent most of his substance in the Fleet Street hostelries where he could consume enormous quantities of whisky without ever getting fuddled let alone intoxicated. He was good company, a droll in his way, always tolerant, and had a fund of racy stories which were very funny as he told them. He knew all the motor magnates and was very useful in working up advertising business with them. He posed as a great authority on cars and certainly wrote the sort of copy of which the motor manufacturers approved, but all the same I very much doubt whether he could have driven a car to save his life.

He liked nothing better than to arrange for the loan of a new type car for me for an outing on a Sunday, he making one of the party. On one occasion when a sister-in-law was staying with my wife and me at Thames Ditton, where we then living, Doug insisted upon borrowing a car to drive down to Harry Preston's famous "Royal York" at Brighton. He duly presented himself with a powerful Napier car, lent by S. F. Edge, and a uniformed chauffeur, an open car in those days, on a remarkably cold day. "Cold," said he cheerfully; "Never mind. We know the way to keep warm."

He had many places of call along the Brighton Road, and as he approached them became very alert for it seemed to be a matter of honour on his part to enter on some pretext or other. In those happy days anybody who was a *bona-fide* traveller, that is to say if he had come a distance of two miles or over from a hostelry, was entitled to enter it and imbibe alcoholic refreshment at any hour. One particularly favoured haunt was the old "George", at Crawley, half-way to Brighton, and here he had some excuse, for the ladies were cold and Doug promised to borrow a second rug for them. Instead of the rug he appeared with glasses of hot Bovril fortified with double brandies. Amused as were my wife and her sister, with his antics they refused this generous offer so it was left to the men of the party to consume them on the principle that it's an ill-wind, etc., but I obtained them Bovril without alcohol, which to Doug was no Bovril at all. After various other drinks, borrowing a rug, and chipping the Phoebe behind the bar who was lost in irrepressible giggles, Doug borrowed the money from me to meet the bill, and on we proceeded. I set my foot down against further stops.

At Brighton he carried off the honours with elegance when dapper little Harry Preston appeared, who gave me a dig in the ribs and a big wink, raised the ladies' hands to his lips, and at once ordered a bottle of the "old and the bold," otherwise champagne, for the occasion. I often stayed with Harry both at the "Royal York" and "Albion," always having great fun, and he also invited me to his parties in town when there was a big boxing match on to which we went after a Lucullan repast. In the sacred name of sport this little publican - as he described himself to me many a time - could assemble round his hospitable board a party including not infrequently the Prince of Wales (Duke of Windsor), peers of the realm, politicians, generals, admirals, trainers, Jockeys, any lion of the hour, and mere Journalists, where all met informally on equal terms.

Meanwhile in Germany von Tirpitz was rapidly proceeding with his feverish plans to build a navy able to challenge us for the mastery of the seas. German dreadnoughts were launched "according to plan" in quick succession. It gave me an opportunity to indicate what the Kaiser was accomplishing, so **The Graphic** published a huge panorama of the entire German Navy built and in process of building. The article on the subject was written by Sir Alan Burgoyne, a leading member of the Navy League, whose book, **The War Inevitable**, at this time had created great discussion.

I followed this up with another on the German Army, and was fortunate enough to induce the famous "Bobs," Lord Roberts, to write it. This great little general was revered by the nation, and at this time he was doing his best to advocate compulsory military service in order to meet the might of Germany. His plea fell on deaf ears as far as the Government was concerned, but had he received encouragement the 1914-18 war would have been prepared with more than seven divisions when it started and might have been over far sooner. It is pitiful to recall what opportunities our nation has let slip through the public faith in its Governments to see the thing through. If the nation has no sense of political responsibility it means that it is passive, and passiveness is half-way to becoming servile.

These special articles and others with punch were greatly applauded by the readers of **The Graphic**. Carmichael Thomas supported me in these endeavours but I began to scent disapproval with two of the other directors, Messrs. Lupton and Davis already mentioned. I had a tiff with them about the Zeppelins.

Rumours were spread abroad that German "Zepps" were crossing our coasts by night. Their engines had been heard. Some reported that they had seen them. Then a clergyman living not far from Hull sent me a sketch of a Zeppelin he had seen overhead at night, had followed its direction of flight, and accompanied his statement with a sworn affidavit. I instructed one of our artists to draw a page of the occurrence, terming it the "Fly by Night," and as a result I attended a board meeting to be reprimanded. The offending page lay before them.

"You don't seriously believe that a Zeppelin flew over our coast, do you?" questioned tall, good-looking Alan Lupton, member of a well-known pacifist family, "for it is absurd, of course."

"Obviously I do," I replied, "or I should not have published the drawing."

"My dear fellow, it is ludicrous! It is impossible that it could fly all the distance from Lake Constance and get home again. Seen only by one person!"

"Come, come, Mr. Lupton," I protested. "Several of the dailies have reported their presence. In this case we have the evidence of a clergyman who not only sent us the sketch hot but swore an affidavit. A Yorkshireman, too - from your own county!"

"Not reputable papers," objected Lupton, "and you can't accept the ha'penny rags," alluding to the **Daily Express**, **Daily Mail**, and others. He looked across at Davis: "What is your view?"

"I concur entirely," said Israel Davis, coldly. "**The Graphic** is not a political organ and such matters as this Zeppelin drawing are dangerously controversial. The Editor's articles upon Germany's naval and army strength are unsettling Jingo propaganda and can only have the effect of disturbing our friendly relations with Germany."

"To warn our country that Germany is arming to the teeth, especially after the Bosnia-Herzegovina episode and other matters, is scarcely my interpretation of Jingoism," I retorted. "But please tell me where you draw the line between what you term 'politics' and events? A Zeppelin over our shores is surely an event of national interest and I as your Editor claim that it is good journalism to portray it."

"I fear you are a warmonger," replied Davis, "and this sort of thing is disturbing to business if no more."

"You do not imagine that Germany wants to go to war with us, Beaumont, do you?" interposed Lupton.

"I am certain of it, and the longer we bury our heads in the sand the more certain they will catch us unprepared."

"What a crazy idea!" laughed Lupton. "Why on earth should Germany want to make war on us? Our markets are open to her. We are her best customers. We finance her mercantile operations. Don't you realise that she would cut her own throat?"

"Unfortunately Germany does not hold the same views," I said. "I discovered some of her manoeuvres years ago when I was living in Switzerland. Her idea is to catch us napping, overthrow us, and become mistress of the world while we are her slaves."

"I have for some time been afraid that you hold reactionary views," said Davis, acidly. "And now I am sure of it. I should like to think otherwise."

"You may think as you like, Mr. Davis," I returned with a smile. "I am a materialist, that's all. Perhaps you can explain why Germany is building vast armaments and especially her navy and against whom. You don't imagine that she is wasting money on them and that they are not for a definite purpose, do you?"

The storm blew over. Carmichael and Hunter stood by me on the issue, but it was only the first round. As far as the Zeppelin was concerned, before long it transpired that one of them had crossed the Atlantic and it was proved that they had paid many reconnaissance and testing visits to our shores. In the war these scientific windbags created much havoc until their vulnerability was proved. But the argument I have reconstructed indicates the opinion of large numbers of educated persons before the last war who were totally incapable of assessing the inordinate ambition of Germany to acquire world supremacy to which Britain and her Empire barred the way. For in those days neither France nor the United States counted. It was Britain who frustrated her and whom they hated as they always will.

Another storm was brewing in the offing. A man named Lucien Wolf wrote a weekly article in **The Graphic** on foreign affairs, called the "F.O. Bag." An elderly red-haired Jew of German origin, he was also the Foreign Editor of the **Daily Graphic**, but his Graphic article, well paid for, helped to augment his income to reach a figure commensurate with his position as an Authority. He often wrote leading articles in the "Daily" and contributed to political reviews of more or less Liberal tendency. He wielded a pontifical pen and was regarded as a considerable authority on such subjects, not by men like the astute Leo Maxse of the **National Review**, most widely read of all the reviews, but by my employers whose knowledge of such subjects was by no means profound.

My visits to the Foreign Office and Mr. Tyrrell every Friday made it clear enough how important it was to popularise the *Entente* with Russia, Wolf's articles worried me. His attitude was a veiled disparagement of Russia as an ally with doubts thrown on the Tsar's loyalty towards us. If they were not pro-German - he was too clever for that - they were harmful. On one or two occasions I criticised his attitude with no notable change and finally I deleted certain passages which were opposed to the trend of the journal. He called on me and expostulated.

"Never before have my articles been tampered with," he said indignantly. "And I must beg you to leave my copy in future as I write it."

"I have told you several times before, Mr. Wolf," I returned, "that this journal supports the Government policy and the *Entente* - and that goes for Russia, too. If you damn it by implication I shall not publish what you write."

He denied the accusation. "Moreover," he went on, "I have written this page the F.O. Bag, for years before you ever entered the firm, and neither Mr. Car nor Mr. Joyce," who had been previously the Literary Editor, "ever dreamed of interfering with my work. I accept full responsibility for my work and will be answerable to the directors."

"No you will not," I said. "I am answerable, not you. The directors gave me a free hand and you will obey my instructions or take the consequences."

"What do you mean?" he queried, giving me a dirty look.

"That I am warning you, Mr. Wolf - for the last time."

He was furious, of course, as I fully expected he would be. An oldish man, with an established reputation on foreign affairs, he naturally regarded me as an impertinent young upstart ignoramus. He believed that he was strong enough to prevail. For a while he showed circumspection but gradually he allowed his anti-Russian prejudices to creep into his work. The day came when I omitted his article and told him that I regarded his contract as void.

He reported the matter to Carmichael and so did I, who appreciated my position but gave me rather a wry smile. "We shall have our friends Davis and Lupton on the warpath, no doubt," he remarked, as indeed was the case. I believe in his heart of hearts he detested both of them, for they were always meddling in matters of which they possessed no knowledge.

Once again I was on the mat. They invited me to explain why I had summarily dismissed so invaluable a contributor as Mr. Wolf. In reply I detailed the circumstances and finally reminded them that they had specifically granted me full editorial control and here was an instance where I had been compelled to exercise it. However brilliant he might be, if a contributor could defy the Editor and run counter to him, it must lead to an intolerable situation for no paper could survive under such conditions. Finally I said that I expected them to support my action in accordance with their own undertaking.

There was something of a pause and then Israel Davis said quite softly, "You appreciate that Lucien Wolf is widely recognised as perhaps the greatest living authority in the country on foreign affairs."

"You rate him higher than I do," I replied.

"Perhaps you are unaware that when he offered his services to the *Daily Graphic* as its foreign editor it was regarded as a great score, for he might have picked and chosen in many other directions. Consequently, to make it worth his while, his weekly article in *The Graphic* was included in the arrangement by Mr. Car here. It has worked hitherto without friction and now you propose to upset it."

"Wolf has upset it, Mr. Davis, not I. You surely don't propose that your Editor is to adapt his paper to fit in with Mr. Wolf's eccentricities?"

"Why should the Editor concern himself with Mr. Wolf's views? He writes as an independent critic and you are not bound by what he may say."

"I agree that a contributor may sometimes take his own line of country but it is a different matter when he consistently adopts a line of policy which in this case if it were taken to a logical conclusion might damage the *Entente Cordiale* with France and Russia. That is the policy of the Government, and **The Graphic**, without being a Party organ, has always supported the Government in foreign affairs."

"Wolf is striving for a better understanding with Germany," remarked Lupton, "and I dare say that like many of us he hopes that with a little good-will on both sides permanent good relations could be established. Obviously the peace of the world will be better assured if we are friends than at daggers drawn. That I fancy is behind Mr. Davis's mind."

"Your sentiments are admirable, Mr. Lupton," I said, "But I am afraid that your views are not those of Sir Edward Grey."

"How do you know?"

"Because I visit the Foreign Office every week and interview Sir Edward's private political secretary, who very discreetly, of course, indicates his chief's attitude. For instance, the Foreign Office are anxious to obtain all the Press support possible to foster the agreement with

Russia. Lucien Wolf is certainly not assisting in the matter. In fact he seems to lose few chances to snipe at the Tsar's government."

I saw that I had scored with this revelation of confidences straight from the horse's mouth it might be said. Lupton raised his eye-brows. Carmichael concealed a smile by lighting his pipe. Davis looked incredulous.

"You have a personal interview with Sir Edward Grey's private secretary every week?" he repeated. "What is his name?"

"Mr. Tyrrell. I have a personal talk and usually a cup of tea with him. He tries to assist editors and is very discreet but I have gathered that Sir Edward labours under no delusions as to the German intentions. Only recently I learnt that the true reason why the Kaiser dismissed the Prince von Bülow from the Chancellorship and put in the nonentity Bethmann von Hollweg was because Bülow was suspected of harbouring friendly feelings towards us," I added, with a laugh. "If his friendliness towards us was like his brother's, the Baron von Bülow, it would be difficult to imagine that they were cordial."

"The Editor," interposed Carmichael, "some years ago was to some extent concerned with diplomacy and he is probably alluding to that period: Am I right?" He looked across at me.

"Yes, Mr. Car. I was private secretary to Mr. Leishman, then United States Minister to Switzerland, now Ambassador to Germany. I knew Baron von Bülow and his wife and I found out then - some years ago - that he was directing secretly espionage on a huge scale, although he was officially the German Envoy he was preparing for the war destined to place *Deutschland über alles*. He had no love for us."

The debate had taken a good deal of the sting out of the Davis offensive. Lupton leaned back in his chair.

"After all," he observed, "if Wolf disregards the instructions of our Editor it is his own undoing."

"Perhaps a warning from Mr Car might meet the situation," said Davis, wavering. "I think it was rash to dismiss him so summarily. We should remember that he has a big following and is an asset to our papers."

I shook my head. "I am sorry that what Mr. Davis proposes is not possible. I have already appointed his successor."

"Rather rushing your fences, isn't it?" ejaculated Lupton.

"Simply precaution," I returned. "I must not have any hiatus between Wolf and his successor and I had accordingly laid my plans in case there was a break."

"And who is your new foreign affairs contributor?" sneered Davis, whose manner betokened his irritation.

"He is Charles Watney, Foreign Editor of the *Daily Mail*: He is highly regarded writes very well and authoritatively. Lord Northcliffe has a high opinion of his abilities."

So the storm blew over. Watney, a carroty-haired, queer person who ambled along a street seemingly in a day-dream, wrote straight-speaking articles in place of the tortuous and equivocal meanderings of Lucien Wolf. The subject, however, was not dead. It remained dormant to burst forth presently afresh.

Some time after this *contretemps* which I have recalled as nearly as possible as demonstrating the mentality of a large section of the business world a few years before the first Great War, I received a message one day that Lord Northcliffe would like to have a talk with me.

Curious to learn what he wanted with me I crossed the street and was conducted to his long room in Carmelite House, where there stood in the window the famous bust of Napoleon on whom he was popularly supposed to have modelled himself. Certainly both had the same hanging fringe of hair and both were ruthless.

Some six years had slipped by since I had last seen him in Scott-Montagu's editorial room sipping a cup of tea handed him by the dainty fingers of Miss Thornton. Then he had been plain Alfred Harmsworth, watched by Fleet Street and the world with a certain suspicion as a cheap-jack newspaper publisher. To-day his vast business had grown by leaps and bounds, he was already a multimillionaire, and had emerged from a plain "mister" first to the rank of a baronet and then to a peer of the realm. Politically he had reached immense stature for besides his control of the *Daily Mail* and a host of other publications, he now directed the destinies of *The Times*, the doyen of world newspapers.

He greeted me with a friendly grin and a shake of the hand and there was nothing patronising as he recalled our earlier meeting with "John," and even remembered the **Car Magazine** which had been priced too highly. When I remarked that I had pressed for a sixpenny but had been over-ruled in the face of so great an authority, he retorted quickly that it was because we did not give the public a shillingsworth of value. "Remember that, my boy," he snapped. "If you want to be successful you must always give the public value for money. That is how I have made my fortune." I bowed but reflected that this was not his purpose in sending for me.

"I have heard that you are having some trouble across the road" he asked abruptly. "Haven't you been falling out with your directors?" Seeing my surprise he grinned. "I always make its my business to be aware of what other publishing firms are doing. Remember that too. It may be useful to you. I am a shareholder in your company and have ways and means of learning what happens. You have dismissed Lucien Wolf from **The Graphic** and have employed my foreign editor Watney in his place. It interests me."

"I hope you have no objection to my having acquired Watney's services?" I asked.

"Not in the least. You show your perspicacity. Assuming that I have first call on the services of my staff and that outside work does not interfere with their duties here - for I pay my people well - I am pleased when they can earn yet more. I am interested in the motives that prompted you to take such at step if you feel inclined to confide them to me."

Whereupon and nothing loath I confided to this remarkable man the difficulties I had experienced with Wolf and certain of the directors. I told him how I had watched Germany's spider-like methods to weave a web to entangle Britain, my anxiety to do what I could to arouse public opinion to a full realisation of the peril, Wolf's anti-Russian attitude and defiance, and I outlined briefly my former experience with Leishman even including my flirtations with the Baroness von Bülow, which seemed to amuse him. When I had ended he said in his abrupt manner:

"Then you believe war with Germany is inevitable?"

"I am sorry to say I do, Lord Northcliffe," I replied.

He took a turn or two in his long room and then paused before me. He looked me straight in the eyes.

"I have been intending for some time to visit Germany and see for myself what is happening there. My **Daily Mail** Berlin correspondent is anxious that I should." With a quizzing glance he proceeded: "I find I can manage a few days next week, and there is a further inducement that my wife wants to visit Berlin for personal reasons. If I were to invite you to come as my guest and we could ferret out the lie of the land for ourselves could you manage to obtain leave without saying anything about this matter?"

"Surely I could!" I exclaimed.

"Would you like to come with us?"

"Of course I should, Lord Northcliffe. It is an extremely generous invitation on your part and I can scarcely thank you sufficiently."

"It may be worth your while, my boy," he said. Then he snapped: "See your passport is in order. You have nothing else to do, for everything will be arranged. George Sutton - I gather you have met him - will keep in touch with you and give you all necessary directions. I rely on your discretion. Are you married?"

"Yes."

"Be discreet!"

Lord Montague of Beaulieu

Mr. Carmichael ["Car"] Thomas
[*From a portrait by Sir Luke Fildes.*]

CHAPTER VI

OUT OF THE FRYING-PAN . . .

"Those principally responsible (for German rearmament) are the Anglo Saxons, with their incorrigible faculty of illusion on the subject of Germany. . After the warmongers of Berlin the principal culprits are the British and French pacifists."

PROFESSOR FOESTER (a German).

TRAVELLING VIA OSTEND we reached Berlin in the early morning of a fine day and drove to the famous *Hotel Adlon*, in the Unter den Linden, where a suite had been reserved. I suspect that it was many years since the Chief - as his staff called him and as he liked to be termed - had travelled with so light a retinue, for beyond Lady Northcliffe, his private secretary Price, a valet and a lady's maid, there was only myself as his solitary guest.

From the balcony of the *salon* one had a fine view of the *va et vient* in the heart of the German capital, a continually changing scene of activity along that great wide thoroughfare with its double line of lime trees down the centre, and on the side-walks, the concourse of vehicles of all descriptions, the clanging of trains, the shops and cafés and restaurants groaning with supplies, while now and again a company of soldiers on their way to and from the Kaiser's Palace, a little higher up the street, would march goose-stepping along. On our left stood the Brandenburg Gate and the Tiergarten beyond. It all looked peaceful.

On our journey my hosts set to work to make me feel completely at ease, and I may say that Lady Northcliffe is one of the most charming and considerate women I have ever met. She happened to have met my sister Muriel and her husband Gerald du Maurier, which made a bond between us. Northcliffe was bubbling over with fun, and possessed a form of Puckish humour when the mood seized him. He painted imaginary pictures of the reception we would get in Germany, darkly mentioned dungeons and fortresses where we would be thrown as spies, talked of secret agents dogging our footsteps, and in short was what the Scots term jocose. As a matter of fact we learned soon afterwards that he - and I, too, for some reason - were continually under close surveillance, for the authorities suspected something was in the wind, but did not know what. Outwardly they were honoured to have so distinguished a guest in their midst and a high official from the *Wilhelmstrasse*, the Foreign Office, called immediately on our arrival and assured his Lordship that anyone he would wish to see or anywhere he would desire to visit, his request was their command. When told that it was purely a private visit, he repeated once more that everything was at his disposal and bowed himself out, convinced that we were in Berlin for no good purpose. From his point of view I suppose we were not.

Northcliffe, with his indomitable energy, was soon receiving callers and discussing newspaper business. Among them was Valentine Williams, the well known novelist, who at the time was Reuters' correspondent in Berlin, and although in his early twenties was an experienced journalist and a linguist. Northcliffe offered him while we were there the post of **Daily Mail** correspondent in Paris, where he was for many years until the last war, when he obtained a commission in the Guards and played a distinguished part both as a war correspondent and as a soldier. In past days I used to see a good deal of Valentine, who married the well-known actress, Alice Crawford.

Meantime, all the while Northcliffe was shadowed by detectives, who dogged his footsteps with grim determination, and occasionally secret service men would brush past us if we were walking along the streets or the Tiergarten, obviously trying to gather some idea of the conversation. It amused the Chief vastly, and he even recognised some of the spies and gave them designations.

"You observed that cadaverous, unfrocked-priest-looking rogue who passed us just now?" he would ask. "Look casually round and see what he is up to."

I looked round casually. "He's just sauntering along."

"He will dodge behind a linden tree and bob up again shortly, you'll see. Next time he will wear a false moustache. We will now turn round again and stalk him."

There was often a curious schoolboy attitude about Northcliffe when he was not absorbed in newspapers or politics. He had a ready wit and a scorching tongue. I soon found that he was most interested in talking of himself and I was a good listener. He possessed a scarcely disguised contempt for other newspaper proprietors; or, if it came to that, for all rivals whether journalistic or business. But what was important about that visit - or seemed to be at the time - was that he saw and heard enough about Germany's secret plans to decide that there were solid grounds for believing her rulers to be preparing a rod in pickle.

He made up his mind that he would use the influence of his papers to rouse the British nation to the danger ahead. This was a big and important achievement it seemed to me and from a purely personal point of view I was, of course, interested when he expressed his intention shortly of starting a national weekly or monthly - a weekly was certainly predominant at the time - to be devoted to preparations for a possible war, and of which I was to become editor. He became enthusiastic about this idea and on the journey homewards discussed all sorts of aspects of this new publication-to-be which flowed from his fertile mind. That it never saw the light of day in the end was but one of many of his abortive Press offspring. We parted company *en route*, for the Northcliffes went to Paris and I to Ostend, and although no decision had been come to it was understood that I had the offer to join the Chief's staff of editors.

In Berlin I had gathered certain information relating to Lucien Wolf - who was regarded by reputable correspondents as a quite dangerous ally of Germany - which would explain why this man was willing to occupy a position as Foreign Editor of the **Daily Graphic**, a publication which possessed no important political influence at home and enjoyed quite a small circulation. On the Continent, however, it was another matter entirely, for there it basked in the reflected sunshine of **The**

Graphic, whose name carried prestige. It could therefore be of considerable propaganda value to the policy of the Kaiser and his naval chiefs if a London daily with a reputation as a Conservative organ of opinions could be used when occasion required to give a fillip to the Kaiser's warmongering policy.

Suppose, for instance, that the German Government needed a further vote of credit from the Reichstag to lay down more battleships and could produce as an argument the old ruse that Germany was threatened with war by Britain, when an agitation was afoot to expand her own (i.e. Germany's) naval programme on the pretext that British Imperialism necessitated it. What more simple than to have an *agent provocateur* in London who could be depended on to pretend uneasiness of German expansionist policy and demand in strong terms an increase in our naval plans? Appearing in a Conservative and respected daily it would be able to evoke a reply from Berlin. Not for a moment do I suggest that the directors of the **Daily Graphic** had the slightest inkling of how they may have been made "stooges" to serve German interests.

Such articles were cabled to Berlin and quoted in full in the newspapers of the Reich as evidence of Britain's intention to keep Germany down. A fresh agitation was then artificially stimulated in the German Press and violent articles were published, accusing us of Machiavellian tactics, crafty diplomacy and all the ready-made stock epithets of abuse in which Germans shine, and thereupon the Reichstag did its stuff and agreed to a huge new credit. It was as easy as falling off a log with a Press *agent provocateur* obeying orders in London.

I learnt, too, that there were more ways than one to make journalism pay. If Lucien Wolf were agreeable to accept a relatively small salary on the **Daily Graphic**, there were plums to be picked in other directions. I was informed in Berlin on good authority that he received a very considerable retainer from a most influential and wealthy international finance house in the City, whose tentacles stretched to all the world money centres. This firm opposed any close military alliance between Russia and Britain for reasons no doubt well known to its partners, and accordingly it was Mr. Wolf's object to throw a spanner into the works. Soon after my return from Germany a young man, who had been my secretary when on the **Bystander**, obtained other employment, and came to me to take parting leave. The conversation turned on Germany and in a rash moment I said something about Wolf and why I had dismissed him from **The Graphic**. To my intense surprise - for I had implicitly trusted the youth - I received shortly afterwards a letter from a firm of solicitors informing me that they were instructed to issue a writ for slander on behalf of their client Mr. Lucien Wolf, and when I received it I found that it was based on an affidavit sworn by the young man who, I may say, had owed his job in the firm to me. It was a pretty good instance of nursing an adder in one's bosom, but his subsequent career made his action less surprising.

As Wolf gave signs of proceeding with his action I came to the conclusion that the Directors should take it over as it was a matter which concerned my position in the firm, so I duly placed the circumstances before them and said my defence was firstly that I denied the accuracy of the statements imputed to me, and, secondly, that anything I said to an employee of the firm was privileged. Personally I hoped to see the case come into Court, for I had collected enough evidence to create a possible *cause célébre*. especially if both the *Wilhelmstrasse* and the famous firm of international bankers had found their names dragged into Court. The Directors, however, refused to assist in the matter. The sat like a certain notorious Biblical character and washed their hands of it. Israel-Davis contended that it was purely a personal quarrel between Wolf and myself. Wolf never proceeded with the action.

There was something of a sequel to it all soon after the outbreak of the first German War of 1914-18. The able and public-spirited proprietor and editor of the **National Review**, Leo Maxse, who year in and year out had criticised the Foreign Office and exposed Germany's machinations, revealed Lucien Wolf's activities, which finished his career as a publicist of value. Carmichael Thomas wrote me a graceful letter after the exposure and said that I had been justified up to the hilt. It came, however, far too late so far as I was concerned, as I had long before burnt my boats and had accepted a position with Northcliffe soon after the Directors of **The Graphic** had betrayed so churlish an attitude in regard to l'*affaire Wolf*. I regretted leaving that famous journal, but it was obvious that Car was not powerful enough to stand up to these two men who were really responsible for the steady decline in its prestige and ultimate demise.

Looking back I think I might have shown Messrs. Lupton and Davis a more conciliatory attitude and with care might have bent them to my outlook. Put it down to the folly of youth. I have always been impatient of insularity and the ostrich attitude of burying one's head in the sand if danger lurks. My faults, I frankly admit, are many, but I have never been a "Yes" man, of whom there have been far too many in Britain, many, alas, who have held key positions in the defence policy of the country and to which I attribute much of the decline of British power and hence prestige in the last few decades.

There has been too much victimisation of men in high positions who have dared to stand up against official shortcomings. The more we prattle about Democracy the more the government seeks to walk by dark and devious paths. It has been seen in my own modest position how efforts to bring any realisation of the serious position into which the country was then drifting were thwarted and how closely Big Business and High Finance wedded to greed played a leading part in an inevitable war. Business magnates uttered immaculately patriotic phrases, so admirably brought out at this time by Guy du Maurier in his play *The Englishman's Home*, which his brother Gerald produced, where complacency was suddenly confronted by a German invasion. Men like Davis and Lupton, typical of their order, were unconsciously defeatists. I have cited them as types, and because such men largely dominated the Press.

I was succeeded, as I mentioned, on **The Graphic** by J. M. Bulloch, a stumpy, gnarled, thick-set son of Caledonia. This Aberdonian, born and bred a strong Scottish nationalist, who adored the Granite Capital about which he wrote various treatises, who imagined himself a Liberal and a Democrat, but was in fact a crusted Tory, was to my mind one of the least-fitted men to edit **The Graphic**, where totally different qualifications were needed, especially a broad outlook. He had been assistant editor of **The Sphere** under Clement Shorter, both being birds of a feather, and was learned in a way, being well-known as a book and theatre critic, the antithesis of what an editor of a national newspaper should be, for the critic merely sits in judgment on other people's creations, while an able editor requires to construct ideas himself from all that goes on and use such to the best advantage. He was terse, spoke with an pronounced Aberdonian accent - *Doric* some term it - and was very ungracious when I assisted him prior to his taking over my duties. It may have been due to a high opinion of his superior abilities or maybe he resented the thought that he was merely walking into the shoes I had deliberately cast off. Many a time subsequently I ran across him at theatrical first nights or at public dinners and occasionally he favoured me with a curt nod, but often not that.

Dr. Bulloch, as he liked to call himself, as an LL.D. of Aberdeen University, doubtless succeeded in pleasing Lupton and Davis, because he reversed my policy. Nothing polemical was allowed to soil the austere pages of the paper, and it no longer offended the susceptibilities of pacifists or pro-Germans, though it failed to attract the instructed classes of the public. Slowly, but surely, the work of our artists was superseded by the employment of photographs, so that **The Graphic** drifted into mediocrity, its circulation gradually dwindled, and it surrendered for ever its artistic supremacy to **The Illustrated London News**, which cleverly attracted the pick of its artists. There may have been some truth in the gibe attributed to Clement Shorter, who was said to have congratulated Carmichael Thomas for relieving him of the "genius" of Bulloch.

When I joined Northcliffe, as he was not yet ready to launch the proposed new national publication, I was put on to edit in the meantime his popular magazine named the **Harmsworth Magazine** and priced at fourpence. Northcliffe decided to change its name to **The London** and to raise its price to sixpence. He told me that the magazine which bore the surname of his family was of great importance and he looked to me to raise its character and tone.

The first idea he passed on to me in the way of contents was to engage a medical expert to write an article on the hygienic excellence of the laws of Moses, which struck me as rather an incongruous subject for a publication which had enjoyed a rather low-browed public. However, there it was. It was to be a temporary job and the firm gave me a contract on a bigger salary than I had received on **The Graphic**, but at the same time it was not the sort of editorial post I had left **The Graphic** to undertake, and I regarded it as no more than a stop-gap until the new national weekly could be thoroughly organised The Chief told me that its appearance must be postponed until he returned from an ensuing visit to the United States. Meantime he entrusted me to produce and edit a book to be placed on the market to be entitled **The German Menace**, its object to place on record what Germany was adding in every direction, containing chapters on her Army, Navy, Diplomacy, Commerce, the training of her youth and so on. Expert journalists and other writers were commissioned to prepare chapters on such of these subjects about which they could write with authority. Very soon after his return from his American tour he sent for me and I saw at a glance that he was not exactly enraptured with what lay before him on his table.

Long galley proofs of type had been blue-pencilled by him. As he had favoured me with several almost affectionate. cables from America I was unprepared to see him turn round after keeping me standings for a few minutes, wearing a scowl on his features. Without a word of preliminary greeting he asked curtly:

"Do you seriously expect me to publish this sort of stuff?"

"What is wrong with it, Lord Northcliffe?" I asked.

"Wrong!" With a snarl he pointed to the blue-pencil deletions. "Look at that, young man! Do you want to see your chief assassinated?"

"Where have I failed to carry out your instructions?" I questioned, "I got the men you named to write in the way you had indicated. They have written up to the title of '*The German Menace*', or so I thought.

"There is enough said in this to cause war to break out to-morrow," he snapped. "I wanted the truth about Germany, not violent diatribes; You must get in touch with your contributors at once and re-write the chapters. Get someone to contribute a chapter on the German *Mädchen* with their pigtails. Change the title. '*The German Menace*' is highly provocative."

When I mentioned that the title was his own given me before he left for America it did nothing to assuage his irritation. Northcliffe. I realised, could be the most charming and disarming person when he wished but he could also be intolerant to a degree.

"Go away and call it '*Our German Cousins*'," he barked. It was, of course an utterly different viewpoint; an entirely emasculated edition of the original, and in such form it duly appeared on the bookstalls and failed to sell. There was no reason why it should, for the Public were not in the least interested in the cousin idea, and were naturally cold in respect to charming *Mädchen* with pigtails. When he realised that it was a failure Northcliffe with his brilliant opportunism seized on a solution, He wrote an article in the **Daily Mail** under his own name and frankly said it was not selling but that in view of the importance of the subject it ought to be in every home and so great was his prestige with the general public that the edition sold out, although it did no one a ha'p'orth of good.

I soon sized him up as a man of great versatility but of volatile and capricious character. He would take up a cause or subject with utmost enthusiasm one day and the next day would drop it like a hot brick. What caused him to change his mind about Germany I cannot say, but I had been astonished to read a cable of a speech he delivered in New York or Washington in which he was reported to have declared that he did not believe war between Great Britain and Germany was either inevitable or likely and that he believed the motives of the Kaiser were peaceable. His attitude when he returned lent colour to his change of front and it explains why he did not pursue his previous intention of starting at weekly of a strong national character. When I asked him about it he said vaguely that "my brother Harold" was difficult to persuade and anyhow I must make **The London** an overwhelming success first. It was not what I had bargained for but I was powerless in the matter, and had to make the best of it.

At this time undoubtedly Northcliffe was far and away the most powerful publicist in Britain, controlling as he did **The Times** as well as his own stable of daily and weekly newspapers. As a journalist he was somewhat of an *Autolycus*, a man who made much out of unconsidered trifles, rather than profound, but he had the wisdom to surround himself with experts on political and technical subjects, and having been a poor boy who had to make his own way in the world he understood the mentality of the masses and in what they were interested. His instincts enabled him to be often more than one jump ahead of his rivals but he was inclined to arrive at conclusions on superficial grounds.

He was a queer mixture of extreme masculinity and yet femininity as well. Apart from jumping to conclusions he possessed a sort of insatiable curiosity about the private lives of the men who served under him, and as a result he had various *Paul Prys* who made it their business to ferret out the weaknesses of the staffs because they thought he relished such tittle-tattle, and here, again, he formed conclusions which were utterly false in some cases at least.

On 29 December, 1908, there occurred the Messina Earthquake, one of the most disastrous to human life of this century or last, for no fewer than 200,000 persons were estimated to have lost their lives on that awful night when large numbers were sucked down into the earth and never seen again. Being interested in the subject of seismic forces and volcanic outbreaks I thought I might gather some material for **The London** and obtained permission to visit Messina at my own expense, and in the following spring visited the scene on the Calabrian side of the Straits and the damaged areas in Sicily. My views on seismic and volcanic phenomena were (and are) by no means orthodox, for whilst the accepted and conventional dogma is that they are caused by internal adjustments of the earth, my contention is that they are entirely external and are caused by meteoric impacts which in turn are related to cometary movements.

the controversial aspect is scarcely one for this book and as I have advanced my contentions in two published works I will leave it at that except to say that Messina entirely supported my theories, borne out by many such occurrences before and since.

The only premonitory warning at Messina was an oppressive airlessness but, a few moments before 4.20 a.m. deep and continuous rumblings occurred overhead and those survivors who watched saw a vivid stream of brilliant light to the north-east beyond Calabria on the mainland. This was followed shortly by a first shock lasting several seconds, and then, after a deadly silence for a few moments which seemed like eternity, there followed the sickening sensation of rising and falling, the roar of buildings crashing to earth, and above them he terrified screams of human beings and the dismal howling of dogs. Yet the town of Messina escaped more lightly than the areas around Taormina and Catania along the eastern, shores of Sicily, where great tracts were devastated, marking the main direction of the meteor which was attracted to Mount Etna. This solid body or a portion of it plunged into the sea between Messina and Calabria on the opposite side of the Straits, and just as big buildings reeled and collapsed, many in flames, burying alive or injuring thousands of the townsfolk who had rushed into the streets panic-stricken - most of them stark naked - the sea which had deserted the harbour and shore now returned as a vast sea-wall of water and thus as a tidal wave hurled itself upon the town to complete the scene of utter chaos.

When I visited Messina it still remained a ruined city. Churches and great stone buildings had collapsed like a pack of cards, many flattened to the ground, The force of the tidal wave had been so great that it had picked up good-sized ships as well as fishing-boats, and had carried them completely over the four- and five-storey solid stone houses on the quay, some being deposited into streets far back. The tidal wave was accompanied by a tremendous cloudburst caused by the condensation of hydrogen and oxygen which are among the gases known to accompany such bodies and which condense after striking our atmosphere. Among the houses at Messina swallowed up in the earthquake was an English bank with all its cash and securities, and a well-known English family resident in the town saw its fortune disappear in a flash together with its villa nearby, although the family escaped physical injury.

It was my conviction that, as is not infrequent, the meteor of considerable size broke in two, the one portion speeding towards the flanks of Etna, and on its way crushing and flattening out houses and orange groves by blast along the line of Ali-Santa Teresa-Castiglione-Taormina with Catania beyond. The houses and groves were flattened by the accompanying blast and the devastation was greater here because the celestial body in its trajectory was plunging downward to earth. The same principle was witnessed at Calabria in Italy, north-east of Messina, where again houses and olive groves were pancaked as though some gargantuan roller had passed over the comparatively narrow area, for the body which struck the sea evidently flashed past very low, and struck the sea thereby creating a great vacuum into which were drawn the surrounding waters and then after it filled up, surged back again with an added and terrible impetus.

These celestial bombs operate, indeed, like high-explosive missiles but on such a grandiose scale as makes comparison seem fatuous, for a meteor, though it may weigh a few ounces, may also weigh thousands of tons. The subject is of paramount scientific importance especially to those who dwell in the danger zone of living volcanoes, for, once they are created and are not extinct, these provide an attracting target through their emissions. Meteoric bodies, almost invariably approach us from the north-east and accordingly areas like Calabria, Messina, Reggio and others lying in the track of Etna's approaches are in constant danger, especially as in the earthquake of 1783, or as at St. Pierre, Martinique, below Mont Pelée, whose entire population of 28,000 were killed in a flash by a blast in 1902.

Before deserting Messina I may recall that immediately, following that disaster the first to arrive on the spot, take matters in hand, succour the wounded, homeless, and starving, was - need I say? - the Royal Navy. British cruisers hurtled to the scene while the Italian Government was wringing its hands. The Navy took supplies, medical needs, and doctors, and began to straighten things out. The

Lord Mayor of London opened a public fund for the sufferers and raised a large sum exceeding half a million. Before I had reached Reggio on my way to Messina and thereafter as far south as Catania, thousands of white bell-tents were visual evidence of British aid, The Italians expressed their gratitude and repaid us with - Mussolini. We rendered even more help to Japan after the great Tokyo earthquake of 1923 when 350,000 houses were destroyed and there were over 130,000 casualties, for the Lord Mayor's Fund exceeded over a million sterling. I fear it is too much to expect that we have learnt wisdom from such base ingratitude and at a future date will let such countries look after their own earthquake misfortunes.

When I was on **The London** I thought for one brief moment that I had stumbled across the biggest scoop in my career, no less than to announce to the world the discovery of the long-lost MSS of the Shakespeare plays and sonnets, other lost MSS of the Elizabethan period, and certain regalia and personal possessions which belonged to Francis Bacon.

It happened in this way. My eye caught one morning a short announcement in the **Daily Express**, at that time and for many years edited by that charming and talented man R. D. Blumenfeld, to the effect that Dr. Orville W. Owen, of Detroit, Mich., had arrived at Chepstow, Monmouthshire, for the purpose of discovering most important relics of the great Elizabethan which he claimed had been concealed in a cache in the bed of the Wye. Owen, in an interview a day or two later, stated that he possessed the key to the mystery in a cipher he had unravelled, and he went on to declare that he expected to find not only the original MSS of the Shakespeare plays and sonnets but also those of contemporary poets including Marlowe, Greene, Edmund Spenser, Peele, Sir Philip Sidney's *Arcadia,* and Burton's *Anatomy of Melancholy.*

Here was romance! A chance not to be missed, indeed! The problem of Bacon-Shakespeare had interested me for some years for I had been converted into a Baconian by a connection on my mother's side, W. S. Lilly, in his day a man of strong literary proclivities and who entertained largely leading authors, actors, and poets in his house at Knightsbridge. Without more ado I hastily threw some clothes into a dressing-case and took the first train to Chepstow. I spent several weeks there varied with my work in London, weeks full of anticipation for what promised to be the greatest literary discovery of all time. There were many exciting hours.

I found Dr. Owen was in residence at the old-fashioned and comfortable Beaufort Arms Hotel, together with his wife and young children, so I stayed there too in order to be in close touch. He was a grey-haired man, strongly built, aged about fifty, genial, alert, communicative except as regarded the cipher he was depending on for his discovery, and absolutely cocksure that he would be successful in the search. He had planned out his course and already a gang of labourers were at work on the section of the river bed when the tide permitted and he had so arranged his campaign that, as he told me, there was no room for error. It surprised me to learn that the search was being financed by no other than the Duke of Beaufort (father of the present duke), who owned most of the land in those parts including Chepstow Castle, surprising because I had regarded the Duke as a sporting nobleman, addicted more to fox-hunting than literary pursuits, but the Duchess was the moving spirit behind the scenes, who occasionally appeared on the scene to see how we were getting on.

There were three or four newspaper reporters staying in the hotel, and also tall, good-looking, and urbane Harry Pirie Gordon, the Duke's representative on the spot, who managed the pressmen, labourers, and Owen himself, whom he handled with great tact, not too easy a task, for the Doctor was unpractical like most visionaries, and in certain matters most secretive. It was Gordon's job to humour the Doctor, provide for his and his family's wants, shepherd the Press, and pay the outgoings. Nothing ever disturbed his equanimity, and as regards the search he was as enthusiastic as any of us. Himself very literary, an authority on the history of the Crusades. he married the daughter of George Buckle, then editor of **The Times**, which he subsequently joined in the Foreign Department. At the present time he holds a position in the Admiralty.

As thirty years have passed since all Britain was agog with the news of this romantic never-completed search, perhaps the present generation not conversant with Dr. Owen's claim may be interested to hear more about it. To Baconians, conversant with Mrs. Elizabeth Wells Gallup's deciphering of the *Biliteral Cipher* of Bacon published in 1901, and Dr. Owen's Cipher Story, published in two volumes in 1894, with subsequent additional decipherments of what is known as the *Word Cipher*, the general claim is, of course, well known. These ciphers contained astounding information and in their day across the Atlantic created a considerable sensation. In fact it was claimed that they had been embodied in the Shakespeare plays and in many other works by Bacon himself in order to tell the future world who he was and why he was compelled to have recourse to hidden ciphers to proclaim himself.

In brief the ciphers - which confirm one another although based on separate systems - contended that he, Francis Bacon, was the legitimate son of Queen Elizabeth and Robert Dudley, Earl of Leicester, born in lawful wedlock, but that Elizabeth for reasons of state and for other motives kept this union a dark secret, although it was well known to high persons of her Court including Lord Burghley, the Queen's Secretary of State, Robert Cecil, his hunchback son and successor, naturally to Sir Nicholas and Lady Bacon, his pretended parents, and was common gossip of the Court itself as well as of foreign ambassadors. It was discovered to Francis, when a Royal Page, by Elizabeth herself in a moment of violent passion, during a *fracas* at Court.

This brilliant youth, possessor of the greatest intellect that perhaps the world has ever known, was deprived of his birthright by his royal mother and remained Francis Bacon, later Viscount Verulam, while she posed as the "Virgin Queen." Any divulgement of the secret on his part was threatened with death and in fact throughout his life his liberty was always imperilled, but chafing under the cloud cast upon his birth and the stupendous injustice imposed upon one who was legitimately Prince of Wales and the heir to the throne of the Tudors, he determined to give the facts to posterity. This he accomplished by devising the ciphers in his own works and many others he influenced even if he did not write them under various "masks."

115

Altogether he devised no fewer than six types of ciphers to convey his meaning, the two principal being the Word Cipher and the Biliteral, the first being discovered by Dr. Owen by chance, the other being actually explained later in Bacon's **De Augmentis Scientiarum**, written in Latin, when he had become a little bolder. In these he tells the secret of his birth over and over again so that the truth should not be missed, together with a fund of information on politics, the Armada, the death of Elizabeth at the hands of Robert Cecil to prevent her from acknowledging his right to the throne, and of events at the Courts of Whitehall and of France. These two brilliant Americans, Dr. Owen and Mrs. Gallup, originally the Doctor's disciple, made the discoveries.

Almost more astonishing than the foregoing claims are those revealing the consummate genius of Bacon. Not only was he the real author of the plays and sonnets attributed to William Shakespeare, used primarily to disguise his true object, but he "masked" himself, according to the statements in the ciphers, under many names, using Edmund Spenser, Marlowe, Greene, Peele, Burton, and even occasionally borrowing the name of his friend Ben Jonson himself, paying the first four at least for the use of their names and making all of them famous but who were in fact merely his "stooges." Owen and Mrs. Gallup, to follow the instructions of the ciphers, had to use original or facsimile editions of all these works, as well as Bacon's admitted writings, with four Shakespeare plays not included in those bearing that name, in order to gather together the much dispersed narrative and present a consecutive story. Sometimes in the Word Cipher he would introduce a diversion in order to prove himself as the playwright and poet by introducing other matters, including a partly blank-verse version of Homer's *Iliad*, his *Odyssey*, an epic on the Armada, and a play on Mary Queen of Scots, for the edification of the decipherer. Apart from the genius of this astonishing man there stands out the amazing industry and determination which this work entailed outside of the writing. He had to transfer his secret stories into cipher from the straightforward work, or to devise his plays and other writings into such a form as could take the cipher. He took a leading part in the printing of the works and the decoration of the title pages which carried a secret meaning. He had to differentiate between two founts of type for the purpose of the *Biliteral*

116

Cipher. All these matters caused an enormous drain on his resources made for the one purpose. Yet, despite, his vast and foreseeing genius he failed in his object, for it took nearly three-hundred years before his decipherers appeared from America and by that time the name of Shakespeare had been so firmly established that no one would listen to Bacon's voice from the grave.

The ciphers were incredulously dismissed by the bulk of people who were sufficiently educated to give the subject a moment's thought and generally they were ignored. Indeed, comparatively few read them in England. It is a sad reflection that few persons care a tinker's curse about truth for truth's sake. They prefer to hug their illusions even if they are quite false.

Owen's discovery of the *Word Cipher*, as I said, was by chance. A G.P. at Detroit, an intense lover of the Shakespeare plays, it was his habit, while being driven from patient to patient to take his mind off his patients by reading the poet from a well thumbed facsimile copy, and one day he was suddenly struck with the incongruity of words in the soliloquy of the Bastard in *King John*, Act I, Scene 1, where *à propos* of nothing he says,

"My dear sir, thus leaning on mine elbow I begin."

This led him to certain key words and instructions and he began the decipherment by pasting the required contexts in duplicate on a great wheel, which was no light task since he was compelled to obtain the original editions or facsimiles. Dr. Owen himself died many years ago but I believe the task of deciphering these voluminous works still proceeds in the United States.

Instructions for finding the chests were contained in the work attributed to Sir Philip Sidney, entitled, *The Countess of Pembroke's Arcadia*, and explains in part at least why the river Wye was chosen as the hiding-place. Lady Pembroke was Sidney's sister, both of whom possessed strong literary tastes, as did also the Earl of Pembroke, the well-known William Herbert of his age who wrote poems himself, was a lavish patron of literature, and to whom, (with his brother and successor Philip), the first folio of Shakespeare was dedicated. He is also believed - but it is certainly doubtful - to have been the "Mr. W. H." of the sonnets, addressed as "*the onlie begetter of these insuing sonnets.*" When later in life charges of corruption were brought against Bacon, and the peers debated whether or no to deprive him of his title, Pembroke constituted himself his champion and spoke convincingly on his behalf. Very wealthy for that age, having an income not £22,000 per annum, he died suddenly leaving behind debts of £80,000. Among his seats was Chepstow Castle.

Thus can be explained why Bacon, so intimate with the Pembrokes, could discover a safe hiding-place for his treasures, and it can scarcely be doubted that they were well aware of all the circumstances. From its now ivy-clad ruins, perched on a rocky eminence high above the rapid Wye, which flows right under the castle walls, Bacon could have viewed the actual site where he concealed his relics which included, according to Dr. Owen, the MSS. of the plays and sonnets bearing the name of William Shakespeare, and in addition those of the other authors already mentioned, all written, it is averred, in his neat and beautiful calligraphy, specimens of which have survived. Also there was supposed to be certain personal regalia, including his coronet, and further proofs of his royal birth. Had they materialised, what a sensation it would have created! Their value would have been beyond any computation.

And here I should say that the Duke of Beaufort had stipulated, in return for permission to search and for financing the search, that they were to be presented to the nation. I was promised for my part that I should edit the publication of the relics and write the full story. In addition I intended to feature the search fully in the London in a series of articles. I said nothing to Northcliffe about the matter until or unless it should materialise. I made arrangements to photograph the relics and all connected with it.

The sensation never broke. The search was abandoned prematurely. Its quest could only proceed under the direct instruction of Owen, worked

118

out by his reading of the cipher which he permitted no one to check, not even Pirie Gordon. He had divided the area of search into a number of squares embracing an area which was intended to cover every possible error in calculation. One square after another was to be tested after the instructions given by cipher in the *Arcadia*. The road from Chepstow to Tintern Abbey runs along a ridge high above the Wye, and about a mile above the Castle ruins an old Roman Road leads to a former ford with the remains of a Roman wall. From the foot of this the cipher instructed the searcher to dig "twice ten times ten feet due east," 200 feet in all, and then look for "the boxes like eels in the mud, boxes swathed in *camlet* and covered with tar," *camlet* being a strong material made of camel's hair. Another instruction was "make a triangle of 123 feet due north and 33 paces," and Bacon gave a clue to direction in the words, "I filled up the shallow water with mud and beams, cut down all the trees, and turned the course of the river." It was further stated that towards the middle of the stream he found a seam of open rock, dammed a narrow rift of this with wood, clay, stones, and rubble, levelled a part of the "three-walled vault" thus formed, and buried the chests, making a triangular roof over them. Bacon had foreseen everything except *anno Domini*! He imagined that the ciphers would be discovered within fifty years of his death. But he had buried his deep secret only too well and truly.

Few parts of Britain are more beautiful than the high road to Tintern Abbey with the silvery Wye winding through richly wooded country with the Black Mountain and the distant Malvern Hills forming a perfect background, but I must confess that the glories of the scenery were lost upon me during the search. The first few months were execrable, cold, with heavy rains and sleet, and thick mud everywhere. The digging operations were over a mile from the hotel, and they proceeded day and night when the tide was out, fair weather or foul, so that we might be on the spot at any hour of early morning or late night. I managed to procure the loan of a push-bike and usually in company with Pirie Gordon, who also had one, together with other enthusiasts, wrapped up as warmly as possible, with rubber boots up to our thighs, we would sally forth to Wasp Hill. There we would deposit our bikes, hunt with lanterns for a slimy rope and descend a precipitous slope as slippery as a greasy pole, slither as best we could to its foot, and then pick our wary way along narrow duck-boards to the scene. There by the glare of oil-flares the gang of navvies would be working with pickaxes and shovels, while in the semi-darkness around the hole one or two previous arrivals would be watching tensely and seeming almost spectral a short distance away. One of them was always the Doctor.

We would join them in the vigil. Few words were spoken. Now and again a pickaxe would strike something solid, sparks would fly, and all the company would stare breathlessly for a few moments, oblivious to the driving rain or cold blasts blowing down the river from the north. Only another false alarm - but a thrill all the same. At any moment a pickaxe might strike the roof of the cache. Hope springs eternal when treasure-hunting.

Then suddenly the rising tide would lap the top of the piles driven in the square where the men worked in the bed of the stream. A word of warning, a muttered oath, and rapidly the gang would clamber out, for the Wye is the fastest-running river in England, and in a few seconds the hole would be filled with water, while the party made a hasty exit to, the shore to avoid being trapped by the rising tide. Sometimes one or another of us would make a false step and be helped out covered in mud from top to toe. After this we would hasten back to the hotel, pass though the ancient Town Gate, and get into bed.

The search had reached what was, I believe, No. 8 square without result. This was a great disappointment, because it was, according to the calculation, "twice ten times ten feet due east" and great hopes had been raised. The Doctor checked up his code and bearings. One night we thought we had struck it. Great excitement prevailed when a solid piece of rock was sounded and the pickaxes found some big stones. The Doctor was an optimist as always. "We're on it, boys, I guess!" he shouted. . . . And just then the tide lapped the lip of the hole.

Unexpectedly the work was stopped. I do not know exactly to this day what the reason was except that the Duke of Beaufort refused to finance the operations any longer. One rumour said that he was dissatisfied with the refusal of Dr. Owen to permit anyone else to check the truth of his cipher. Another was that owing to certain discrepancies in the finances of his estates amounting to a considerable sum, for which he blamed his chief agent who had been in favour of the search, he threw up the matter in disgust. Whatever the reason the Duke buttoned up his pockets and we were perforce compelled to pack up our traps and depart, hoping that the ever-optimistic Doctor would obtain financial aid from the U.S.A., for which he was angling. It was a great disappointment to everyone concerned and not least to myself.

My dreams of editing the official story of the discovery vanished into thin air. I had lost the great "scoop" with which I had hoped to stagger Northcliffe. I had spent a good deal of my own money fruitlessly, for I paid my own expenses, and everyone in Carmelite House persisted in asking me if I had enjoyed my "holiday." I had nothing to show for it all except a vile chill. To add to it all I got on the wrong side of my brother-in-law, to whom in a purple moment I had sent a wire saying that we were unearthing the Bacon relics, and he had passed the information round to all his cronies in the Garrick Clubs. He said I had made a fool of him, and I don't think he ever quite forgave me; Gerald had a queer dislike of the Press and journalists. He added me to his black list, I am afraid.

I have been asked many times since whether I was such an ass as to believe that Bacon did conceal the alleged MSS. in a cache in the middle - or nearly middle - of the Wye. I do believe it, and I feel confident that somewhere in the region are the chests, unless some seismic disturbance disturbed the site. It was a hide-out which only a genius such as he would have devised, to conceal his treasure in a cache in a rock and even turn the bed of the river upon it at that spot. It must be recollected, too, that for some forty-five years of his chequered career he lived in daily dread of sudden arrest by day or night, not least on the orders of his own mother. In one of the passages in the *Word Cipher* he describes the circumstances whereby the Queen made the discovery that he was the author of *Hamlet*, when he was only twenty, and regarded it as a veiled attack on her Throne:

121

"Fool, I have heard this mangled tale," she cried scornfully. "Hamlet's a prince out of thy star . . . thou playedst most foully to show the death of the Danish king and Hamlet to my enemies. They murdered their king in the heaviness of sleep and the violent harm that the chiefest princes of Rome did put upon their emperors I doubt not shall be put on me." She threatened then to have him executed for treason. As to the MSS. of the Shakespeare plays and sonnets, and those of the various poets and writers said to have been Bacon's "masks," not one has ever been found.

It is a great pity the search was not completed for lack of a few hundred pounds. I possess copies of both Ciphers and of other works bearing on the Bacon controversy, and I declare that if Owen and Mrs. Gallup could have faked up all their deciphered work they were almost as marvellous as Bacon himself. Besides which anyone interested can work on the ciphers himself if he acquires a facsimile copy of the First Folio of Shakespeare, as I have done, to test their accuracy. I consider that the Doctor made several errors in his deciphering, but they do not impugn the general value of his work.

I used to think that in justice to Bacon and his claims, and to Shakespeare, too, that some intellectual body like the Royal Society, or the Royal Society of Literature, or the combined Universities, should take steps to institute a full inquiry into the question, or even better still that the Government should set up a Select Committee of public men to complete the search in the Wye, that is, after they had ascertained the genuineness of Dr. Owen's *Arcadia* Cipher, which must exist still in America. But to-day I am not quite so sure.

I have learnt since that far more important than even truth and justice to the bulk of Englishmen is the maintenance of existing institutions, and that their preservation counts infinitely more in their eyes than rendering tardy justice to the memory of England's greatest genius, a man whose mind outshines any other in the history of mankind, and who happened to have been the rightful heir to the throne of England. That Queen Elizabeth was the "Virgin Queen," that the

Tudors were worthy sovereigns instead of arrogant, rapacious, and niggardly tyrants, and that Shakespeare was such a Heaven-sent genius that he possessed a consummate knowledge of ancient and modern history, of the procedure of royal courts, of languages and law, of science, a vocabulary never equalled elsewhere, and a consummate mastery of phrases although he appears to have had great difficulty in signing his name, all these are time-honoured beliefs and institutions, and if the props that support them are rotten we avert our eyes.

We British have a simple way of coping with inconvenient problems, whether political or literary or scientific, if they worry us, as anything new does. We just boycott them. The Press is barred to such and if their names are mentioned it evokes a shrug of the shoulder. That is why we always lose wars until we sink enormous treasure and priceless lives in finally winning them. We simply won't learn.

Whether Northcliffe would have viewed the search for the Bacon relics in this light I cannot state, for I never mentioned. the matter to him. Why I did not was because I had realised that he worshipped success and despised failure. *Fiat justitia, ruat cœlum* was unlikely to appeal to his particular brand of genius.

Viscount Northcliffe - when aged 45

My sister Muriel and Gerald - photographed at Cannon Hall on the occasion of their Silver Wedding.

CHAPTER VII

THE ACHILLES' HEEL

"Under every stone a scorpion sleeps,"
(GREEK PROVERB)

THE NORTHCLIFFES used to spend a good deal of their time at stately Sutton Place, a historic mansion situated between Woking and Guildford, which had been leased from the Duke of Sutherland. Approached from either the Portsmouth or Woking roads one entered the park through ornamental bronze gates, flanked by lodges, and then drove for over a mile over the private road until the handsome Tudor mansion of red brick, with high spiral chimneys, emerged from behind a protecting copse. Usually massed outside the entrance was a collection of various cars belonging to the Chief and to callers.

The main front contained the great banqueting hall with deep, long windows, a panelled hall inside, hung with armour and medieval weapons, and flanked east and west by deep wings leading to other apartments. Used as a lounge, it was comfortably furnished with rugs, divans and easy chairs, having a refectory table in the centre looking almost like a bookstall with its collection of periodicals. In two immense open fireplaces big log fires were always blazing.

I was often at Sutton Place, perhaps due to the fact that I then lived at Thames Ditton not far away and could easily motor over. Northcliffe would ring me up at home quite early and say, "The Chief speaking. What are you doing to-day?" It mattered little what I had designed to do for he would invite me - a sort of royal command - to go over perhaps for luncheon or for a game of tennis or what not. Sometimes Lady Northcliffe would request me to stay to dinner and sleep the night for I was convenient if an odd man were wanted. Northcliffe took violent likes or dislikes and one was either in his good books or his bad.

Perhaps it was his method of sizing up the worth of a man, but if so he set about it wrongly as far as I was concerned. He was dictatorial, and that does not lead to an independent interchange of views. I had to be always on my guard, which frustrates frankness. None the less he had a winning and most fascinating personality and could be charming when he really relaxed and unbent, especially at meals which were made the occasion of a good deal of chaff and jocularity, usually personal of someone and with a spice of malice - for his wit was barbed.

His mornings were generally occupied and in his private suite where he kept a couple of secretaries and he was perpetually on the telephone to one or other of his employees, issuing orders, putting over ideas and other matters which passed through his restless brain. Men like Hamilton Fyfe were among the many journalists to be found round his Lordship's board, Fyfe, grey-haired, distinguished-looking, with a fine voice and presence, had been travelling over the world writing descriptive and penetrating articles for the *Daily Mail*. In the last war he was one of that paper's war correspondents and then directed anti-German propaganda at Crewe House for the Ministry of Information.

Whether or no the ducal trappings of Sutton Place jarred on the nerves of Hamilton Fyfe, he nourished great scorn for plutocracy, and became in due course anti-capitalist, a champion of the under-dog, and a pillar of the Socialist Party. The T.U.C. and Labour Party offered him the editorship of the Daily Herald and he made a respectable journal of it, but I fancy that he was disillusioned with the Party chiefs. To an intellectual like himself their crass ignorance, must have jarred on a highly-strung temperament, for the Socialist Party have never yet displayed the least comprehension of world affairs. or ever shown the faintest conception of a national outlook, being merely sectional. They were stubbornly Free Trade when the working-man was starving through unemployment, plumped solidly for disarmament during the MacDonald-Baldwin regime, were solid supporters of the League of Nations long after intelligent people had realised its decline, detested the Empire and wanted to have everything run by the State hence leading up to a gigantic bureaucracy which seeks, to lower everything to one level. The mental make-up of the Socialist is usually governed by envy and spite, unless he becomes a cabinet minister, when chameleon-like he makes a first-class autocrat, and all thoughts of equality vanish.

On one or two occasions Tom Marlowe, then editor of the **Daily Mail**, was present. A big, bluff man of few words and with a booming voice when he did speak, he looked like a prosperous farmer. Northcliffe treated him with marked respect, although I was told that in the early stages of his paper Marlowe was nearly driven to desperation by, his proprietor's onslaughts and pinpricks. Another constant visitor was Evelyn Wrench, later knighted, founder of the Overseas Club and Circle, subsequently editor of **The Spectator**. He was head of the publicity of the Amalgamated Press, his job being to boost the firms productions and thus it was his task to feel the public pulse which he did uncommonly well. With great diplomatic tact and charming manners, he was *persona grata* with both the Chief and Lady Northcliffe.

One Sunday, Gordon Selfridge and his entire family came to luncheon, soon after he had opened his famous store on Oxford Street, bringing from Chicago a dazzling new outlook on salesmanship, which made the big London shops sit up and gasp, so revolutionary were they to conservative ideas. His slogan "the customer is always right," delighted the public and put rivals on their mettle in place of the former "take it or leave it." His expert window-dressing and other innovations drew immense crowds, who made his store the excuse for a day's outing, as he intended they should do, without being pestered to buy. Usually they bought.

He ploughed his deepest furrow in his publicity and advertising, spending immense sums to make the name "Selfridge" a household word as he did rapidly. His advertising was brilliant and compelled his rivals to pay him the compliment of imitation, but he was always a jump ahead. He would pay big prices for new ideas and was always accessible. It was a great loss to the store when this vivid personality retired.

Selfridge interested Northcliffe greatly and I do not doubt but that the luncheon party given in the Chicagoan's honour at that ducal seat by the leading newspaper proprietor of England made an equal impression upon Mr. Selfridge. Certainly the Northcliffe publications did not lose any advertising allocations as a result of this hospitality, although the Chief affected an indifference to advertising, as he maintained that when his papers gave certificated sales the rest must follow, in which he gave the lead to the press but it does not always follow. The class of reader is more important than mere hordes.

Northcliffe's life has been written by more able pens than mine. It is commonly known that he was the eldest of fourteen, his father, a barrister of the Middle Temple, being a Hampshire man, although Alfred Harmsworth was born in Dublin. His first chance to see the world offered itself when he became secretary and companion to the son of a peer and travelled with him over most of Europe in comfort, and I have little doubt but that he owed much to this fortunate chance, for it gives youth a better balance and cures insularity. He got a job on a magazine named **Youth**, but his health suffered in London and he went to *Iliffe's* at Coventry as a sub-editor on their daily. Returning to London he worked, I believe, for a short time on **The Sphere** under Clement Shorter, about whom he used to joke with me. He then took his luck in both hands and started **Answers**, under the cumbrous title of **Answers to Correspondents**, intended to be a sort of popular "Notes and Queries."

Through the grounds of Sutton Place ran the delightful little River Wey and one beautiful summer afternoon I paddled him along the silvery stream in a Canadian canoe whilst he dilated upon how he first faced ruin and finally triumphed.

Answers made its first bow in a golden cover at the price of one penny. Although snappily written in which unusual matters and curiosities were stressed quite in accordance with Northcliffe's Autolycus-like disposition, it proved no great rival to George Newnes's **Tit-Bits**. Circulation dwindled and advertisements were a minus quantity. The offices were blocked up with returns. The capital, mainly borrowed, was small, and failure stared him in the face. He wrote and made up the paper, brother Harold looked after the business end, Harry Ebden, an old friend of mine, doyen of newspaper publishers and with whom I am associated to this hour, was the publisher, Miss Mary Elizabeth Milner, subsequently Mrs. Alfred Harmsworth and later Lady Northcliffe, was his secretary, and a youth named Sutton, his typist, to-day Sir George Sutton, *Bart.*

When matters looked desperate his quick mind, always alive to improvisation, suddenly saw a possible chance. In the canoe he told me his version:

"One morning I was looking through **The Times** when my eye caught a small paragraph in the financial page. It mentioned the value of gold lying in the coffers of the Bank of England on the previous day. Suppose I were to offer a tempting prise to the reader of **Answers** who was nearest to the exact amount on a future specified date! Such newspaper competitions that existed were wearisome and offered small prizes. My offer was glittering, for nothing like it had ever been dreamed of - it was the freehold of a seven-roomed house, completely furnished, and valued at a thousand pounds. The effect was electrical. The public fought to buy up copies and fill in the form. We could not print sufficient to satisfy them. The value of the prise and the equal chance offered to all dazzled. them, and although the figure was pure guess-work - as yet the law had not stepped in to forbid guessing competitions - I printed figures of previous amounts as some guide, but even I failed to realise how immensely it appealed to the public imagination."

"It was customary," he continued, "for one of the liveried porters of the Bank to paste the figure on a board outside the main entrance in Threadneedle Street. Generally a few interested parties would glance, at the amount and pass on, but on the date of the competition the big open space between the Royal Exchange, the Mansion House, and the Bank was a vast struggling, surging concourse of the public all eager to learn the figure. Traffic was blocked and great excitement prevailed. After that I never looked back."

Just an idea treated boldly - some might say recklessly! How little indeed is often the dividing line between failure and success! To Alfred

Harmsworth, then aged twenty-three, it gave him a bride as his first reward, and before long out of the profits of *Answers* he was able to purchase Elmwood, St. Peter's, Thanet, a comfortable country house in large grounds, for which both his wife and he had the deepest sentimental affection. There, within sight and sound of the sea, he used to retire to work out many of his deep-laid schemes.

Six years later, another live-wire, Kennedy Jones, then a reporter, subsequently his partner, a Baronet and M.P. came to him with the suggestion that the **Evening News** was in the market and could be snapped up cheaply. Alfred had observed its weaknesses and had his own ideas of how to popularise an evening newspaper. He found the capital, reorganised it, and within one year had turned a loss into a profit of £14,000. It became a gold-mine to "K. J." and him. His appetite whetted, he determined to revolutionise the daily newspaper market and two years later created the **Daily Mail**, which first saw the daylight on 4 May 1896, before he had attained his thirty-first birthday. An eight-page paper, with new ideas in setting, type, headlines, and contents, and a news service perfectly organised for home and foreign affairs, a leading article crisp and outspoken, costing only one half-penny, it took the town by storm. It looked readable and it was, while most of the dailies were heavy. Women took to it, and that as much as anything was the secret of its success, for from the first it gave space to women's special interests like dress. Within three years it attained a sale of 600,000 a day, prodigious in those days, had become a most powerful organ of public opinion, and in the van of every new idea and movement.

Northcliffe said something about the start. Although Tom Marlowe was appointed editor-in-chief and the entire staff had been most carefully selected, he arranged personally everything down to the smallest details. Before the **Daily Mail** was officially published he had a week's rehearsal with every member of the staff working as though the paper were being actually published and then he criticised the production with his usual pungent method for nothing escaped his eagle eye. A friend of mine who was on the staff during its birth-pangs told me that the Chief, on the night of its real date of publication, lay on a couch most of the time in a state of nervous prostration and more than once declared that the new venture, with its tremendous stake, would prove his ruin. The year after it started Arthur Balfour, the Conservative Prime Minister, gave him a baronetcy, and a barony in the following year, pretty good proof of how the Government valued his support. Nevertheless, although a strong Imperialist, he was never a Tory Party man, was often its sternest critic, and he threw in all his weight on the side of Chamberlain when he preached the gospel of Tariff Reform.

He possessed an unerring instinct of comprehending the public taste but he never played down to it. Rather he endeavoured to educate it to a realisation of the trend of the future. He travelled a great deal and placed picked men in key positions in all parts of the world. He kept the Empire before men's eyes. No man did more to popularise motoring and he was the outstanding pioneer of flying from its very infancy. More than any big newspaper proprietor he edited his newspapers in the sense of actively directing their main talking points or stressing, their policy or running a campaign. Most of his work was done by telephone. Any man on his staff might be rung up at any hour day or night at his office or home and woe betide any editor who failed to rise to the occasion after a jolt. If he paid his staff well he certainly took it out of them in kind. He was excessively dictatorial, as he had a right to be, but no man serving under him could call his soul his own except maybe the printers, who, with their strong trade union, are always a law unto themselves.

John Scott-Montagu first taught him to drive a car and enthused him with his own exuberant confidence in the future of the motor. Although Northcliffe owned a fleet of cars I never saw him drive, although more than once I drove him - once on the road when his Daimler broke down - in my then 12h.p. *Gladiator*, a good French car of its time.

That reminds me of my first car in 1907. It was second-hand, very much so, a 6½h. p. two-seater *Humberette*, with a single-cylinder engine, which we christened "Garbage." A plausible advertisement of a wonderful bargain, "very little used, almost like new," price only £35, tempted me, and with the cash in my hand I repaired to a big garage in the Clapham Road. The manager sized me up at once as a mug, knowing full well that infatuation for a car is as blinding to the truth as infatuation for a woman. I doubted whether "Garbage" was all that was claimed for her, for she looked shabby, but he guaranteed her for six months subject to "fair wear and tear," and I made the purchase. As I had never driven a car before, my first journey to Thames Ditton was a perfect nightmare. In those days one had no bother about licences, registrations, or insurances.

Since then, although I have owned high-powered and fast cars, and have tried out many others writing up my experiences for the Press, "Garbage" gave me thrills like no other and taught me more about the mechanics than the rest put together. She had an unconquerable habit of always breaking down at unexpected moments with some part or other going wrong and what I did not learn from roadside repairs - sometimes failing and having to push her for distances to the nearest garage - was nobody's business. I reckon that I could have obtained a job as a garage hand at any time.

Motor transport on a large scale was a new thing then. In 1911 the Automobile Association carried out a test transport of a battalion of the Guards to Hastings, the idea being that an enemy force had landed in the vicinity and reinforcements had to be dispatched by road. Members of the A.A., of which I was a member, carried their allotment of husky Guardsmen with full kit, ran them down to Hastings according to schedule and brought them back. The journey out was accomplished, with few breakdowns, in under four hours which was considered good going. The scheme, originated by the **Daily Mail**, and under the aegis of the War Office, was, of course, widely publicised, and Kent, always the most patriotic of counties, made it a public holiday. The route was closed to other vehicles, police kept order, and the towns and villages crowded along the highway all along the route, waving Union Jacks and handkerchiefs and cheering enthusiastically. It was whispered that the test was intended to give the Kaiser a taste of what England could do if he asked for trouble. The leading organisers of this undertaking were Arthur and Harvey du Cros, Col. Charles Jarrett - since the moving spirit in the patriotic Society of St. George - and Sir Stenson Cooke, the energetic secretary of the A.A., always a cheery, friendly, and endearing sportsman, both of whom have, alas, recently passed away, and both of whom I knew as friends. Behind it was the hand of Northcliffe.

134

In those years coming events were casting their shadows before. Foreign trade was suffering heavily while alien goods were being dumped in the country and unemployment increased. Mr. Asquith's Government, despite its immense majority in the House of Commons, was losing caste and also by-elections with increasing regularity. Nor did it increase its prestige when the Prime Minister first paid Members of Parliament a salary, then followed it by taking away the power of the Lords in regard to monetary Bills and when it refused to consent to be shorn of its powers threatened to create a large number of coupon peers. In the realm of foreign affairs the outlook was not too happy. Efforts to hold out the olive branch to Germany were not liked by the nation, to put it mildly I have never known the policy of appeasement to appeal to my fellow-countrymen or to know them ever to be remiss when they are asked to agree to extra taxation in order to support a strong Navy, and Army.

As for Sir Edward Grey, during those years preceding 1914; he was well aware of Germany's ambitions and that she was like a young cuckoo in a nest of fledglings; He never showed great firmness towards her although it was recognised later that had he boldly warned the Kaiser, that if Germany attacked France we should undoubtedly fight, Wilhelm would have hesitated to cast the die in 1914. Yet in the spring of 1911, Germany certainly had a warning from Mr. Lloyd George, then Chancellor of the Exchequer, who had been regarded as the Prince of Pacifists.

Indirectly the outcome of Lloyd George's warning led to the Anglo-French *Entente*, and the agreement which conceded France Protectorate rights over Morocco. Irritated by the dispatch of a French military mission to Fez, the German Government sent the gunboat *Panther* to Agadir on the pretence of protecting her nationals although she had none there. A state of extreme tension was created and war loomed between Germany and France until Lloyd George, speaking at the Mansion House in June, warned Germany that any attempt at interference would mean war with us. The crisis passed but the tension remained, and early in the following year France and Britain came to the significant arrangement that the French Fleet would defend the Mediterranean while the British Fleet assumed responsibility for safeguarding the Channel in the event of war. It was generally welcomed.

The truth of the matter was that the European cauldron was beginning to boil over. The Young Turks had started it, and Turkey's weakness was Italy's opportunity. Inspired by her characteristically greedy policy of grab she declared war on Turkey, seized Tripoli and the Dodecanese Isles without the slightest justification or right, stabbing Turkey in the back as she did France in 1940. Then Greece, led by Venizelos, with Serbia, in the following year, seizing the opportunity when Italy was engaged with Turkey, in a six-weeks' campaign practically divided up all European Turkey outside Constantinople. The Balkan League sounded the knell of the Young Turks' ambitions and was the true beginning of the first World War. Sir Edward Grey, it is true, with the approval of the Powers, summoned an International Conference and with the Treaty of London in May 1913 succeeded in staving off war until August 1914. It marked the high-water mark of evasive British diplomacy.

In 1912, Mr. R. B. Haldane, the professorial Minister of War, visited Berlin at the personal invitation of the Kaiser with the object of restoring tolerable relations with Germany, but his mission was doomed to failure. In almost all his conversations with Wilhelm, von Tirpitz was present, not the Chancellor, and what the Kaiser demanded was practically a pledge of unconditional neutrality on our part, which would have meant betrayal of the *Grande Entente*. The inwardness of it was apparent, for it was unmistakable, namely a free hand for Germany to pick a quarrel with France, absorb her, and then polish us off! Haldane, who had been partly educated in Germany and was indiscreet enough to describe it as "my spiritual home," sabotaged his own career and retired with a Viscountcy as a *salarium*.

Such then was the political horizon with an inevitable war looming nearer, and I, anxious to be at least a mere small cog in the wheel, not even that. It was demoralising to reflect that I had joined Northcliffe's staff for the very purpose of doing my best to arouse the nation, and had been side-stepped by an erratic genius who had changed his mind, a man of varying moods. Hints were ignored or I was bluntly told that he regarded my work on **The London** as of great importance. Yet I was still apparently in his good books for he had me around a lot, but I began to suspect that the notorious "whispering gallery" was busy, and a small incident gave point to my doubts.

I was spending a week-end at Elmwood, near Broadstairs, where special guests were alone invited. The only other there was Sir Max Pemberton, a very old friend of the Northcliffes, and on the Sunday morning the four of us had strolled along the beach. On climbing up the cliff, I was walking behind with the Chief when he said suddenly:

"I am told you can't make a decision, young man."

I looked at him in surprise for it has never been a fault of mine:

"Who on earth told you that?" I asked.

"That is my business, What have you to say about it?"

"I say it is sheer nonsense, Chief," I laughed. "It is the first time I have ever been accused of such a weakness."

"It is a serious matter. The men I trust must know what they are doing and not go to others to see them through."

"I don't."

"Did you not show your cover of **The London** to Evelyn Wrench and ask for his opinion of it?"

"Certainly. Wrench directs the publicity of your publications and it was a natural, and I should have thought praiseworthy, motive to seek his reactions as to whether in his opinion it was a selling cover."

"Evelyn is not my editor of **The London**. You are. You must stand by your own judgment. Hesitation is a sign of weakness."

"I had decided," I replied, "I only wanted to see if he approved. Didn't you tell me not long ago that you did not disdain to ask the opinion of an office boy?"

It was a Parthian thrust. Northcliffe stopped in his walk and vouchsafed me a droll glance.

"That depends on the office boy," he snapped. "Reports I have of you are that you are not sure of yourself. It has been said that you are merely a society editor. Do you appreciate what great opportunities I have given you by placing this magazine, which originally bore my family name, in your charge?"

"I do," I answered lamely.

"Then in future act on your own judgment and don't go round inviting others' opinions. Hitherto I have been too busy to give **The London** my close personal attention but I intend to do so in the future."

Such was the way Northcliffe criticised his employees. It was brow-beating even though he intended it kindly. He invited retorts which it were unwise to make if one valued one's job. Necessary as was his patronage, and generous as he was, he judged many men on superficial grounds and he listened too frequently to distilled poison poured into his ear by those of his entourage who held his favour and who did not intend to permit an outsider to edge them from the Presence if they could help it.

He was as good as his word. He kept a sharp watch on **The London** for some time, a type of magazine with articles of a popular nature and largely comprising fiction. I had raised the level of the magazine considerably and had justified its rise in price from fourpence to sixpence. I cannot pretend, however, that I was enamoured with this class of work.

Some time later George Sutton told me that his Lordship, who was fishing in the Tay near Perth, wanted me to take all my plans for the next two or three issues to him and discuss them. He was staying alone at the *Station Hotel* and I found him in excellent spirits because he had hooked a large salmon, was apparently satisfied with my plans as a whole, made certain alterations and suggestions and was altogether affable and jocular. Most of the time he was closely occupied with an important member of **The Times** staff who had also paid a flying visit on a matter of high policy. He and I returned to town together.

We had scarcely taken our seats in a smoking carriage and settled down when the corridor door was flung open and Winston Churchill entered. He greeted my colleague with a grin.

"What are you doing here?" he inquired.

"Interviewing Northcliffe," was the reply. "He is staying at Perth and salmon fishing."

"I heard something about it. Has he had any luck?" He produced his cigar case, offered it round, and sat down with us. "I want to talk to Northcliffe directly. We may have fish, too - to fry!" He stayed with us until we reached Edinburgh.

Churchill was about thirty-seven at the time, podgy, urbane, wearing as always eclectic hats and having small, neat feet encased in boots with *suéde* uppers then very fashionable. He had recently been prominently in the news when as Home Secretary he had taken a prominent part in the Sidney Street siege where a number of murderous gangsters were cornered and finally shot up under his eyes. He had always, as he remarked not long ago when at Casablanca, "knocked around a good bit." I met him again years after when he threw over Liberalism and fought the Abbey Division of Westminster as an Independent, which he lost after an exciting by-election to the official nominee of the Tory Party.

If I never felt quite at home with Northcliffe, the same could not be said of Harold, then Sir Harold Harmsworth Bt., later, of course, Viscount Rothermere, who was genial, kindly, and good-humoured. He liked to play lawn tennis with me - he was a much better player than brother

Alfred who was slow about the court - and I recollect a week-end visit at Highcliffe Castle, a show place set in lovely grounds in Christchurch Bay overlooking the Needles. It had been lent to the Kaiser when he took part in Cowes Regatta and it was while here that Wilhelm II was grossly offended with my old chief Lord Montagu, who at his own request invited him to luncheon at Palace House, and received him wearing old tweeds. This act of deliberate disrespect, as the Kaiser deemed it to be, caused him to complain to King Edward, who was probably highly amused knowing well John's contempt for formality.

Although Rothermere was overshadowed by the genius of his brother, his was the business head to which Alfred owed so much and frankly admitted. Few men of our time have devoted themselves more completely than he to the service of the nation without thought of reward. From the beginning of the uprise of Hitler he realised its potential peril, and tried to bring about a revision of the weaknesses of the Versailles Treaty especially those clauses relative to Hungary, and in gratitude the Hungarians actually offered him the crown. Had he accepted it and eliminated Admiral Horthy, history might have been written somewhat differently.

Travelling extensively over the entire world, accompanied by able publicists like Ward Price and Collin Brooks (now editor of *Truth*), he and they did their level best to arouse the nation and Empire to the danger not only of Hitlerism but of the Rising Sun in the Pacific, all of which fell on deaf ears as far as the Government of Mr. Baldwin was concerned and from all accounts not at all to the liking of Big Business, who would apparently rather chance war than "unsettle" the public mind, which might mean a slump in trade! Like Northcliffe, he took the deepest interest in aviation. In 1917, when Minister for War, he declared himself whole-heartedly in favour of reprisals when many timid souls were afraid of the result. In 1935, when the Baldwinites were utterly starving the Royal Air Force, he ordered from the Bristol Aircraft factory a fast bomber made to special designs and presented it to the nation, naming it significantly, *"Britain First."*

This bomber, faster than our few then existent fighters, played a big part in revising British design of aircraft, and was the forerunner of the *Blenheims*. He gave large sums to philanthropic institutions, and was a great but self-effacing Englishman.

I could see that my number with Northcliffe was up. I don't know what I did to get into his black books, but anyone who did simply had to get out; I ascribed it to the "whispering gallery" and in fact the régime rather resembled a petty German court with its heel-clickings, grovellings, slander, espionage and jealousies of those who so ardently desired to bask in the sunshine of patronage. I fancy I fell out of favour when in an unfortunate moment I was tricked into a gamble where my losses in having rashly purchased many bales of cotton on a marginal rise amounted to four figures, although I thought I had limited liability. The bottom fell out of the market, the brokers left me in the lurch and as I had to find the money I asked my employers to advance some of it without giving the reason for it. An advance of a few hundreds was given me, but it doubtless got to the ears of the Chief through his "ferrets" and I imagine he came to the conclusion that I was leading a double life! He hated that sort of thing and was rather prone to such beliefs.

Anyhow, on quite another matter I had a hectic interview with him, he accusing me of having given a job to a distant relation by marriage, which was quite untrue, and I retorted that had I dreamt that instead of creating a big Empire publication I was to be side-tracked on to a mere popular magazine I would never have quitted **The Graphic**. He was white with anger. The only pleasant memory I possessed was in taking leave of Harold, his brother, who shook my hand and said how much he regretted that I had fallen out with his brother.

Let it not be said that I fail in admiration of Lord Northcliffe. Every man of genius has his Achilles' Heel. As a director of newspapers and a creator of publicity he outshone all others. Nothing was too big as nothing was too small to engage his personal attention. His enterprise, his ingenuity, and his creativeness, added to his amazing energy and drive, made him practically the dictator of the Press, controlling, as he did, so huge a "stable", from the pontifical *Times* down to little publications with immense circulations. He was extremely generous and free-handed, and no man better appreciated the importance of his editors having the benefit of seeing the greater world, and shaking off the trammels of insularity. He was a pioneer in every progressive new enterprise such as motoring and flying. He was a really great business man, although he pretended to disdain the sordid side of finance.

His mind worked with the quickness of streaked lightning, but he was superficial in thought. He jumped rapidly to conclusions with almost feminine intuition and his judgment was not infallible, but he grew so powerful that few dared question it. I have mentioned how he vacillated from one extreme to another over the question of war with Germany and it must be said that he showed none of the qualities of a great statesman. Yet it may be added that he did more than any man to save the situation in the last great war, for he had the ability and the courage to expose the muddles and inefficiency of the High Command at a critical hour without which we might have lost the war. He was totally indifferent to the savage abuse levelled at him for daring to tell the truth. Alfred Harmsworth, Viscount Northcliffe, had his foibles, but he was a bold and tremendous figure, in a period when outspokenness and daring were considered almost indecent.

CHAPTER VIII

GAMBLING IN NEWSPAPER OWNERSHIP

"There's a sucker born every minute."

CHICAGO GANGSTER APHORISM

I MUST CONFESS that I left the atmosphere of Carmelite House with a sigh of relief. I felt as though I had escaped from a foetid and insufferable atmosphere. In an interview with Mr. George Sutton, Northcliffe's manager and keeper of his conscience, now a baronet, he said frankly that since the Chief and I evidently could not see eye to eye it would be better if we parted company. I was only too delighted to agree and we came to an amicable settlement of our affairs.

I had, however, left the Chief with a sagging bank account and a wife and young family dependent upon me. While I was angling for the editorship of an Anglo-Indian daily, I received a telegram from an unexpected source, signed "Elias," and inviting me to call upon him without delay.

At some public reception I remembered that I had met Julius Salter Elias, head of a firm of printers named Odham's. I duly presented myself at his offices, not then gargantuan as to-day, and found my hand warmly grasped by a little fellow with fair, slightly sandyish hair, a slight figure, a quick perhaps nervous manner, a big, wide smile, and remarkable perception. He looked little more than a boy, so youthful was he in appearance, although the brains of a business growing rapidly from very small beginnings. To-day he has become Lord Southwood. He is still "J.S." to his oldest friends.

To-day Lord Southwood has also emerged - and for many years past - from being a printer of other owners' publications into a newspaper proprietor, head of a huge capitalistic concern built up of small beginnings, all entirely due to the energy, enterprise, and brilliant business perspicacity of one man. Socialists may talk of the lack of opportunity offered to the working man, but, given the genius, the opportunity makes itself. Southwood began life as a poor boy, his wits being his sole capital, and he has reached the top of the tree by ability, merit, and great diligence. He works something like eighteen hours out of the twenty-four. He is just and considerate to his employees, pays them well, is interested in their welfare individually, and is always accessible. He sacked me once, so I can praise him without prejudice.

Elias had as clients two men of position, tyros in the intricacies of newspaper management, who had purchased two weekly newspapers as a speculation. He had heard that I was free at the time - he evidently had his scouts! - and wanted to know if I would be interested in editing and managing them. He kindly said that he believed that I could make a success of them. When I heard their names I was not so sure.

My heart sank when it transpired that the first of the two journals was **The Throne**, a threepenny illustrated weekly which had burst out with a huge flourish of trumpets a few years earlier as a most exclusive socialite weekly costing half a crown, for which scarcely anyone below the degree of a Countess was permitted to write. It was badly printed, execrably made up, hopelessly snobbish, and utterly dull. Its blatancy and amateurishness made it the joke of Fleet Street. Gradually it descended in the social scale until it had fallen into the hands of William Lotinga, a racing tipster, with a biggish following under the pseudonym of "Larry Lynx," and was now a liability. The other journal was a woman's weekly named *Madame*, which had a certain vogue among the middle classes, and also a losing property, although it was claimed to be paying its way.

The Throne, it appeared, had been purchased by the Hon. Charles Bateman Hanbury, a jovial sportsman, well known in racing circles, who, as I learnt subsequently, bought it up presumably from Lotinga for a hundred pounds in cash with the idea of refurbishing and reselling it at a handsome profit. Bateman-Hanbury, as a matter of fact, was in a low financial condition, but his brother-in-law, Mr. (now Sir) Samuel Hill-Wood, then M.P. for the Peak Division of Derbyshire, reputed to be very wealthy, was put forward as his backer. How or why Bateman-Hanbury added **Madame** to his bag I never ascertained, but she turned out a jade of the first water, for the journal should have been either a "class" woman's weekly, produced on art paper, catering for Society and its following on sale at sixpence, or made a popular middle-class home weekly at one penny, aiming at a large circulation. Priced at threepence it fell between two stools.

Neither of these two properties offered any attraction to an editor of experience and on the face of it there lay a path of peril. At first I hesitated. On the other hand I was attracted by the prospect of an up-hill fight and I believed sufficiently in my lucky star to imagine that if the papers had sufficient new capital behind them they might be made successful if well edited and produced.

At a conference at which both Bateman-Hanbury and Hill-Wood were present I was asked what capital I would consider essential. I said £20,000 should do it on the assumption that little need be spent on **Madame**. As the outcome of a discussion this was agreed upon, and I was appointed managing editor of both journals as well as a director of the company, being allotted a quarter of the shares. We had offices in Essex Street, the staff was appointed, and with little delay the enterprise started.

My plan of campaign was to concentrate first upon **The Throne**, which was in a more desperate state of health than the other and yet offered the best chances of financial success if it could be pulled through and restored, and meanwhile to run **Madame** as economically as possible until we had put **The Throne** on its feet. The business manager agreed enthusiastically to this plan and I took over the editorship of **The Throne**, dropping its other title, *And Country*, which seemed meaningless. Rennie Byles, the business manager, who had been a director of a publishing business, one of the most conscientious and honest of men, but inclined to worry overmuch - indeed, he worried himself into a premature grave - worked like a Trojan, but before long an abyss opened at our feet which neither had foreseen.

To begin with we made fair sail. I was fortunate enough to obtain Olive Viner and her husband, Maitland Davidson, as joint editors of **Madame.** for few women journalists could vie with Olive in regard to the interests of her sex, while Davidson had been thoroughly trained on dailies. Tommy Sapt, a well-known and efficient Fleet Street reporter, was the assistant editor of **The Throne,** While its Advertisement Manager was John Gibson Jarvie, a young dark-haired Scot, a super-optimist, who was convinced that we should gain big advertising support. At that time advertisements were a minus quantity.

Gibson Jarvie is to-day well known as a banker and financier, even a partner of the Bank of England, who came prominently before the public during this war as Regional Port Director of the Liverpool Docks, where he proved remarkably successful in taming the tough dockers. After leaving *The Throne* he went to America, grasped the big idea of car purchase on the instalment system, returned to pioneer it and established his powerful financial combine *The United Dominions Trust.* Possessing enormous energy and drive from small beginnings he has risen to considerable financial heights.

Among artist contributors was the well-known **Daily Express** cartoonist Sidney Strube. On one occasion he submitted a cartoon which I could not use and remarked, "Why don't you offer it to the **Express**? It seems to be down their street."

"Do you think so?" he asked dubiously.

"You can but try. They won't skin you alive!"

He took my advice, the cartoon was accepted, and so paved the way for him to become their staff cartoonist, and the best-known of his craft in Britain, who, with David Low, the Socialist-minded New Zealander of the *Evening Standard,* is probably the highest-paid draughtsman in the world outside the United States, which shows you what Lord Beaverbrook thinks of the value of a cartoon to influence public opinion. Personally I dislike Low's political views intensely, but he's a brilliant artist.

Before Strube attained eminence, when in fact he was a free-lance humorous artist, he found it difficult to reach the editors through a string of minor myrmidons and so hit on the device of having large and somewhat expensive cigarettes made specially for him, the paper bearing a caricature of himself and the words, "Strobe, Cartoonist." Beginning with office-boys, he gradually offered his lure until he reached the "high-ups" - at least such is the account he once gave me.

"I don't seem to remember your super-cigarettes," I commented.

"No, George," he replied, for everybody is George to him. "I had reached the goal and then came the time to economise!"

The abyss I hinted at was this. Bateman-Hanbury never breathed a word to me about the liabilities incurred by his two precious periodicals, and when I had stipulated for twenty thousand pounds new working capital I naturally anticipated that the papers' liabilities were fully met and that we had the minimum amount estimated as essential to success at call. Finance is always a tiresome matter to my mind and I had my hands very full editing the one journal, keeping close watch over the other, and endeavouring to produce a sixpenny weekly at the price of threepence, at the same time exercising all economies possible. It was some little time - for Byles kept silence in regard to the matter - before I realised that we were uncommonly short of funds. Odhams reminded me that a big bill was outstanding and that they would be glad to receive a substantial cheque.

I saw strange men hanging round the general office and discovered that they were duns who had been promised settlement and could not get it. Photograph agencies began to be shy and I ascertained that they found it difficult to obtain payment of their accounts. I interviewed Byles, who looked more worried than ever, and let the cat out of the bag.

The company was owing between five and six thousand pounds before I took over, and since then he had only been able to collect some two thousand of the promised twenty, but he expected a big amount within the next few days. When I asked him why he had kept me in the dark, he

147

replied that he supposed that I had been acquainted with the facts from the first. Here was a pretty kettle of fish! Importunate creditors were on the doorstep from morning to night, for in addition to all else both **The Throne** and **Madame** had rotten reputations, especially the former, and Fleet Street regarded them as shaky so credit was becoming more and more restricted. Our promised new capital was only coming in by drips and drabs and when it was paid over it only served to settle the more importunate creditors. Indeed, our financial position steadily deteriorated instead of improving and it needed great tact on the part of Byles to allocate the limited funds in his possession and enable us to keep going, while in addition it entirely prevented us from carrying out a projected publicity scheme which was one of the main planks in my programme to establish the papers.

Mr. Hill-Wood was a busy man and difficult to track down, and in any case Bateman-Hanbury was the responsible party; so I got hold of him. He was entirely unimpressed by protests.

"We are doing the best we can," he said. "You don't expect that Hill-Wood has twenty thousand pounds lying idle in his bank? It means realising securities and that takes time."

"Surely it would be easy for him to instruct his bankers to advance at least a moiety of the amount, Hanbury?" I protested. "If we don't get it I shall have to refuse to accept responsibility for the consequences. Twenty thousand in one sum, or the ability to draw on it as needed, is a very different matter to these driblets. Moreover, there is this other serious matter of the pre-existing liabilities. It means that we shall, require at least another five thousand pounds, for I named the lowest amount of new capital when we discussed the finance with Mr. Elias. Mr. Hill-Wood must be asked to supply it."

He laughed in my face.

"Not a hope!" he said. "He only agreed to put up twenty thousand to oblige me. Besides, you are getting on very well. You'll make a success of the papers all right."

148

It was true that the net circulation of **The Throne**, which had proved to be infinitesimal, was steadily on the up-grade, and at least a few genuine advertisements were being obtained; We covered events with a sturdy independence and were definite critics of the Government. It might sound cynical to assert that after a Government has been in office for a few years it is sound journalism to oppose it, but there is a good reason for it, namely, that no Government ever lives up to its promises, and can only be brought up to scratch by strong opposition. A Government in our country, no matter how it may prate of democracy, gradually leans towards nepotism unless it is severely reprimanded. Of course in a paper lacking a gleam of prestige, as was **The Throne**, it was not easy to acquire, any influence, but we employed sarcasm and satire, lampooned Ministers, and met with growing success. It is true that the public remained for the most part foggy-minded and were more interested in knowing who won the three o'clock race than their own stake in the country.

I wrote certain articles about Germany and here I was on safe ground. My co-directors, so far from finding fault, applauded any action. Moreover, some three years earlier, Sir Eyre Crowe, the most perspicacious Under-Secretary for Foreign Affairs for many a long moon, had anticipated the intentions of the sword-rattling Kaiser and his advisers, and lamented the feebleness of the British Government.

"The action of Germany," he declared roundly, "towards this country since 1890 might be likened not inappropriately to that of a professional blackmailer. . . . There is one road which, if past experience is any guide to the future, will most certainly not lead to any permanent improvement of relations and which must therefore be abandoned: that is the road paved with graceful British concessions made without any conviction of their justice or of their being set off by equivalent counter-services."

Eyre Crowe said what everyone of insight knew only too well, but his reproach, which reflected upon Lord Lansdowne and Sir Edward Grey, fell on deaf ears. The million had no power - they never have after they elect their M.P.s - business, and especially Big Business, followed their old game of endeavouring to discount war and rumours of war, but daily the cloud loomed nearer, and when the Balkan Concert was destroyed war became inevitable with the disruption of Turkey, added to the grabbing action of Austria-Hungary and Italy.

With all the heavy disadvantages from which we suffered those two papers survived for over a couple of years and with any luck we would have pulled through when a final disaster scuttled the ship. We had to face a libel action against **The Throne**, a futile action in which we were the victims of a marriage imbroglio without the least intent. It was not due even to a slip-up, which so often mulcts a paper of damages.

In the page of book reviews we published a photograph of a very well-known woman novelist, who was known generally as the wife of another equally well-known novelist of the day, Ford Madox Hueffer - later he dropped the surname of Hueffer and added another Ford - and this gentleman wrote an introduction to his "wife's" novel, calling her his wife. **The Throne** in perfect good faith described the lady as "Mrs. Ford Madox Hueffer," the next we heard of it being a writ for libel, issued on the instructions of the real wife who had her marriage lines.

I was the more surprised because I had dined with Ford Madox Hueffer and his "wife" at their Kensington residence, while Byles was frequently their guest and knew both of them well. He saw them and assured me that all would be well, that Hueffer had obtained at divorce against his first wife and had married the authoress in Hanover. Hueffer had promised him, likewise the authoress, to give evidence on our behalf if the case came into court, although I was assured that this would not happen. The matter dragged on and we were in the difficult position of not being able to mitigate any damage by an apology because Hueffer claimed that his marriage was good. The injured wife engaged silk and we had to do likewise, briefing Mr. Ernest Wild, later Sir Ernest Wild, M.P., the Recorder of the City of London. In court the injured wife obtained the sympathy of the judge, to which she was no doubt entitled, and since our defence was vitiated by the disappearance of Hueffer and his lady friend, the plaintiff obtained £400 damages and costs.

It was no defence in law that we had accepted the *ipse dixit* of the erring husband, although the judge expressed some sympathy with our position. He posed a question to me, when I was in the witness-box, rather on the same lines as the old tag, "When did you last beat your wife?" He asked, "If you had known that Miss X was not Mr. Hueffer's wife would you so have described her?" I tried to parry the question by replying, "I can't say what I might have done. The point never arose." Pressed for a more explicit answer, I said, "I should probably have evaded the subject. The private relationship of these two persons was merely a side issue to a literary critique. We only quoted the book."

The laws of libel have been so strained and the damages awarded against a newspaper can be so preposterous that to-day newspapers insure against actions for libel. This case seemed a particularly dangerous trap, for after all a newspaper, like an individual, can only accept the relationships between private persons as they are known generally to the world. Hueffer and his lady lived in good surroundings as husband and wife and the ass had gone to the length of publicly labelling her as his wife in the introduction to her novel. The only way to ascertain such relationships, as our counsel suggested, would be to ask persons for their marriage certificates, which was absurd. Why Hueffer stirred up mud and victimised us I never ascertained. Ernest Wild advised that we had a strong case for an appeal.

But the damages and costs - these amounted to about a thousand pounds - were our undoing. Bateman-Hanbury said that neither he nor his brother-in-law were prepared to finance the papers further.

I decided that since the judgment, if allowed to stand, would prove a perilous trap for newspaper proprietors, to see if a number of newspaper proprietors would agree to subscribe to a fund to enable us to appeal. It was suggested that I should first call on Clement Shorter, then Editor of **The Sphere**, who regarded himself as in the foremost ranks of literary critics. I knew that Shorter was an inordinately vain man, but he was a protagonist and might be expected to support an appeal. At one time he was enthusiastically pro-Irish, probably inspired by his wife, Dora Sigerson, a vehement *Sinn-Feiner* as well as a poetess. He was also a

151

turgid devotee of the Victorian Brontes, whose genius he was never tired of extolling in ecstatic and fulsome adulation. He being as it were a supporter of lone causes, I thought that Shorter might welcome the opportunity to advance the freedom of the Press. His reception was more than frigid. It was uncompromising.

"I read the report of the case in **The Times**," he said, bestowing a quite malignant eye upon me, "and I am not in the least interested in your proposed appeal."

I stared at this strange little man in some surprise. His appearance could not be said to be impressive. Squat, thick-set, with a mulatto-like skin and unkempt black-grey hair rebelliously sprouting out like porcupine quills, he might have been a descendant of Caliban.

"You will realise, Mr. Shorter," I expostulated, "that if a judgment such as this stands unchallenged it will be a never-ending source of anxiety to an editor like yourself who may quite innocently be trapped into an expensive libel suit."

"If you make mistakes you must take the consequences," he returned, "and not expect others to help you out of the mess."

"It is in your own interests," I retorted. "And as **The Sphere** is a more important journal than **The Throne** you stand to be hit harder than we. It is my object to ask newspaper proprietors and so yourself to subscribe to a fund to enable an appeal to be entered. Mr. Ernest Wild advises that we have a strong case. Are you prepared to guarantee, say, fifty pounds?"

"No," said Shorter bluntly, "I will not."

"Oh! Well, thank you for your exquisite courtesy, Mr. Shorter," I said, rising from the chair. "And congratulations on your public spirit."

It annoyed him intensely, as I naturally intended to do, for surely he asked for it. I did not know then, as I learnt subsequently, that **The Sphere** had perpetrated the same error as we by calling the authoress "Mrs. Ford Madox Hueffer." If I had known it would have been a useful weapon in my hands.

Shorter looked daggers at me.

"I wish to waste no more time with you, Comyns Beaumont," he snorted. "I disapprove of you and all your views. I think you are a war-monger."

"What do you know about war?" I gibed. "Confine yourself to something you profess to know - such as the Brontes!"

So that interview took me nowhere. Other efforts also proved abortive, and so that strange judgment still stands as an axiom of British jurisprudence that if a woman calls herself Mrs. Smith, and is known as Mrs. Smith, a newspaper by giving her the name she is commonly known by as the wife of Mr. Smith is thereby libelling the unknown discarded wife. A strange world, my masters!

Apart from this particular libel case, which only had the effect of throwing a lot of innocent people out of employment and stopped a paper - or did soon after - which was trying to be useful, I will confess that I regard the existing state of the libel laws in this country to be a menace to freedom of opinion. They appear to have been devised to protect the evildoer and the harpy generally, for such is the loose fabric of our law of libel that as a legal friend confessed to me once, "practically everything that is published about persons contains a libel in some form or another." He may have been a super-optimist, for libels rejoice the heart of the brethren of the wig and gown. If a newspaper makes the least slip which might by the widest stretch of the imagination reflect upon a person, there are wide-awake firms of shoddy attorneys ready to pounce upon a newspaper armed with a writ, they having ascertained the address of the alleged maligned one and promise to obtains them adequate damages often on a fifty-fifty basis, knowing that in nine cases out of ten the newspaper will make a cash offer to avoid litigation. I knew a journalist on a big-circulation daily whose job was to forestall these harpies by arriving first on the scene with a pocketful of bank notes and settle any possible case of action off-hand.

It would almost seem as though the existing law of libel had been drawn up by legal-minded poltergeists whose mischievous object was to produce confusion, muddle, irresponsibility and wanton damage, rather than protect the honest person whose reputation has suffered by an untrue charge, for the effect of it is to place a strong weapon in the hands of swindlers and blackmailers who desire to follow their pernicious callings without the glare of publicity. It is quite a serious matter from a national point of view because it exerts a severe restriction upon the ability of the Press to criticise a variety of subjects in the public interest.

The legal editors or advisers on newspapers frequently refuse to permit any exposure, even though the facts can be well established, because of the loopholes and the not uncommon aptitude of judges to award enormous damages to a litigant where a newspaper is the defendant, for somehow the legal mind appears to regard the Press as a danger to society. There still stands the judgment where a litigant brought a libel action against a journal which published a short story about a purely fictitious person to whom the author had given the same name as the alleged libelled one and although neither the author nor the personnel of the journal had ever heard of the plaintiff, he obtained heavy damages - I believe £10,000 - and it has since compelled every newspaper publishing fiction to protect itself by stating that all the characters are imaginary.

I know from experience the restrictive effect of our law of libel, for I was on the staff of **John Bull** for a time and edited it for a short while. From its commencement it adopted the laudable principle of exposing rogues and dangerous characters who prey upon the simplicity and good-will of the public, and it has performed this duty with its eyes fully open to the heavy risks it has entailed. Apart from leading firms of solicitors who act for it, **John Bull** employs a distinguished barrister - indeed two of them - who reads everything in type before publication after preliminary conferences and who cancels at his discretion anything which may give the slightest opening to a libel action. In addition, on the staff are expert criminologists, including Sir Wyndham Childs, formerly Chief of the Criminal Investigation Department of Scotland Yard, and, let me add, the journal possesses a dossier of the records of criminals and crooks which Scotland Yard detectives are often pleased to consult.

Yet, with all this safeguard, the expense of lawsuits costs **John Bull** thousands a year. The year before the war, with no very heavy damages given against it, its legal costs exceeded £20,000, so the paper's chief barrister informed me. It has won innumerable actions against crooks who have taken it into court and who never pay a penny piece of the costs awarded against them because they are not worth powder and shot. I know of many instances where it has been found cheaper to pay a rogue a sum of money when he issues a writ, although the man's dossier exposes his shady past, owing to the queer leaning of judges in favour of the "oppressed" classes. If an application be made in court by a defendant newspaper for some security for costs, although the plaintiff may be proved to be a man of straw it is rarely granted above fifty pounds although the costs of the defence may run into four figures.

I went personally with **John Bull**'s crime reporter to visit a mushroom farm in one of the home counties, for we had a great deal of evidence to prove that behind the existing evidence was an enormous swindle being perpetrated on the investing public. We satisfied ourselves that although the farm was a show place and producing the mushrooms it was indeed a real "mushroom" concern, the farm being worth a few thousand pounds whereas the share-pushers were selling shares approaching seven figures. Having run the main instigators to earth in an hotel and with a complete story and dossiers, we placed the matter before our legal editor, who vetoed the proposed exposure because the swindle had not yet come to light and he said we must give the gang the benefit of the doubt. The sequel was that the conspirators a little later realised the game to be up and fled across the Atlantic with their ill-gotten gains, some being eventually rounded up, extradited and tried, and sentenced to long terms of imprisonment. It was a case of closing the stable-door after the horses were stolen. One objection to publication by our legal editor was that if we exposed the racket the culprits would almost certainly serve a writ for libel which would seal our mouth *pendente lite* and would probably cause the enterprise to crash whereas there was always a bare possibility of a reconstruction if it were trading honestly although over-capitalised.

Editors therefore cannot be blamed if they hesitate before exposing graft, and the public, who are exploited, are the sufferers, for sharks flourish everywhere as there are millions of gullible small fry around. A revision of the law of libel is one of the reforms I hope to see if we are going to face the future with a hopeful set of new ideals because if the law is going to protect the dishonest elements in our midst and derive fat fees from libel actions it undermines one's belief in equity. Personally I should like to see the whole procedure of the administration of the civil law overhauled from top to bottom. It rarely bestows what it exists to do - give justice.

It was a distressing sequel to all the efforts we had made that by reason of this absurd libel action **The Throne** enterprise came to an end. A few months longer and we should have established it as a go-ahead and independently minded journal, which was badly needed at that time with war looming on the horizon and the Press mainly occupied with sport and the antics of the Suffragettes added to Asquith's starting the perilous road of paying Members of Parliament, thus destroying their independence. I believe that Mr. Hill-Wood actually put up more than the agreed on twenty thousand pounds but as it came in doles it was of small avail. I dare say he was sick of the drain on him, and as for Bateman-Hanbury he had taken on a gamble not at his own risk, and had calculated that having bought up two papers, saddled with liabilities, at what he fondly imagined was a bargain price, he could turn his money over many hundred times in a few months. An astute young man, with considerable charm of manner, at humorist with a twinkling eye, when it came to newspapers he was no better than a babe in arms.

It taught me a lesson, namely that it is tempting Providence to reconstruct newspapers which have been suffered to deteriorate, unless very large capital is available and in such a case it is far cheaper to let the dead bury their dead and create a new journal. I made up my mind never to be trapped into such a situation again, and yet in the future I was destined to have to make similar efforts with four other such publications!

Such was the disheartening climax to **The Throne** and **Madame**. The former was purchased by a young super-optimist who had recently come down from Cambridge and had little or no experience of newspapers. A scion of a wealthy York family and with rich backers he possessed the youthful impetuosity and the superiority complex often a product of such seats of learning wedded to a sublime innocence of the real world. He was Harold Terry, who became a close friend of mine, and blossomed into a playwright of some repute. **The Throne** soon sank unhonoured into its grave. So did **Madame**.

The eclipse of all my plans was necessarily a disheartening and even serious matter to me from a professional standpoint, for this world is prone to forget quickly a man's successes and to keep a close tally on his failures - unless he is a prominent politician. However, I carried on with certain free-lance work, and edited part-time a tariff-reforms journal whose proprietor was no other than my old acquaintance Holt Thomas, squeaky-voiced, parrot-faced, elegantly-tailored rebel of the Thomas family, showing how deceptive often are personal appearances, for he had brains, initiative, and courage.

And then World War Number One burst unexpectedly upon us.

It burst like a sudden cyclone to the paralysed astonishment of almost everybody. If the Foreign Office had suspected such a situation - as it should have done, for that war was inevitable was evident three years before - it had shown laggard footsteps.

Big Business - the hordes of Luptons and Davises - was, of course, washed up by the tide, although many contrived to flourish by battening on the nation's sufferings.

CHAPTER IX

THE FIRST GREAT WAR

"The Government remained in that total ignorance reserved for those who govern."

ANATOLE FRANCE

WAR FELL UPON US in 1914 more unexpectedly than in the later and yet more terrible war, for the assassination of the Archduke Ferdinand of Austria at Sarajevo - since established as the dirty work of German *agents provocateurs* - seemed to most people just another bubbling-up of the hellish cauldron of the Balkans.

It was a lovely summer, and part of the British fleet lay peacefully at anchor off Kiel, being entertained by the Kaiser during Kiel Regatta, where yachts were competing with Wilhelm's Meteor. It was difficult to associate hostilities so near in the offing when the warships of Britain and Germany were moored side by side decked in bunting from bow to stern.

War had daily loomed nearer. Germany ominously announced her intention of standing by her ally Austria-Hungary whose senile emperor, Franz-Josef had unleashed the hounds of war on poor Serbia, despite her expressed regrets. Russia in honour bound took her stand by the side of Serbia, and France, true to the Dual Alliance, threw in her lot with Russia. Only Italy, although a member of the Triple Alliance, stood aloof as a neutral, waiting to see what England did. In London, Cabinet meetings were watched with anxiety and everyone wondered when we would be drawn into the vortex. Then came the German ultimatum to little Belgium demanding the right to march through her territories to get at France, a demand refused point-blank by King Albert, who Immediately called upon Britain to come to his aid. The fat was in the fire. England had guaranteed the integrity of Belgium, but the Cabinet had not yet shown its hand.

The fourth of August 1914 was a blazing hot Bank Holiday. Enormous crowds blocked Whitehall and waited apprehensively for the expected decision of Mr. Asquith's Cabinet. British mass psychology is simple and direct, based on instinctive desire to do what is right and just. The nation is intelligent enough to detest the thought of war, a destructive use of brute force in which might becomes right, but all felt confident that if it came to fighting that Germany would receive the chastisement she deserved. Their sentiments were clear enough by their cheers whenever they caught sight of an army or naval uniform, for it meant that the only path which we could tread with honour was to stand side by side with little Belgium and France against the bullying transgressors. Apart from the huge crowds everything seemed so peaceful on that day, with no roar of London's traffic, and war, with its bloody harvest, far beyond the horizon of the azure sky above us.

Hush! What was that? From Downing Street a car emerged. Cheers arose from near by . . . . It meant that the Cabinet had made its fatal decision. *War*! A fight to the death with the bullies of Europe! England would stand by her pledge to Belgium, and the rumour passed round that already an ultimatum had been dispatched to the German Government amounting to a declaration of war should Germany cross the Belgian frontier. War "for a scrap of paper," was the contemptuous description given by Prince von Bülow, the German Chancellor, to our Ambassador who handed him the ultimatum. A brief sentence, but one showing the vast chasm between British and German conceptions of honour.

Later, a rumour spread that there had been some dissension in the Cabinet. John Burns for one resigned office. But Lloyd George, hitherto placed in the ranks of the Peace-at-any-Price Party, had declared unequivocally for war, and from being the most execrated, in a day became most popular. Which shows you! Our Army - small, but said to be admirably equipped - was ready. Churchill, then First Lord of the Admiralty, with "Jackie" Fisher as his First Sea Lord, was fully prepared, and promptly set up the Dover Patrol which executed such splendid work.

Nevertheless, on land, defeat and unpreparedness soon began to loom up. Inefficiency in the War Office "High-Ups," and poor generalship in the field on the part of certain generals, led to a dangerous situation which gallantry by itself could not overcome. The War Office thought that shrapnel was good enough for the forces while the enemy employed high explosive shells, and the casualty lists became a terrible nightmare. In another direction we were faced with heavy defeat by Turkey in our attempt to force the Dardanelles, and despite tremendous heroism and resource at Gallipoli we had to withdraw, to defeat Turkey in 1917 by land. There was lack of cohesion between the Army and Navy in the Dardanelles campaign, a half-hearted affair, but behind it lay the utter incompetence of the Foreign Office from 1907 onwards, whose successive Foreign Ministers and Ambassadors had permitted one of our oldest allies to be wooed and won by Germany. As regards the Western Front, fortunately the blunt exposure by Northcliffe in the **Daily Mail** saved a situation steadily deteriorating. He revealed the pitiable obstinacy and stupidity of the War Office and fixed the blame directly on Kitchener, the Chief of Staff. Though a blaze of anger shot up and the incorrigible humorists of the Stock Exchange publicly burnt a copy of the **Daily Mail**, the Chief serenely stood his ground, and reforms were instituted. That shows what resolute leadership by the Press can effect.

Conscription was yet to come into force, but Kitchener's call for volunteers met with incredible support. Recruiting booths were packed by long queues of men of all shapes and sizes, hoping to have a knock at the Hun. The war was expected to be settled with Germany's defeat in three months. The War Office was supercilious about accepting recruits, at a shilling a day, and at first more were rejected on medical grounds or on the score of age than accepted; Before long, however, we had the poster of Kitchener plastered throughout the country, pointing a fore-finger at the observer and saying, "*Your King and Country Need You.*"

Like many others, I made various efforts to join up as a Tommy, and was ignominiously rejected by the doctors. I was at the time just over thirty-five, the age limit, but a little later I scraped through into the

Armoured Car division, commanded by Commander Oliver Locker-Lampson, a force ranked as A.B. sailors attached to the Naval Brigade. In due course part of the force was landed at Antwerp and thrown into action against the Germans, who had brought up heavy guns. The attempt to take the enemy in the rear and defend Antwerp proved abortive, but the idea of using armoured cars was sound enough had they been adequately supported by artillery. The remnants were brought home. Churchill himself was in Antwerp with the Brigade. It was his original idea.

After this, it was high time I got a new job. We had let our house furnished and were economising in a flat at Margate when a good angel in the shape of Elias came to my rescue. He wanted to start a new weekly which would republish world cartoons of the war from all sources, and invited me to edit it. Thus was born the *Passing Show*, which quickly developed its own outlook and became a remarkable success for many years. It was, I fancy, the first publication actually fathered by Odhams, excepting for **John Bull**, which had started under the independent auspices of Horatio Bottomley. Elias took a great personal interest in **Passing Show** from the first, and I was in close touch with him.

Other people's cartoons soon took a back seat and the paper produced its own cartoons and outlook on the war. It was a twopenny weekly when twopenny Weeklies were general. Its letterpress was amusing, up to date, and always cheerful. It held up the Kaiser and his generals to constant ridicule, as also the Sultan, but it was never vulgar. It published three topical cartoons in each number and did not hesitate to quiz the Government's shortcomings. If we did not possess a "Mr. Punch" to emphasise the paper's personality, Leo Cheney, a brilliant humorous artist on the staff, created the *Showman*, a genial figure with a very tall, white beaver hat and a ruffle, who answered our purpose admirably. Our black-and-white artists were men whose names were household words, and our jokes were second to none. The Services selected it in preference to any other humorous weekly and the Government placed a large permanent order. It was regarded as important propaganda.

Cartoons were a main consideration, and we held a weekly conference to decide them. Present usually was Vernon Woodhouse, an old friend, assistant editor, a playwright and our dramatic critic, a man of most kindly temperament, with an impish sense of satire and considerable knowledge of the technique of composition The art editor was Owen Aves, a very tall, droll personality, with a deep voice, extremely deaf, and a genius for roughing out the baldest ideas into a composition. Leo Cheney, a famous poster artist and a wonderful cartoonist, invariably cheerful although he new well that his days were numbered, who did more than any man to make the paper outstanding. He was a master of the art of pictorial satire and could ridicule mercilessly without being vulgar or blatant.

Besides Leo we had George Whitelaw, a young man who had made a mark as cartoonist on the **Glasgow Herald** and whom I induced to come to London - if a Scot needs inducement! - another fine draughtsman with a delicacy of touch and very versatile. There was old E. T. Reed, the erstwhile **Punch** artist, a master of caricature of Ministers, who had Worked for years in the Press Gallery of the House of Commons. His weakness was sometimes in anatomy, never portraits, and here Owen Aves often improved on the original. If Reed realised it he never said anything, nor did we, so all were satisfied. He could produce laughable cartoons lampooning Mr. Asquith, Mr. Balfour, or anyone else.

There were others, too. We had the whimsical George Studdy, well-known creator of the "*Bonzo*" dog, who made the funniest remarks in a melancholy drawl, and whose one happiness was fishing anything from salmon to flounders in a small sailing boat. There was Charles Crombie, a tall cheery fellow with carroty hair and a very white skin, who shone in colour work of humorous character, also David Wilson, a glutton for work, an Ulsterman with a big, round Irish face and a soft burr, who always wore a black stock which gave him the appearance of a *dominie*. We had Welsh humour represented by gay little Bert Thomas, whose irrepressible mirth bubbled over at all times at the Savage Club, to which I belonged for many years. A quaint artist frequently appearing in our pages was Thomas Maybank, a bachelor with a big brown beard, who adored kiddies and was never happier than when drawing comic little gnomes and elves, forerunners of Walt Disney's creations. D'Egville, a droll, now Major D'Egville, was excruciatingly funny at times, whose work is to-day a feature of **Punch**. He was a leading winter sports enthusiast, who would be found in Switzerland every year. No journal could approach our staff of artists and we were a cheery band.

Our cartoons lampooning the enemy had a considerable political value as propaganda, and were widely reproduced throughout the civilised world, in the United States, Italy, France, Holland, Spain, and the Scandinavian countries, even in India and Japan, as well as throughout the Empire, cited as London's view of the war. Copies were sent to neutrals like Holland and Spain to offset the clever but coarse German Weeklies like **Simplicissimus**, **Jugend**, **Kladderadatsch** and others which worked hard to disparage our cause and our war leaders.

In those days the power of, the political cartoon was considerable, but since then it has largely deteriorated owing to the lack of punch and the timidity or lack of insight of editors, whose job it should be to provide the theme. The only man to-day with a powerful outlook is David Low, a genius with the pen, but unfortunately he vitiates much of his work by a one-sided partisan outlook. **Punch**, on the other hand, is of an ancient epoch in its too reserved and hesitant attitude in cartoon work. It is true that forty years ago a cartoon in **Punch** could create reverberations throughout the world, such as the famous cartoon by Sir John Tenniel of *"Dropping the Pilot"* when Wilhelm II dismissed Bismarck. To-day such a type of cartoon would fail to arouse the least emotion.

Mention of **Punch** recalls an amusing little contretemps with that journal. Odhams advertised **Passing Show** as the "Twopenny **Punch**." and the proprietors of that dignified periodical wrote protesting against the wording, which they considered was in poor taste. J. S. replied wittily, saying that he regarded the advertisement as a tribute to the excellence of **Punch**, and added that he had no objection to **Punch** proclaiming itself as the "Sixpenny **Passing Show**." In our art and humour we regarded ourselves as a jump ahead of **Punch**, but then, as our esteemed contemporary remarked dryly about itself, it was never so good as it had been.

On the literary side we also were in good company. Alfred Berlyn, a former editor of The World, wrote first-page quips on passing events, always witty if sometimes a little acidulous. Vernon Woodhouse was an amusing dramatic critic. W. A. Darlington, the discriminating dramatic critic of the **Daily Telepraph**, first made his name with Alf's Button, both dramatised and filmed, which the **Passing Show** published originally. He served with the Northumberlands in a battalion commanded by my brother-in-law Col. Bertram Gibson, who was killed in action on the Somme, and later joined my staff. Our leading contributor was T. W. H. Crosland, whose weekly article scintillated with brilliant and sardonic humour. He was no respecter of persons.

No writer for the Press could wield a more caustic pen than Crosland. Poet, satirist, cynic, Bohemian and patriot, he walked out on many editors who had tried to curb his tendencies towards free expression of views palatable or otherwise. He was untidy, his clothes hanging about him anyhow, and his uncombed hair falling rebelliously, but he always had a twinkle in his eye. One of his peculiarities was that he never removed his hat even in my sanctum (a peculiarity he shared with Hannen Swaffer), unless it were to scratch his head, and when talking he subconsciously kept tilting it from one side of his head to the other, accelerating the movement when he was indulging in some diatribe against newspaper directors, all of which tribe he cordially distrusted.

Crosland first gained a public reputation by his daring book **The Unspeakable Scot**; written with great vigour and wit; having his tongue in his cheek, of course, to which Scottish humour did not respond. The more they attacked him the more copies were sold. He was also a remarkable poet although his output was small. Not long ago my old friend Philip Page, discussing in the **Daily Mail** the lack of vigour in our war poets of the present time, expressed the opinion that that "good hater" T.W.H. Crosland was the greatest poet in the last war.

He could certainly write powerful - and perhaps prophetic of this war - verse as in his "**Chant of Affection**," composed as a reply to the Hun "**Hymn of Hate**," as witness:

"How shall we hate you back
We who are England; we
Who are to big for hate,
Too careless and too fine,
Too good-tempered and too proud?

From icy hidden peaks
And far off fastnesses,
From chambers of the South
And in the unconquerable heart
Of England, ware and wake.

The tempest gathers up
That shall be flails for you,
And break you in your place
And scatter you like straw;
Instead of 'Hate, Hate, Hate'
You shall cry 'Doom, Doom, Doom,'
And you shall wail and mourn,
With none to comfort you
But sprites of murdered babes,
And ghosts of women raped,
And wraiths of great dead men."

Prophetic, I repeat, of this wanton war, but not of the last, where the professional disturbers of the peace of the world got off only too lightly, and there were far too many persons in this country anxious to shake them by the hand and say "let bygones be bygones." Crossland used his gifts to castigate the Huns, knowing full well that any sign of generosity towards them would be treated at once as evidence of weakness and fear on which they prey.

In my spare time I assisted the Department of Foreign Propaganda directed by C.F.C. Masterman at Wellington House. In his day few politicians obtained more Press publicity than he, but I should add that it was not of a flattering character. What time Lloyd George Was fluttering the dovecotes by attacking the landed classes for the ostensible benefit of the working classes and sneering at dukes with uncultivated deer forests, Charley Masterman was accused of licking his master's boots. His flamboyant speeches even outdid his leader's and accordingly the Tory Press belaboured him unmercifully and cartoonists depicted him as a little cur yapping at the heels of "L. G.". His trouble was that Just before the 1914 war he had been given the post of the Duchy of Lancaster and a seat in the Cabinet, but was unable to find a constituency which would accept him. His own, Bethnal Green, firmly rejected him when he stood for re-election and at two or three by-elections where he tried his luck he was decisively defeated. He never obtained a seat and became a public joke.

I found him agreeable and accessible. Untidy in appearance, with black lank hair drooping down one side of his forehead, he strode through the streets with an air of absent-mindedness, usually wearing a shabby astrakhan-collared overcoat giving him the appearance of an old-fashioned ham actor. He had been Literary Editor of the **Daily News**, and was in fact a clever publicist. He conducted foreign propaganda with great skill and at considerably less expense than the Ministry of Information attempts the same sort of work with greater staffs and far less effective results. Perhaps he knew too much about Civil Servants to engage them for he employed journalists almost exclusively. He came to quick decisions and those who worked under him were enabled to get down to the business in hand without any interminable red tape.

It seemed to me that it would be valuable foreign propaganda if we could produce some rival publication to the German satirical cartoon weeklies of **Simplicissimus** and **Jugend** character which flooded neutral countries by enemy subsidy, and which we could only partly offset by our own and those not subsidised by the Government. The German publications were distributed free especially to hotels, cafes,

167

and *estaminets*, and they played cleverly upon the psychology of neutral subjects. Generally, it may be said, the Continental mind possesses a very different idea of humour than does the Anglo-Saxon, leaning more to the grotesque, or rather crude vulgarity, and by no means shunning what we should term sheer indecency. Still . . . in Rome one must do as Rome does!

Owen Aves and I set to work to produce a counterblast to the enemy cartoon offensive with its reiterated innuendo that a haggard and scared John Bull was sitting on his money-bags and forcing the French and Italians to do his fighting for him. We, too, took the gloves off and were thoroughly scurrilous, with coloured cartoons front and back and in the centre pages, bold in treatment and holding the Kaiser and his fighting machine up to ridicule carefully avoiding the subtle. We collected and prepared jokes apart from war politics designed to appeal to the Latin temperament, and we provisionally got in touch with likely contributors who could write stories from the angle needed. Finally, with a couple of completed specimens or "dummies" I placed the proposal before Masterman together with a plan and estimates of cost I obtained from Odhams. It Was to be printed in two languages, French, for French-speaking countries or those understanding French, and Spanish, for Spain and South America Where German influence was strong. Its title **Caricature**, **Caricatura**, or **Karikatur** was a blessed word, practically the same anywhere. . .

Masterman saw great possibilities in the idea, approved it, and recommended it to Northcliffe, who was then Director of Propaganda in Enemy Countries, and he consented to the scheme being given a trial. It was to appear under private auspices, not official propaganda or even a smell of it, and plans went ahead. Unfortunately - from my point of view - the sudden collapse of the enemy knocked the scheme on the head.

In the first few weeks of this war, observing the feeble efforts of the Ministry of Information to employ any satirical weapon against the Germans, I thought I would resuscitate the idea and talked it over with my friend Kem, one of the most versatile and widely travelled of cartoonists and publicists, whose knowledge of Mediterranean countries is intimate and embraces the Arab lands as well. A sturdy young man of medium height, black-haired, round-faced, with merry brown eyes, Kem is a phenomenon, Born in Cairo, with a Greek father and an English mother, he was educated in Cairo, in Athens, and in England. He speaks over half a dozen languages fluently, is erudite, artistic, and has created and edited journals in Cairo, working as well for Arabic papers. He is not merely a cartoonist, but a first-class publicist with a profound knowledge of world affairs and within a few minutes can design a cartoon, serious or humorous, on any topical theme, understands the psychology of the public to whom he is appealing for he is a true cosmopolitan, and by Jove! how invaluable as an offset to red tape. Add to this a devotion to the British cause and you have this young man, probably with an eye-glass screwed into one eye, the very versatile Kem.

So Kem and I - mostly Kem - elaborated the idea of a resurrected **Caricature** and it was duly offered to the Powers-that-be at the M.O.I., who, with their usual appreciation, carefully pigeon-holed it, together with our careful estimates of cost. It was submerged in the hidden purlieus of bureaucracy. Both Kem and I endeavoured to track it down, as it apparently passed from one committee to another, some of which with inane notions interviewed Kem. I had a friend in an important position, who intervened and discovered the scheme which he promised to bring personally before the eyes of the Director-in-Chief, but that functionary resigned, as did my friend, so at last I applied directly to Lord Camrose, at the time Minister of Information, who courteously gave Kem and me an interview for nearly an hour, and promised that he would see that the scheme should be fully considered. I am certain he would have done so, too, for he is an experienced journalist and publicist besides being a leading newspaper proprietor, but a few days later he resigned from the job of cleaning up the Augean Stable, and wrote me a personal note regretting that he could not do more in view of circumstances. After that the plans and dummies were lost apparently for good and all.

Doubtless they are reposing in someone's pigeon-hole to this hour, and may come in for the next war!

However, the scheme had one good effect. Someone in that huge rabbit-warren behind the British Museum discovered the virtues of Kem. To-day he works in a great room as official cartoonist to the Ministry, and his cartoons are sent to all parts of the world, he working some eighteen hours out of the twenty-four and apparently enjoying himself. He persists in calling himself plain "Kem," as he does in **Who's Who**, thus rather shocking the susceptibilities of the M.O.I. authorities who consider he should figure as K. E. Marengo. But here Kem is adamant.

*   *   *

Armistice Day! With church bells clanging, cheers resounding everywhere, November the eleventh, 1918, was made an occasion of universal gaiety and rejoicing. The vile Hun had been beaten to his knees, and the only disappointment was that the Allies, apparently at the instigation of President Wilson, did not march on to Berlin and there dictate terms of peace. If they had done so history might have been written very differently and certainly Hitler could not have boasted as he did that the German army was never defeated. I hope that this time we shall proclaim our victory with a great military parade through Berlin with loud speakers retailing the crimes of the Nazi gangsters. You cannot rub in defeat too often to the Prussians, or be too blatant. They must be humbled to the dust before they will understand.

The last war was nearer to us than this one, at the time I pen this. The bulk of our armies fought on the Western Front and hence it was a usual sight to see men home from leave trains carrying their rifles and equipment, often dusty and tired out. Long strings of ambulances awaited the trains at the railway termini. We did not experience air raids such as London and many other cities, towns, and villages have suffered in this war, but London did not escape scathless. I recollect especially one night when I visited a theatre in the West End with a woman friend where Seymour Hicks was starring in *The Man in Dress Clothes*. A severe raid was in

170

progress. The restaurant where we dined was full, also the theatre, but nobody dreamed of quitting. We are a bad nation for quitting.

Our defences were pretty hopeless. On that same night Odhams received a direct hit, my own office was partly destroyed, and a large number of persons who had used the machine rooms as a raid shelter were killed or injured. Then, as now, directly there was an alert all the foreign population who lived around Long Acre fled panic-stricken to the Tube station for refuge. These aliens in our midst, whose offspring become *ipso facto* British subjects, whether their parents are naturalised or no, merely because they are born on British soil, rarely make very desirable citizens. They are no asset, with few exceptions, and I trust the day will soon dawn when to obtain naturalisation will be rendered far less easy than the desultory filling up of a few forms and paying a slight fee. We should require some definite proof of service to the State and unimpeachable testimonials of character before admitting them to our birthright. In the last war, as in this, the Tubes were choked with these same so-called "friendly aliens", who pushed and hustled for safety regardless of others. One would commonly see hefty young alien males not in the least interested in aiding the nation which has accorded them protection against persecution and has donated large sums to support them, and who show their gratitude in such ways. Their growing numbers undermine the British stock.

I know very well that what I say is a view held by almost all who come into contact with them. You find them at the back of most shady happenings, such as receivers of stolen property, and prominent in the Black Market. It is nauseating to realise that they possess friends in high places and big finance. Not long ago a Member of Parliament, a former well-known editor of a big daily, in a debate on the Black Market, drew attention to the high record of convictions registered for illicit trading against these "friendly aliens." He warned them and suggested that their leaders should discipline their erring brethren. He was immediately accosted by another M.P. in the Lobby who is a wealthy member of the same race and who apparently told him that he would hear more about it. My journalistic friend mentioned the

171

matter to a leading newspaper proprietor, a peer of the realm, to one of whose journals he was contributing a series of special signed articles on the war under a contract. The peer looked worried. A few days later a strange coincidence took place, in which his employer proposed a cancellation, on generous terms, of the contract. It was rumoured that the newspaper proprietor was visited by a group of advertising magnates who threatened to withdraw all their advertising support for all his newspapers unless he dismissed his M.P. correspondent forthwith.

This sort of pressure is a serious matter. It undermines the independence of the Press and brings it into disrepute. Unhappily few editors have escaped the unseen but severely felt hand of Big Finance when a journal dares to stray beyond the dotted line and the animus shown by these "friendly aliens" when their misdeeds are exposed is astounding. There is indeed an *imperium in imperio* with a sinister power of big finance behind it, and news editors take refuge behind the euphemism of "friendly aliens", although the public know perfectly well who are meant in most cases. This money business is behind the political party war chests, a Hidden Hand which the Press should unite to smash.

In 1919 with the enemy defeated and large numbers of men receiving their gratuity and returning to civil life, a desire everywhere to turn one's back on the grim past four years and to give gaiety and laughter an innings, added to an artificial boom with huge sums being spent in amusement and entertainment, I put an idea before J. S. of a new sixpenny weekly, called **Pan**, which I believed could captivate a big public. Its scope was an illustrated satirical journal using colour and black and white art, mainly intended to amuse, cosmopolitan and a social but not socialite weekly.

At this precise period Clarence Hatry, the then financial wizard of the City, had purchased a famous old weekly, **The World**, really for his friend De Wend Fenton, a sportsman well-known in the world of racing as one of the most prominent of gentleman jockeys, and who, I believe, much assisted Hatry in the formation of his stable. De Wend

172

Fenton had an idea that he was a great authority on foreign affairs and insisted on writing a weekly article on the subject, but he also contributed the racing notes which were much more to the point. He was not capable of editing the journal and had asked J. S., whose firm were to publish it, to find a capable editor. He hit on me.

The World was living on a fast-dwindling reputation of its triumphs in Victorian days when, under the Yates family, it had been a staunch supporter of Royalty, High Society, the Church, the Services; the Tory Party and Old Port. Formerly thought racy, the more sparkling illustrated Weeklies had usurped its place and its present circulation was wobbly to say the least of it. J.S. expected me to restore it to a state of health, reconstruct it, infuse it with new energy, and make it a paying proposition. It was a compliment, but a back-handed one, for once more I looked like being the mug to take the risks.

"If you insist, I cannot refuse," I expostulated. "Surely you have not forgotten the fate of **The Throne** and **Madame**? Besides, what about **Pan**?"

"Your **Pan** can wait awhile. To succeed with **The World** will be a feather in your cap. You can do what you like with it, have a free hand, for neither Harry nor De Wend Fenton will bother you, and I need scarcely say that there will be no question about finance this time."

I certainly disclosed no great anxiety to jump at the offer. J. S. laughed. He has a most persuasive manner and none can say him nay. He lifted the receiver.

"Put me through to Mr. Hatry," he said to the telephone operator.

"Now, Beau, I am going to tell Hatry to put out the red carpet for you, that you will call on He is in your hands and you can ask him any salary you like in addition to your contract here."

He spoke to Hatry, made an appointment for me, and hung up the receiver again. His attitude had been generous.

"All the same," I said, "I'm doing this for you. I don't propose to accept any salary from Hatry."

"What!" He stared at me in amazement. "Refuse to accept a salary from Clarence Hatry, a multi-millionaire! What's the matter with you?"

"Nothing at all, except that I want to place it on record that it is a temporary job and that I am employed by you and not by Mr. Hatry. Then, when I have reconditioned **The World** I shall have a pull on you to let me start **Pan**."

"Well, you may please yourself," grinned J. S., "but I think you are cutting off your nose to spite your face. It is foolish to throw away good money for a whim."

"Maybe it is more subtle than you think, J. S." I said. "For I prefer to hitch my Waggon to your star than to Hatry's! If I were not careful I might find myself caught up in the vortex of the City - and I should hate that!!

All I did was to charge a small sum for my expenses, which gave me a feeling of certain independence when I interviewed Hatry and De Wend Fenton, although probably neither of them knew of my resolve, and would not have cared a button either way.

I paid various visits to Clarence Hatry at his palatial offices by the Stock Exchange, and although he was invariably courteous, he gave me a definite impression of not wanting to be bored with the paper, although it was losing him several hundreds a week. He regarded me rather as the embodiment of the managerial side than as the potential editor.

I would be conducted to his private office, a long, panelled room, carpeted with Turkey rugs, with easy chairs, a table covered with periodicals and other materials, a large desk, many telephones, and usually pretty full of various friends discussing high finance. Hatry, slim, young-looking, with a slight dark moustache, carrying a cup of tea in his hand, would disengage himself from the group and approach me with a quick, nervous movement.

"Let me see," he would say dubiously, "you are - "

I would tell him.

"Yes, of course. Odhams, aren't you? Have I any criticisms? I don't think you printed the last issue too well. I did not care for the frontispiece either."

"I will bear in mind what you say, Mr. Hatry, But do you approve of the policy we have adopted? The new style in make-up? The many new features? Is the style too flippant or - in a word - are there any suggestions or instructions you care to give?"

"You must really improve on the printing, Odhams," he would repeat, as he paced up and down with his cup of tea. "I have complained before, you know."

"I will report what you say to Mr. Elias. The control of the printing is not really in my hands although I watch it. I am the editor, you know. Would you like more sport, for instance?"

I don't think I ever got anything decisive out of him, and so I would take my leave to his evident relief, whose mind was full of operations in mounting millions and was too fully occupied to give any thought to such a trivial speculation as **The World**. I always rather suspected that his reading of newspapers other than financial ones, or perhaps sporting journals, was strictly limited and that **The World** was not on his reading list. It was merely a toy which he presented to his friend De Wend Fenton in return for the aid he gave him with his racing stable.

This reminds me that his horse "Furious" won the Lincolnshire at 33 to 1 in 1920, and I scooped in a good win. Not that I have ever been addicted to betting or am a student of form. Far from it. It so happened that a small sweep was got up in Odhams and I happened to draw "Furious." Putting two and two together it seemed a good omen, because I was associated, if slightly, with the Midas of the times, was editing his paper and had drawn his horse in a sweepstake. Accordingly I risked a fiver each way at starting price.

My customary restaurant for lunch was the well-known *Ivy*, near Leicester Square, not so fashionable then as it has since become, the rendezvous of all theatrical celebrities, but from the first the stage had patronised it, and, in fact, Fay Compton first took me there. On that particular day, I had invited a friend to lunch, and was greeted by the courteous Abel, its proprietor, and his smiling manager, Mario, both of whom I am glad to say are still in receipt of custom at the same old stand.

"Who will win the Lincolnshire, please, Monsieur?" asked Mario as he brought the bill of fare.

"How on earth should I know, Mario?" I queried.

He shrugged his shoulders and smiled: "Well, Monsieur, you are an editor and . . ." Believe me, there is little these *restaurateurs* do not know about our private lives, and I imagine that somehow they associated me with inside information.

"All I can tell you," I said, "is that I have backed an outsider. He will probably be among the also ran. It is Mr. Hatry's horse 'Furious'."

Mario whispered in Abel's ear, my friend and I enjoyed an excellent luncheon, had lots to talk about and I forgot all about the race. We still lingered over our coffee when in the distance newsboys could be heard shouting the winner. The doorkeeper then rushed into the restaurant with an afternoon paper, Mario snatched it, his face wreathed in smiles, and, followed by Abel and others, equally delighted, handed me the paper.

" 'Furious' has won, Sir," almost screamed Mario. "thirty-three to one, Monsieur Beaumont!"

"Splendid!" I cried enthusiastically, for a rapid calculation showed that I had won over two hundred pounds. "I should like to celebrate this lucky occasion by inviting you all to drink - "

"No, no, Monsieur Beaumont," interposed Abel, waving his hands delightedly. "It is on ze house! We have all back 'im, too!"

So, indeed, I believe they had. With consummate faith, little knowing the genesis of my gamble, my tip had been passed round the entire staff including the chef onwards, and never was a small community more delighted than my Latin friends. M. Abel honoured us by producing his most priceless cognac and choicest cigars and, one might say, laid down the red carpet in my honour. It became a little embarrassing in fact later for I was regarded as an oracle in racing knowledge and nothing I could say would change their opinions. My friends Abel and Mario may remember that pleasant little encounter of twenty-three years ago.

I am not going to dilate on Hatry's downfall, much as it distressed and angered me at the time. Whatever sins Clarence Hatry may or may not have committed against some particular code of high finance, in my opinion he got a raw deal from the Bench. It was a great pity that Hatry pleaded guilty to the charges brought against him, for it vitiated his defence and it placed him at the mercy of his judge who was vindictiveness personified. I allude to Mr. Justice Avory, who, it was said, especially requested to take the Assizes at the Old Bailey in order to try Hatry. A prisoner on a criminal charge should have a right to object to a judge if there is reason to believe that he is prejudiced.

Avory looked what he was, a hard, remorseless, prejudiced man. He was, I fancy, the son of a horse-keeper and looked like an ostler himself. Parchment-faced, without a vestige of sympathy, not taking into account the fact that Hatry had given the prosecution all the help in his power to get to the bottom of the labyrinth of involved negotiations, harshly he pronounced a sentence of fourteen years, yet without Hatry's own voluntary aid it was said that the prosecution might have found it difficult to prove its case. That sentence left a nasty taste in the mouth, and the shame of it stuck to the scarlet and ermine gown and long-bottomed wig of Mr. Justice Avory rather than to Clarence Hatry, for it was spiteful and vindictive. British justice has long been extolled, but I have noticed in the past years more than one instance of equity being subordinated to other interests. The "Contempt of Court" weapon has been sometimes over-stretched. We don't want any more Judge Jeffreys, thank you.

If Avory snapped out his savage sentence in order to restore the then waning prestige of City finance he failed of his object. The impression spread abroad that the sentence was less influenced by the desire to insist upon the purity of financial dealings than to avenge certain powerful corporations which had been stung by Hatry's collapse. It seemed to me that more than one victim would be wanted to clean the Augean Stable, for in that *milieu* of international finance and many accents it had been instrumental in lending the nation's savings to foreign countries like Germany and Japan, and had struck hard against the Empire's interests. And what is this "paper" worth now?

Another famous man connected with the Old Bailey, a well-known journalist, but a very different type to Hatry let me hasten to add, was Horatio Bottomley, the man with an enormous leonine head and squat legs. The machinery of the law never got him to plead guilty, no matter how black his case, and no judge or counsel could browbeat him. On the contrary, his knowledge of legal procedure and his eloquence enabled him to make rings round wig and gown. He was a man of great ability but bravado, in some ways almost a genius, but unfortunately for him and those too closely associated with him he had a kink of dishonesty. He could not run straight.

Outwardly urbane, generous, and genial, there were no heights to which he might not have attained. He claimed to be the natural son of Charles Bradlaugh, a brilliant orator and a noted politician and revolutionary of Victorian days, most famed for his support of atheism and attacks on the Church. Horatio, with whom I came into contact on many occasions, always gave me an impression of absolute self-confidence and the ability to carry almost anything through on which he set his heart. A great orator, a man who knew no finer feelings, revelling in finding opposition and defying conventions, he had a huge following and might at one time have gone far in politics. Yet somehow he never rang true to me. His vices, wine, women, and racehorses, led inevitably to his downfall. He made money so quickly and easily that when financial difficulties threatened to submerge him he always believed in his lucky star, until once too many a time.

I was first disillusioned about him when I once heard him haranguing a recruiting meeting. His silky voice and his expressions of patriotism were impeccable, unless your happened to know, as I did, that he was being paid large sums by the Government to stump the country for volunteers before conscription was introduced by a trembling Liberal Government. He mixed his patriotic strains with a lot of maudlin sentiment, played on the emotions of his audience like a Paderewski at the piano, and yet behind the scenes was haggling for the big fees he demanded in return for his services, although he was drawing a princely income as editor of **John Bull**.

After the Bottomley *débacle* it became no easy task to restore confidence in a journal so completely identified with him, and it was generally believed that its days were numbered. Those who thought thus did not know the resolute Elias. He nursed it through a dangerous period, skilfully selected his editors, built up a character for integrity with the middle and working classes, provided them with a succession of services, and triumphantly pulled his own child, if ever a man could claim a journal as his own, into greater prosperity than ever before.

When Bottomley had served his seven-year sentence he tried to resuscitate himself and started a rival to **John Bull**, which he called **John Blunt**. But the magic of his name had departed. He descended gradually into the gutter, and at length, broken and penniless, was taken to hospital to die.

Brig.-Gen. Nevile Campbell, C.S.I., C.M.G., D.S.O.
[*Caricature by Autori*]

Lord Southwood

CHAPTER X

WAR'S AFTERMATH

"I console myself with this, that the dogs bark, but the caravan passes on."
MONTAGU NORMAN

BEFORE VERY LONG, I was relieved from the necessity of editing **The World**, beyond keeping an eye on it, and J. S., true to his word, permitted me to go ahead with **Pan**. I threw myself into the work and revelled in it.

It was a gay and audacious periodical, eschewed politics, which were taboo anyhow just then in the mood the nation was passing through, published artistic coloured pages of satirical character, caricatures of leading personalities, and kept abreast of movements. Its cover, in full colour, was changed weekly and was always enticing, its contents light-hearted and sophisticated with a leaning towards irreverence of our supposed elders and betters. It tilted at snobs, prigs, and hypocrites, and reflecting the widened outlook of the men now released from the services became a popular periodical with a large circulation for a Weekly priced at sixpence. It obtained a circulation topping 100,000, quickly became a household word, but never gained the advertising support it should have expected.

Michael Arlen, then little known, was one of its contributors, my right-hand man as chief sub-editor was Victor MacClure, who had fought on the beaches at Gallipoli and had brought away as a souvenir a bullet still lodged in his heart. This most versatile Victor had sailed before the mast, had established a reputation as a scenic artist, was a playwright, and wrote a delightful series of short stories for Pan set in the atmosphere of the Parisian Boulevards and the Latin Quarter, which he knew intimately, always ironic and perhaps daring. He is known to a wide public in a score or more of novels and other works, of which perhaps the more outstanding are **Nicolette of the Quarter**, **The Secret Fool**, and **The Engadine Cypher**.

My art editor was an extremely engaging young ex-officer in the R.F.C., with dark chestnut hair, a caressing voice, immaculately dressed by Savile Row, and with a penchant for leading theatrical ladies. A bachelor of artistic tastes, he rented a luxurious mezzanine-floor flat in St. James's Street, where in his dressing-room his valet would show you with pride over a hundred pairs of expensive shoes, many unworn, and wardrobes full of new suits by firms like Anderson and Sheppard. I will call him Jack.

The salary paid to Jack was scarcely more than a drop in the ocean compared with his expenses, which commonly included luncheons, dinners, and supper parties given to his *inamoratas* at such resorts of gilded youth as the *Embassy Club, Ciro's, The Ritz, Savoy, Berkeley*, and other places; He strove to make both ends meet by gambling at nights in various clubs and parties, where sometimes he had a stroke of luck and cleaned up a few hundreds and at other times lost, which meant that he had to dash round at his lunch hour from place to place cashing cheques and paying in the sums before the bank closed. Of course he came a crash in the end, which was a pity in more directions than one. I did my best to save him from these extravagances, but it was useless. He had implicit faith in his own lucky star.

There was no honest excuse for Jack, whose love of being on familiar terms with theatrical stars - male as well as female - brought him down, but there was an explanation. Men who had been face to face with death hourly, like Jack, a pilot, were inclined to kick over the traces and go the whole hog. Theatres, hotels, and restaurants, with all the good things of, life again procurable, did a thundering trade. Money was thrown about with prodigal recklessness. To hell with the war! Jerry was down and out and there would never be another war, no sirree! Let's get that nightmare out of our heads! Eat, drink, and be merry! The unfortunate thing was that Jack's escapades began to leak out and an impression got round in certain managerial circles that Beaumont and his staff were indulging in wild orgies. A stealthy community of Little Bethelites spoke with horror of abandoned actresses who called at the office and were given tea and cocktails. All that really happened was that a few of Jack's girl-friends among the stars occasionally dropped in to see him.

In the Spring of 1920, as a big publicity scheme, I decided to run a big fancy-dress ball at Covent Garden called the **Pan** Ball, in aid of St. Bartholomew's Hospital, to which J.S. gave his assent. The professional direction was under Margaret Chute, an accomplished journalist and a wonderful organiser, who formed a committee of famous theatrical stars - **Pan** was very much to the fore as a theatrical journal - tickets costing three guineas including supper and drinks. It proved the high spot of the season. All tickets were sold out before the day and fancy prices were offered for them.

The theatrical world, always to the fore where gaiety and charity could be combined, rose nobly to the occasion. Nearly every London management rented a box costing from twenty-five to a hundred guineas apiece. Two leading dance bands were hired, so there was non-stop dancing throughout the night. The huge auditorium was decorated with flags of all nations and hung with festoons of large coloured balloons which were released after midnight. Gifts of fans, chocolates, scent, and the like were distributed as prizes, and except for myself, who had to wear evening dress to be distinctive, and J. S., who arrived late, every guest wore fancy costume, among whom Pans, Fauns, and lovely Nymphs and Sylphides were prominent. As a result St. Bartholomew's benefited by some £3,500 and Lady Henry Somerset's Homes by £500, while **Pan** gained added fame.

With all this gaiety, with plenty to eat and drink, there were few *contretemps*. There were several gate-crashers, usually well-known theatrical artists who said they had lost their tickets and got the benefit of the doubt. Some exuberant young Naval officers in an upper box began to take cock-shies at their friends on the dance floor, using empty champagne bottles to the danger of the public below. Gerald du Maurier and I visited them and they got the talking-to of their young lives, and next day, as might be expected of the Royal Navy, they called on me with profuse apologies, saying the "electric" atmosphere upset them! A very famous leading actress, who saw her boy friend dancing with a rival, set up a piercing shriek and swooned in her box, causing some consternation. These were minor troubles with such a party.

At midnight, preceded by a blare of trumpets, there appeared on the stage, amid concentrated limes, a classically beautiful Aphrodite, Gladys Cooper, a ravishing red-haired Mercury with his wand, delightful Fay Compton, introduced by a small winged Cupid in white silk, my own little daughter Diana, to-day well known on the stage and screen. The two goddesses selected the prize-winners - there were many good prizes - from the dancers who promenaded slowly round the floor and Cupid performed the task of giving them to the winners. A little later a somewhat indignant Aphrodite tackled me in my sister's box.

"Is that mite your daughter?" she demanded indignantly.

"I've always been led to believe she is," I replied.

"Is your wife here? She is even more to be blamed for bringing a small child here at such an hour. It's heartless!"

"Her aunt brought her only a short time before midnight," I said meekly, "and she is probably in bed and asleep by now."

"Is she?" laughed my sister. "There she is on the floor dancing with Gerald."

Diana was being snatched by man after man and whisked across the dance floor until at length her mother rescued her in the zenith of delight and took her home.

I was heartily congratulated by J. S. on the success of the Ball, but clouds were beginning to gather about my head. The expenses of production were heavy and advertising support continued to be shy, as it always is with a new publication. To meet to some extent a growing discrepancy we had to raise the price of **Pan** to a shilling, not

186

formally, but by producing a series of "special" numbers, an irritating trick on the public, who soon get tired of paying a shilling for a publication listed at sixpence. We should have reduced the colour pages or economised in other ways, but with all this the journal maintained a circulation of about 70,000, far beyond any of its rivals. It eventually resulted in a hectic interview between J.S., the Advertisement Director, and me.

The Advertisement Director complained that he could not get large agents to recommend **Pan** to their clients because of its moral laxity. Several had said that they would not take it to their homes because their children's morals might be corrupted. I denied that there was anything in **Pan** which entitled the critics to make such sweeping charges, and added that all said and done **Pan** was a topical journal of the time for adults and, while denying any charges of moral laxity, said it was not produced for small children and could not be judged from their level. I suppose I rather added fuel to the flames by alluding to the Nonconformist conscience.

I was told that the advertisement manager of a large West End jeweller and silversmith had cancelled an important contract because of a suggestive combination in the current issue. "I will show you what I mean," said my advertisement friend, who held up a copy of the offending journal to the light, where two page drawings backed on one another and to the coarse-minded gave the impression that the god Pan in a rustic scene was behaving rather after the nature god he was supposed to represent with a nymph in the other picture.

"It was pointed out to me," complained the Advertisement Director, "and my client said it must have been deliberate. So my order is cancelled."

"I assure you that no such idea ever entered our minds. No one, and certainly not I, would ever dream of faking two pictures for an obscene effect. Someone must have a very prurient mind."

"It has gone the round of the Stock Exchange at any rate," protested the Advertisement Director.

"The Stock Exchange! My dear fellow! Surely you won't use the notorious character of the Stock Exchange against me. They spend all their leisure time looking for dirt!"

"You may not have known about it," I was asked "but what about your Art Editor?"

"Send for him if you wish, but he hasn't a mind like a sewer and I am certain the whole thing is a coincidence. Permit me to point out another side to this. The war has opened the minds of intelligent men and women to the cant and hypocrisy of the past. **Pan** is essentially modernist, and is the reason why it sells. Are we to be restricted to the narrow outlook of a number of elderly men who direct advertising businesses, who still live in the Victorian age, and who will apparently only patronise papers that publish pap? It seems like it."

"Unfortunately," said J.S., "they are the men who handle the business."

"Yet," I returned, "they are the prurient-minded ones, who see smut everywhere, and make false charges. The world is moving on. It is growing out of the nonsense about the abandoned Continental Sunday, the shocking *Moulin Rouge* of Paris, and the attempt to pretend that sex doesn't exist. I have met these men, usually brought up in a small Bethel in Wales or Scotland, ignorant of the world, but knowing all the scandal about their neighbours and gloating over it, who go to chapel or church because it gives them respectability, and yet whose minds are often sinks, although their precious brats must be brought up in innocence of the facts of life until their stupid daughters get into trouble and are turned out of their homes by their strait-laced parents. Must we tamely surrender to such hypocrites and prudes who live in an artificial world of their own and forces the Press to be as mealy-mouthed and full of inhibitions as themselves?"

I think they were rather shocked at me. Probably they concluded that I was abandoned. All they said was that my remarks were not very helpful.

"Perhaps one day," I said, "someone will start a paper which may be small in contents, but is not the slave of advertisers. It could indulge in plain speaking. I don't know, gentlemen, whether you realise that we English are regarded throughout Europe as as nation of hypocrites and humbugs because we tolerate the sort of cant I have outlined!"

A black mark was registered against me for these views. They were too rebellious. **Pan**, of course, was never obscene, but it did not pretend that the world was composed of lollipops, and refused to accept the outlook of the young miss of fifteen as its criterion of sophistication. **Pan** by ridicule was waging war on bigots and kill-joys who have had far too long an innings in this country, and are merely a bad hang-over from Puritanical days.

The problem of advertising revenue and the influence of plutocratic patrons upon the freedom of the Press is a gigantic one, of which the parochial outlook of certain advertisers in regard to a paper like **Pan** was only a minor matter, instructive as it was in its way. Ever since the day when newspaper production became an enormous business, with vast overhead charges, and competition led one paper after another to give the public bulk in place of brains, it meant that the Press must be led in chains since the advertiser held the whip hand. Not all, but some put the screw on in regard to policies.

Those who have marvelled why the "National" dailies before the present war and prior to the last German war pursued such flabby attitudes on foreign affairs and in regard to national defence, rarely showing any disposition to criticise and turning a blind eye to Ministerial neglect, need not have looked far beyond big and international capitalism able to exert its influence on the Press by the power of advertising. The reason was simple. Anything which upset the existing Government might cause a grave slump. A General

Election which might return a Socialist Government with predatory instincts presented an appalling vista to their eyes and might prove a prelude to the bogey of Bolshevism, which gave Big Capital the cold shivers to contemplate. Perish the thought! Any political subterfuge - even a forged Zinoviev letter - rather than let the wreckers in!

The very thought of WAR was consequently taboo, and any newspaper which stressed the neglected state of the national defences and demanded a rearming of the nation and preparedness for war was going more than half-way, in their view, to stage a war! Their hearts went out to men like Asquith with his "Wait and See," which was all wait until we saw only too clearly; or the "my lips are sealed" and "Safety First" of Stanley Baldwin, who deliberately kept Winston Churchill out of office because he exposed our nakedness; or Neville Chamberlain, who prated of "Peace in our time" while Hitler was feverishly re-arming day and night, and who also kept Mr. Churchill rigorously out of office until circumstances forced his hand - these were the men backed by big money, not because they were anti-British, but because the money-bugs were purely and simply sons of Mammon with no prescience at all, who mistook war preparedness for militarism.

Thus the Unseen Hand operated in the Press by using the weight of money. Newspaper staffs were not all ignorant of what was being prepared in Germany and a few to their honour exposed it, but most of them, terrified of a crisis, threw dust in their readers' eyes. We have it on record that continued warnings by well-informed newspaper correspondents in Berlin were deliberately ignored by a certain most important management who no doubt had their reasons for playing Hitler in a minor key. The War-Mongers and Jitter-Bugs must not be permitted to raise a scare! Bad for trade, bad for the share markets, terrible for capital values as assessed in their books.

"Why should Germany want to go to war with us?" chorussed the present-day Luptons and Israel Davises as they had thirty years earlier: "Are we not Germany's best customer? Have we not lent her millions?"

So we left the French in the lurch by walking out of the Ruhr, and looked on with equanimity when Hitler walked in at his convenience. Adolf was a friend of Britain, had praised us in his **Mein Kampf,** and if he rearmed, well, what of it? Wasn't he building up Germany as a buffer state between the awful Russian Bolshevists and International Capital? Keep friendly with Adolf Hitler, make concessions to him for the sake of peace, and let our Trusts prosper with their monopolies and their chain-stores! I do not exaggerate. How came it that after Lord Rothermere, with Ward Price and Collin Brooks (then editor of the **Sunday Dispatch**) had travelled over the world and proceeded to write articles, as did all three of them, drawing attention to the undermining of British prestige and certain ominous factors operating against the future peace of the world, someone or something clamped down on the campaign? Fleet Street rumour had it that Rothermere was threatened by certain big interests if he pursued his policy. The only daily newspaper which never hesitated to publish the truth about Germany fell by the wayside - the **Morning Post** - for reasons which do not make very agreeable reading. I know something about it because then I was on its staff. It was called "a reactionary Tory organ."

The fact of the matter is that advertising interests or big finance controlled the Press, and that Frankenstein monster grew into a vast diabolical machine with an unwieldy body and tiny brain, so that the public fell more and more into the clutches of trading combines and monopolies. I should be happier if I could see any indication that in the near future these harpies would be given their deserts, but I must frankly say that they seem at present to be increasing their power in all directions. I am not a pessimist by nature, but at the present time it looks rather as though they will play at ball with he bureaucracy, the unhappy ball being the Big Public, and be in effect the nation's rulers, unless, of course, they sell out at a stupendous price to the bureaucracy and leave us with an additional staggering weight of debt.

The only hope I see of stimulating public opinion to fight for its own rights and interests against these ogres is the establishment of a few journals which will take the gloves off and expose the Unseen Hand wherever it shows up. It needs a bold and single-minded millionaire to take up the cudgels, a man who will institute weekly papers - independent of advertisers, or certainly unprepared to bow the knee to them - like Henry R. Luce's policy in the United States. He must be a man too big to be bribed with honours or be blackmailed by money interests. He must be blatantly and unhesitatingly pro-British, an upholder of our rights and a champion of the Empire - including India. His publications must be bold, outspoken, carefully prepared, attractively illustrated, and with unquestioning sincerity gain the confidence of the nation, being sold at a price within the reach of the million. Perhaps Lord Nuffield, a man of great public spirit, might entertain the idea.

Whether such a type of weekly journal will come about, only time and opportunity will prove. I am certain of but one thing. The nation needs forceful and honest papers; The Press has it in its power to become the overwhelming force in forming public opinion and lead us onward to prosperity - if it is British first and last. If it is British first and last it will have to unite and smash the Money Power. I mean vast trusts and monopolies which are undermining our independence. Don't mistake my meaning, I am not anti-capitalist. On the contrary, men who risk their capital to produce goods or foodstuffs, or anything else advantageous to national prosperity, become consequently employers of labour and add to the wealth of the nation in my view are public benefactors; My war is against international capital used to acquire monopolies and exploit us. Furthermore - since I am airing these views - the royal road to national prosperity in business must be in the future a big scheme of compulsory profit sharing. If I were to stand for Parliament it would be a main plank in my platform.

One evening in summer in 1920 I was enjoying a game of lawn tennis at home when I received a curt note by special messenger. I. was sacked forthwith. The directors of Odhams regretted that they must dispense with my services and offered to pay my salary for a certain period. Not a word was vouchsafed as to why I was summarily dismissed after having worked with the firm for some eight years and not unsuccessfully. Had I robbed the till my dismissal could scarcely have been more brutal and brusque. I had a pretty shrewd idea of what lay at the back of it all. The firm were losing more money on **Pan** than the directors liked and they laid the blame on my shoulders. There had been a coldness ever since I had expressed my opinion about advertising, when I had also had the temerity to say that they did not know how to organise advertising for a class paper like **Pan**, which was a very different proposition to **John Bull**.

I have reason to fancy that there was behind it another divergence of opinion with my chiefs. They had rather the mentality of those advertising managers I had arraigned so tactlessly. I think they were convinced that I had fallen under the spell of my art editor "Jack" and that my outlook was dissolute. They had learned to look askance at *Pan* as something polluted, a horribly distorted view limited to those whose outlook was - well, different from a now sophisticated world. I fancy they must have built up visions of the Scarlet Woman of Babylon and other abandoned nymphs who had bewitched the editor and his staff. My wife and I could not help laughing at the circumstances despite all, for what it came to really was that my dismissal was due to the fact that what I thought was versatility had become vice.

I did not care a brass farthing about **Pan** except as a newspaper proposition and never had. I thought it an opportune time to establish such a journal and I am convinced that I was right. My motive was to establish that paper, add to my prestige, and then hope to rise higher to another paper of more importance with the Odhams backing behind it. If I had mixed to any extent with my friend "Jack's" theatrical stars it was less from infatuation than a desire to enter into the spirit of the time and build up the gaiety which gave it youth and was a big asset. It is strange what queer ideas some newspapers directors hold - or held - about the versatility of their editors. I remember "Car" Thomas saying quite seriously to me after I had edited **The Graphic** for about a year, "I don't suppose you would be able to return and edit **The Bystander** again after this, would you?"

193

It apparently seemed impossible to him that a man concerned with serious matters might also be capable of a flippant outlook, or *vice versa*.

I am afraid that my friend "Jack's" escapades were the true source of my undoing, on the supposition that we were birds of a feather. Even innocent Victor MacClure, whose sole offence was that he wrote ribald and witty sketches round the *Quartier* of Paris, must have appeared vicious in their eyes. At any rate, both of them received similar missives to mine. I learnt by telephone next morning that a cleaning-up party had arrived and taken over, all having been arranged *sub rosa* in advance. They took over with a vengeance. A purity crusade was established. **Pan** deserted the woodlands and he with his nymphs was banished from the henceforth Little Bethel shocked outlook of the reformers. The weekly was transformed into an anaemic monthly magazine of conventional pattern lacking entirely any audacity, gaiety, or life, in which uncongenial atmosphere it quickly languished and departed this life for happier glades of Arcady. **The World** struggled along for a while but some of my friends resigned and in an emasculated form it duly expired. **The Passing Show** under the same management was developed into a lethargic, dull, would-be humorous journal afraid to be sprightly, and slowly slipped down hill. A few years later large sums were lavished on it, it was reconstructed, considerably enlarged, printed in colour photogravure and made to look attractive but it possessed no flair, no personality, no outlook except the commonplace, was just a medley of collected material, and so duly met its appointed end. The Little Bethel mind in this century has become an expensive luxury to those newspaper proprietors who indulge in it.

Strange how frequently men holding important administrative positions in newspaper offices select editors for purely technical reasons in preference to flair. They discourage independence of outlook and seem to imagine that journals can be made successful by pleasant innocuousness. Brigadier-General Campbell, the head of **Illustrated Newspapers**, said to me once, "Why can't you build up a big circulation by pleasing all your readers?"

The half-wit! I replied, "If you don't offend some you fail to please others. One must know where to draw the line." "How?" he asked. I felt like bawling at him, "By having a policy and running it strongly." I actually said, "By coming down to one side of the fence and staying there."

Another important director said to me, "Keep politics out of your paper. They merely annoy your public." I asked him what he meant by "politics," considering that the Journal in question was concerned with persons in the public eye. What he really intended was that it frequently lampooned Mr. Baldwin, who in his eyes was sacrosanct. He was incidentally a distinguished lawyer and I have never yet met a lawyer who was not a compromiser in the big field of politics with the exception of Lord Carson, but Carson was a versatile Irishman, and as a statesman he threw the law to the four Winds of heaven.

I was certainly irate with Odhams in regard to this cursory dismissal and the insulting manner in which they had displaced me. I rejected their offer and brought an action against them for wrongful dismissal. It so happened that when the case was down for hearing I lay in a hospital at Swanage having been operated on for appendicitis with a burst abscess and in a precarious condition. My luck held. The surgeon was brilliant, the hospital-on-the-hill skilfully managed, and when I became conscious my darling wife sat at my bedside and smiled encouragement every time I opened my eyes. In all my vicissitudes never once has she ever reproached me or hesitated to stand by me even when I was hopelessly wrong, and how often wrong she knows well enough, God bless her. Odhams paid money into court and finally on the advice of my lawyers I accepted it.

The sequel was a happy one. I lunched one day with J.S. who frankly admitted that he regretted the action taken with **Pan**, for he learnt later that it was on the verge of success. My friend the Advertisement Director handsomely admitted the same thing. They considered it was a bit in advance of the public taste but the truth was that they had misjudged that public taste. Some years after when I wanted a newspaper job Lord Southwood at once made one for me and at this

195

moment he is still my chairman. He is very fair and no one is more alive to new ideas than he.

For several years I ran a variety of jobs. I became a publicity agent, ran a weekly paper of my own called **The Watchman** on a small scale, edited a Civil Service journal, directed the publicity of a great national organisation in the event of a general strike of which Earl Jellicoe was President, edited and reconstructed another woman's paper, **The Gentlewoman**, and was for a time picture editor of the **Morning Post**. In those years I also wrote two books on meteorology - a pet subject of mine - and kept close touch with politics.

They were not prosperous years.

Europe had been so devastated and impoverished that while its peoples ardently needed everything they could not afford to trade with Britain because costs of production were too high, with heavy taxation and the great rise in the cost of living, some hundred per cent above pre-war. With growing unemployment, house shortage - because large numbers of aliens had come as refugees to our hospitable shores, many of whom had set up in business or had otherwise displaced men serving with the forces - rapidly rising rents, a slump in agriculture, and trading difficulties owing to world impoverishment, dissatisfaction was rife.

There had been an incredible spending mania when men had been demobilised, followed by an extraordinary speculative mania which finally crashed on the gamblers. The unemployed became tremendous and by May 1921 the Coal Strike brought up the number to over two and a half millions. The Government showed no resource. The war was over and those who survived had a medal or so, a small pension if wounded or a gratuity, and meanwhile the unemployed, mostly ex-service men, toured the streets and begged for bread, while others formed small street orchestras, played everywhere and half menacingly carried round the hat.

The plight of our demobilised soldiers and sailors was altogether deplorable, many reduced as I say to begging in the streets. Others accepted any sort of job to keep the wolf from the door, and many a gallant ex-officer was hawking goods from back-door to back-door. It was a ghastly humiliation for the nation whose rulers had termed them heroes while they fought and died and cynically turned their backs on them when they were no longer wanted. If these men had united and hanged a few politicians on lamp-posts in Whitehall they might have had their wrongs remedied. Applications to pity were a waste of time. Had they used fear, the result would have been probably otherwise, for the Government would have had to think twice before daring to turn machine-guns on them. I trust earnestly the same situation may not be attempted at the end of this war. If it should be this time they must not stand aside. I could tell them what to do to the politicians.

It might be recalled here what sacrifices the men of Great Britain and the Empire Overseas made in the last war largely because the politicians had proved themselves neglectful of our defences. We lost 1,089,919 lives killed, 2,400,988 wounded, of which totals 812,317 killed and 1,849,494 wounded were from the British Isles. The British Isles, accused by the Huns of fighting to the last Frenchman, suffered only 222,000 fewer losses than France, but if the Empire were included they exceeded them by over half a million dead and wounded. In this same war the Americans lost altogether; 321,000 in dead and wounded. It is worth recalling these tell-tale figures because we were told over and over again that France was bled white, whereas her population was only some four millions less than ours and her losses included her Colonials whereas ours did not. The U.S.A. only entered the war in 1917, came in fresh at the end and claimed to have won it, and at the same time had amassed enormous wealth whilst we were fighting for the liberty of the world. These facts should not be forgotten.

About 1922, I came into contact with Civil Service methods through an organisation of ex-service men who had obtained what were euphemistically termed "temporary" jobs in various Government

197

departments. Although the Lloyd George Government had promised preferential employment to ex-service men, as a matter of fact there was a movement by the chiefs of departments, some worse than others, to get rid of the men, a policy with which the Treasury were in silent agreement. Many had been discharged on grounds of redundancy, and so some of the men thus threatened formed a defensive organisation which came to be called the Association of Ex-Service Civil Servants, their objects being to fight discharges and to demand fairer terms of wages and conditions. The Service heads as a whole disliked these men, whose manners were inclined to be too independent, and partly because they had not entered the Service by orthodox means, in fact were not sufficiently pliable and subservient, and not trained in the official etiquette of Bureaucracy such as "passed to you" and avoidance of responsibility.

In 1922 there were 173,000 men and women "Temporaries" employed in Government departments, of whom only 24,000 were ex-service men. Every week these men were being discharged while the non-service remained. They were paid at lower rates than the permanent staff (who had entered through examination), and they had no pension rights. This ex-service Association was very energetic and defiant of service big-wigs, and had recently launched a monthly periodical named, not inaptly, **Live Wire,** which I was invited to edit and also act as publicity director. For ten years I edited **Live Wire** as a side line and am to-day the honorary editor of the Association. When I joined them their General Secretary was an ex-artillery lieutenant named George O'Connell, a man of restless energy and dauntless resolution, a man with a big grin and a huge and obstinate chin. The Assistant Secretary, Harry Fenn, a man of great resource and charm of manner, is to-day its lively Chief.

My respect for O'Connell grew by leaps and bounds when I saw that he was not in the least intimidated by the imponderable power of the bureaucratic machine. He had been employed in the Ministry of Pensions himself but had resigned to fight the Civil Service for ex-service men. The Treasury disliked him intensely. At Kew where thousands of Temporaries worked in great hutments of the Ministry of Labour some hundreds of O'Connell's men had received their notices, while non-service personnel were retained. George met the menace in two unorthodox ways. Firstly he staged the original stay-in strike, whereby the men. refused to leave, picketed the entrances and exits, harangued the men in their luncheon hour, and defied the authorities to throw them out. The heads were nonplussed and anxious to avoid calling in the police.

Secondly he dressed up a number of his members in long ghost-like white overalls, cowls covering their faces and only leaving slits for eyes. These men, with the mystic letters "K.K.K." on their chests, paraded Whitehall carrying sandwich boards denouncing the Government and the Ministry of Labour. They attracted wide attention for the idea was novel, borrowed from the American Ku Klux Klan, which the wily O'Connell adapted into *Kew Klerks Klan*. The daily Press became interested and photographs appeared in the papers, much to the annoyance of the Civil Service heads who were powerless to intervene. They thought it a most undignified and ungentlemanly manner of fighting a dispute. Worse still, questions were asked in the House until finally the Treasury were defeated, for the notices were withdrawn and the men reinstated. Guerrilla warfare, skilfully executed, can defeat the bureaucracy and is worth remembering.

O'Connell's greatest triumph perhaps - in conjunction with W. J. Brown, the irrepressible Independent M.P. and General Secretary of the Civil Service Clerical Association - was the actual defeat of Mr. Baldwin's Government in 1924. These two men arranged a debate on the subject of the ex-service men's starting pay, then a grave scandal. By adroit lobbying of M.P.s and the fear of the latter of being attacked in their constituencies for neglecting their pledge to ex-service men, they actually defeated the Government by five votes, large numbers of Government supporters having refrained from voting. It created a sensation and compelled the unwilling Mr. Baldwin to set up a Special Committee under Lord Southborough to inquire into the whole question of ex-service men in the Civil Service. As a result the bulk of the men were granted permanent employment, some with, others without pension rights, opened the doors to promotion, and obtained better terms of pay. Some 40,000 men were eventually given permanent posts in the Civil Service.

Personally I am opposed to permanent jobs in the Civil Service under the existing system as against the interests of the State. No one should obtain a permanent job for an hour later than he is wanted, but if this continues then ex-service men, subject to their efficiency, should have the first claim, and the best jobs.

The history of this organisation is valuable as showing what may be effected by a comparatively limited number of persons provided they are efficiently organised and learn how to wage political guerilla warfare. The A.E.C.S. had scarcely more than 10,000 members at any one time, had no funds other than subscriptions, and most of the work was voluntary. Its electioneering committee took a prominent part in Parliamentary and local elections, had its system of training speakers, learnt to deal with hecklers or to heckle with damaging questions, and took a considerable part in supporting Parliamentary candidates or opposing them according to their promise or refusal to support the ex-service claim. O'Connell was the star orator, a fluent and witty platform speaker, amusing, caustic and sarcastic, who could sway an audience like few men. Many prominent private M.P.s were members of he A.E.C.S. Parliamentary Committee, and there again the procedure of the House was mastered and questions to Ministers were prompted. The Parliamentary Secretary was "Jimmy" Hogge " (formerly M.P. for East Edinburgh), a man gifted with a rich sense of Scottish humour and a deep soft voice. His death was lamented by us all.

Once, O'Connell and his boys stormed the Outer Lobby. After a big rally he sent them in twos and threes to call out M.P.s on an important question. The Lobby became crowded, M.P.s complained, and finally the police on duty sent an SOS to Scotland Yard who dispatched a strong detachment under a superintendent to expel the intruders, who were difficult to remove. The police chief who knew O'Connell - as all Scotland Yard did - was indignant at an act which he thought was taking an unfair advantage.

"This is a dirty trick, O'Connell," he complained.

"Isn't this a free country, Superintendent?" grinned George.

"You know well enough that if you want to invade these precincts it's understood that you advise us first."

"Oh, yeah! - take us for mugs, eh?" sneered George. "Let you pack the Lobby with your men and prevent us from our rights. You want your job made cushy, don't you?"

For a considerable time an extra posse of police was permanently on duty in the Lobby in case the invasion was repeated. I repeat that a determined body of persons can circumvent bureaucratic methods if it is not afraid of officialdom which *au fond* is the servant of the nation but has been allowed to become its master through our easy-going tolerance.

I thoroughly enjoyed my work with the A.E.C.S. and threw myself into the campaign with zest. It was a friendly H.Q. in Victoria Street, with lots of fun and a deal of plain speaking. Long hours were observed, what with various committees, and work, often continued until nearly ll p.m. but nobody minded. I was admitted into the inner counsels, took part in meetings there and in Government offices, and sometimes formed part of a deputation to the Treasury, whose "high-ups" disliked me because of my attacks on them.

I was given a free hand in writing and editing *Live Wire,* which was read pretty widely throughout the Civil Service, and I used facts to indulge in hard hitting sometimes. One such article I wrote attacking four Chiefs of the Board of Trade recoiled on my head during the General Strike of 1926.

At that time the daily Press was paralysed except for the **Morning Post** which alone did not employ union labour, and which published a daily sheet of strike news for the Government. I had just enrolled as a special constable when a friend of mine, who held an important position in the Board of Trade, and who had largely organised food supply, asked me to take over a daily column in order to report its activity. It appeared that the Department of Supply was not getting adequate publicity.

I agreed, was provided with a special pass badge and was conducted to Hyde Park, the main centre of supply for the metropolis, and wrote up a vividly descriptive article. Next day I was scheduled to visit the docks a night where there was some rioting. My friend, however, asked me to call on him immediately.

"I am afraid the job is off, old man," he said, with some embarrassment.

"The Board has decided to use its own official publicity man."

"Why didn't they think of it before?" I asked.

"Well - the truth is they discovered that you were the writer only this morning. They asked who had written the column."

"Did they disapprove of what I wrote?"

"On the contrary - but they disapproved of you."

"Why should they disapprove of me?"

"Can you remember an article you wrote in **Live Wire** some time ago in which you pilloried four heads of the Board and called them 'Four Unjust Men' ?"

"Rather. They deliberately victimised an ex-service man and left him to starve in the gutter. What has it to do with this?"

"Everything, my dear fellow," replied my friend. "Two of them are prominent in directing supplies, and I am afraid that they harbour a grudge against you. I am very sorry indeed."

Personally I did not care a tinker's cuss whether I wrote up the Board of Trade or not. I had not even discussed payment and was willing to work *pro bono publico*. These men showed, however, how petty and small-minded civil servants can be, ready to pay off a grudge at a time when the nation was in the throes of what was intended to be a revolutionary General Strike to overthrow the Government of the people and impose the tyranny of the T.U.C. instead. They were thoroughly thrashed in 1926, but they will try it on again if we are not on the alert.

For many years I have watched with growing apprehension the increasing grip the Bureaucracy has been fastening on the nation, and since the advent of the present war how it has grown both in numbers and appetite until to-day it has become in effect a totalitarian form of government ruling almost independently of the House of Commons by means of Orders in Council, until the freedom of the individual is a thing of the past and we are all in the grip of a vast imponderable machine, which dictates to us through the enactments of men like the Four Unjust Men. It is like some huge prehistoric monster which sucks all initiative and strength from the nation. Laws and new offences grow with rapidly increasing velocity and good citizens find themselves convicted for offences which they were unaware existed, and even lawyers confess that they cannot keep abreast of the spate of new enactments. The most trivial contraventions of the laws bring upon the head of the offender to-day savage fines if not imprisonment and tens of thousands of persons writhe under the oppression.

All this directed by these bureaucrats who with a few exceptions have never travelled or widened their outlook, and whose sheltered lives proceed peacefully despite the sufferings of the nation, obtaining promotion automatically, making themselves eligible for knighthoods or other honours, never sacked no matter how grossly incompetent they prove, unless they commit some misdemeanour, living year in year out in a stifling atmosphere where originality and initiative are taboo. They are mostly listless semi-robots, lacking mental and nervous energy, showing only great resourcefulness of inaction. Only in one respect do they reveal energy - increasing their staffs by involved processes of duplication. A department chief can only aspire to the dignity of a carpet in his room and first-class travel voucher when he can control a staff of at least sixty, and in fact the importance of a head is commonly judged by the presence of a carpet! One says to another, "Is he a carpet man?" Naturally in the bureaucracy it needs two or three to do the work of one in ordinary civilian business.

The brain of the monster reposes at the Treasury, whose task it is to control all public moneys. It used once upon a time to exert a jealous watch on the public purse, but within this last twenty years or so it has shown extraordinary profligacy and only niggardliness where the national defences are concerned. Millions have been thrown hither and thither with a quite staggering profusion and recklessness. For example, apart from the astronomical cost of the war, the greater proportion of which is being added to the National Debt - whose chickens will duly come home to roost - outside loans guaranteed by the British Treasury or other obligations entered into by it, amounted to £772,000,000, in 1940-1, which of itself exceeds the entire National Debt before the 1914-18 war by £122,000,000, and yet is mere make-weight to our prodigious liabilities. The National Debt has reached the staggering figure of some £20,000,000,000, if you can grasp its meaning, and is still mounting. You may put it simply in this form:

Before the first great war, when Britain was prosperous and had big oversea assets, every baby born into this world of woe owed £16 at birth. After, the last war it was born in chains to the extent of £150. To-day, although supremely unconscious of its horrid responsibility, it starts life owing over £450.

Well, well, well . . . it is satisfactory to learn, however, that Lord Halifax, our Ambassador in Washington, accepts no salary other than his £5,000 a year as a Cabinet Minister, but receives something like £17,000 a year for expenses, with much the same system supporting Sir Samuel Hoare, our Ambassador in Madrid. There is a queer system of "allowances" for prominent proconsuls and others too, whose total would make us shudder no doubt if it were known, but a mere drop in the ocean to this astronomical public expenditure going seemingly unchecked. So the Bureaucracy is crushing us financially as well as in freedom of action - and the Socialists and "Planners" devoutly wish to to see it assume yet greater powers of control over our lives and greater expenditure of our money. Of course, this super-taxation and expenditure will continue until such time as the people flatly refuse to pay - as one day they must do and will - and then the balloon will go up, for if it is wide-spread the whole fabric will collapse.

I managed to keep my head above water during these difficult years, frequently doing two or three separate jobs at once. At the request of several friends, I endeavoured to start a weekly of my own and certain capitalists promised to assist the scheme, but I found that going hat in hand to found a national weekly did not interest them overmuch. I started, however, in a small way, naming it **The Watchman**, priced at threepence. It had at personal subscription of about a thousand, somewhat after the style of the later successful **K.H. News-Letter** except that it covered both the home and foreign fields. It was hard work for I had to write it almost from cover to cover. It had a number of fervent supporters who gave limited financial help, and if I had found time to hold meetings it is possible that sufficient capital might have been raised, but after some eight months I closed it down.

For some time, too, I edited **The Gentlewoman**, an old-established woman's weekly, another of those Herculean tasks of endeavouring to reconstruct an old-fashioned journal which had outrun its usefulness. The moving spirit of it was Charles Stewart, an aristocratic cosmopolite with a great sense of humour. He was - and is yet - one of the best-dressed men-about-town, and he and I got on splendidly together, but our hopes of resuscitating the paper were killed by the General Strike. At the same time I was very busy as publicity director of the *Organisation for the Maintenance of Supplies*, its secretary being Gerald Fiennes; Here we had everything so complete that when the General Strike suddenly fell upon the country like a thief in the night, the O.M.S. was ready with operatives in practically all key-points, and the entire system was taken over by the Board of Trade, which was the reason that for once it showed efficiency.

Then I became picture editor of the **Morning Post**, where I might have remained perhaps indefinitely but I felt cramped there, and suddenly an unexpected offer came my way. I was invited to return to the editorship of my earliest offspring, **The Bystander**.

"Lucy" - Lady Houston - taken when Lady Byron

The Earl of Birkenhead, G.C.S.I.

CHAPTER XI

"CLASS" PUBLICATIONS

"No single newspaper gives its readers all the truth as it knows it. . . . Each is subject to behind-the-scene influences and interests which prohibit the publication of this, or lay misleading emphasis on that. . . . Their owners almost always receive those coveted titular adornments which are in the gift of the political parties."

DOUGLAS REED

BRIGADIER-GENERAL NEVILLE CAMPBELL received me in a long, heavily-carpeted room with many windows situated on the corner of the Strand and Aldwych, overlooking Waterloo Bridge in one direction and facing the Gaiety theatre on one side with the Lyceum on the other. He was the Managing Director of **Illustrated Newspapers**, the class shilling-publications of which the firm held the practical monopoly.

The slogan of the firm was "The Great Eight," and, sure enough, they confronted me in full array on a table arranged in order of over-all size. Hence on top lay **The Bystander**, then **The Tatler**, **Eve**, **The Sketch**, **The Sporting and Dramatic**, **The Graphic** - a very different proposition to my time - **The Sphere**, and finally the dignified **Illustrated London News**, with its famous woodcut engraving of My Lord Mayor's barge in a water procession on the Thames in 1842, the year of that journal's birth. The General's pet, as I soon learnt, was **The Tatler**.

Campbell was very tall and thin, stooped, possessed an inordinately long neck which he encased in a stove-pipe upright collar, a small head for so long a trunk, with silver-grey hair, a clipped moustache, and, as he paced up and down the room to pause momentarily to fix me with deep-set eyes under shaggy black eyebrows, gave me the impression somehow of a human giraffe. Though he liked to be thought in his prime, and always had an eye for a pretty face, he was then seventy-ish. He could be irascible to a degree but on this occasion he was extremely affable and had just invited me to take over the editorship of **The Bystander**.

He was not satisfied with it. The paper was in a rut. It lacked liveliness and *savoir faire*. It wanted somebody with ideas and originality who knew the world for which it catered and who better than the man that had first created it, eh? Quite so. He would like to welcome me on his staff, where I would find many of my friends. Such was the theme as he paced his room smoking a series of cigarettes at the end of a prodigious holder half the length of a walking-stick.

I hesitated. Mentally I calculated the numbers of publications I had been forced to reconstruct since the day I had left **The Bystander**. There was **The Graphic** for one, **Harmsworth's** into **The London Magazine**, **The Throne**, **Madame**, **The World**, **The Gentlewoman** - and now the wheel had turned full circle to **The Bystander** once more! Nor was I enthusiastic at the idea of editing a society weekly again. My ideals were set higher!

"Well?" he asked, wheeling round on me. "What do you say?"

"Rather another instance of calling in the doctor when the patient is *in extremis*, isn't it, sir?" I countered. "I have probably had more experience in this sort of task than any other editor, and have found it very thankless. One has to risk one's reputation in what is usually a hopeless task."

"I shall not expect the impossible, Beaumont. I shall not expect to see any change for at least three months. You may do what you like subject to your not exceeding the allowance in expenditure. I never interfere with my editors unless their circulation demands it."

He made me a tempting offer of salary in the circumstances, and I saw before me the prospect of entering the portals of a firm with a capital of many millions, owners of periodicals of proved reputation carrying stacks of high-class advertising, and round me all the signs of opulence. Moreover, **The Bystander**, although it was in a groove and outmoded, was not discredited, and I hoped with energy and a free hand to restore it to its old position as an amusing and topical journal. The immediate problem was to get rid of the present editor, who had originally come on the paper through me, but was no particular friend of mine. That, however, was the General's job.

I had scarcely hung up my hat in the room allotted temporarily to me than the General sent for me. He had a very special task which he wanted me to undertake before anything else. He had suddenly had. the weekly, **Britannia**, put under his control, and matters were in a pretty quandary. It was not then owned by the "Great Eight" but serious difficulties had arisen, Frankau's agreement as editor had been cancelled, and he had entered an action against the proprietors. Gilbert Frankau, eminent author as he is, was not exactly fitted for this particular job in the opinion of Mr. William Harrison, its founder.

Frankau had engaged a large staff at high salaries and this paper occupied the entire upper floors of Inveresk House where we were housed. Campbell asked me to "go upstairs to that damned paper **Britannia** and take it over."

"Do you mean edit it?"

"Yes, edit it - clean it up - make up the paper - cope with contributors - do what you can," he replied. "It's in a bloody mess!"

"What about **The Bystander** in the meantime?"

"It can continue as it is provisionally," he returned impatiently. "The other cannot wait. Will you go upstairs at once? I will ring them up and tell them to expect you? "

Many will recollect **Britannia**, whose advent created quite a furore in its day. It was the project, and a sound one too, of Harrison, a strong Conservative, a fervent believer in the Empire and an ardent

Protectionist. Then in the early forties and a lawyer by profession, proud of his native Yorkshire, he had been brought up by an uncle who had been in the paper industry for many years, and William, following in uncle's footsteps, had built up the Inveresk Paper Company Ltd., which by 1921 controlled the largest paper-making group in Europe. It was very prosperous at this time and had purchased the Great Eight Illustrated papers from the late Sir John Ellerman. Harrison became chairman of **Illustrated Newspapers** which operated this group. The genesis of **Britannia** was in this way. He was accustomed to visit America every spring and was an intimate friend of Condé Nash, the great American publisher, who persuaded him of the great opening in England for an Empire weekly on the lines of the **Saturday Evening Post** of Philadelphia, and being on the look-out for publications to provide a market for his paper he decided to go ahead. Sir Charles Higham, the late well-known advertising publicist, suggested Gilbert Frankau as editor of the new weekly who got the job at a high salary. When the first issue came out it was evident in Harrison's opinion that his editor had not produced anything resembling the **Saturday Evening Post**, and to say that he was disappointed is to put it mildly. Nevertheless, **Britannia**, as produced by Gilbert Frankau, having been brilliantly publicised in advance, obtained an initial circulation of 175,000 copies sold at sixpence. I believe that Campbell had objected to bring **Britannia** into his group for he feared more than all else successful competition from a sixpenny weekly, knowing well that a shilling for illustrated weeklies was an inflated price. However, circumstances had been too strong for him.

Frankau's scheme was a good sixpenny weekly concerned with national affairs, carrying illustrations - but not primarily an illustrated - with an independent national outlook. It was my own ambition in every way. It was lavishly publicised and had acquired a circulation of well over 100,000, and had it only been well-produced technically and not been too ambitious by endeavouring to cover too much ground, it should have established itself as an important organ of opinion. It was outspoken and Frankau's articles were badly needed in those lullaby years when the world was marking time, Mr.

Montagu Norman, Governor of the Bank of England - yes, he is still there, an indispensable - had industriously thrown us back on the gold standard, business was sagging and unemployment was becoming ominous. As it was **Britannia** looked dull, was top-heavy, and badly printed. The truth was that Gilbert Frankau was an amateur as an editor, and was largely surrounded by other amateurs, as well as weighed down by injudicious contracts.

Fleet Street has many geniuses and also many hangers-on, and unfortunately many of the latter had succeeded in obtaining fat contracts out of the editor, with the result that when I went "upstairs" I was staggered at the sight of a list of writers on every conceivable subject all requiring space to be found for their output. They were all as pressing as Penelope's suitors and snowed under with this spate of contributions I saw that considerable firmness and some plain speaking was essential.

My first step was to try to pull the paper together and cut down those contributions which were not essential and so display those more important. My first tussle was with my old colleague Maitland Davidson, who had obtained the contract of theatre critic. His article was tedious and without originality, and in Britannia in any case the stage was a secondary consideration. I cut down his "copy" to a column. He came to me indignant.

"I hear you have cut down my theatre copy to less than a half, C. B." he complained.

"Sorry - I'm afraid I have to. You wrote two pages."

"It's in accordance with my contract."

"I can't help that. Space is congested and I must ration the less essential articles. Besides there has been no first night of any importance."

"That isn't my fault, is it? I have conformed to my contract and I look to you to do the same," he said acidly, "Otherwise I shall have to complain."

"Listen, David," I exclaimed impatiently. "I have no time to enter into a discussion. We are not reducing your fee. You will receive your cheque in due course in full but I warn you that if you and others cling to the letter of your contract there will be no *Britannia* and you will lose your job."

"Why should my article be lacerated? I am being treated very unfairly."

"I intend to look into this precious contract of yours, David," I said, nettled, "which you hug like a Shylock."

He was not the only one with whom I had trouble. I had to be rough or chaos would have resulted. Birkenhead caused us the greatest trouble of all. He was a great friend of Harrison and had managed to obtain a contract for nearly £10,000 a year for a weekly article supposed to be concerned with his outlook on important national affairs. Birkenhead's star was already on the wane, but nevertheless had he written strongly on current affairs his name would have been worth a good deal, although half the fee would have been sufficient, but, as a matter of fact he wrote on unobnoxious and past subjects, without a spark of controversy, and in addition was late with his copy. He had to be worried on the telephone and even then was difficult to find. I spoke to his secretary and said flatly that if His Lordship's article did not reach me by such-and-such a time the paper would go to press without it. The secretary said sharply that Lord Birkenhead would have something in that case to say to Mr. Harrison, and I retorted that he could say what he liked but the article would be omitted - and the fee. It reached me.

With all these doings I innocently fell foul of my esteemed friend W. H. Crawfurd-Price, who had been appointed assistant editor under Frankau, and was properly in control. Crawfurd-Price had had a distinguished career as correspondent firstly of the **Daily Mail**, and then of **The Times** in Turkey, Macedonia, Greece, and in Jugoslavia in the last great war. He had been foreign editor of the **Sunday Times**. and in questions relating to the Balkans was admittedly one of our greatest authorities. Contributors complained to him and he naturally asked me what my authority was for joining the staff and taking over control of the paper's contents. It was a difficult situation.

The fact is that the General had never mentioned Crawfurd-Price to me when he had pitchforked me upstairs to try and pull things together. I gave C.-P. my authority and said that I felt sure he would agree how necessary it was to brighten up the paper. I told him that I had, only been sent to assist temporarily as I had my own problem downstairs, and observed that Britannia was being strangled by contracts which in many instances must be cleared away if it were to succeed.

For two or three weeks I tried my best to settle conflicting interests. I believed, and those about me, that if we were left free to clean up the mess, get to press on time - which the surfeit of work and late deliveries of copy prevented - print the paper well, and induce Harrison to issue an ultimatum to Birkenhead to the effect that he must write on current political matters, we could pull *Britannia* through. However, finding myself obstructed, and realising that to save it someone with a full knowledge of events and the technical experience must take full control, I reported to the General.

"In short," I said, "It may be pulled out of the fire yet, but time is also running short. We must cut down editorial expenditure, get strong talking points, improve its appearance, and give fewer pages. Contributors must be reduced enormously and also the inside staff which is far too great."

He looked at me queerly under his beetling eyebrows, fixed a cigarette into his long tube, lighted it leisurely and sprawled into a chair.

"How could you get rid of the contributors?"

"By transferring the bulk of them into one article a month instead of each week."

"They won't agree. Why should they?"

"I think they will if it is a question of spinning out their contracts to four years as against the shutting up of the shop. I think they all appreciate that as matters stand they are not likely to get a long run."

He pondered a few moments and then queried, "And what if they should agree?"

"The paper must be reconstructed from cover to cover. Birkenhead must write on real issues or be cancelled. It must be far better illustrated and printed and space found for articles by public men dealing with live issues."

"H'm. I am told," said the General, blowing a cloud of smoke in the air, "that you have antagonised several persons upstairs."

"I'm afraid I have. I had to. On the other hand, I have to some extent brightened the paper and made it look more a professional production. You did not give me a cushy job, sir!"

He grinned: "I particularly asked you to avoid any unpleasantness, didn't I?"

"You expected me to make bricks without straw, General. I have now come to the conclusion that I can only save **Britannia** if you give me a completely free hand. The present divided control merely leads to chaos. I am checked everywhere."

The General picked himself up on his long, spindly legs and paced up and down the room. Finally he spoke.

"I can't agree to your plan, Beaumont. Certain persons would undoubtedly walk out on us, and I cannot afford to let that happen, for they are essential witnesses on our side against Frankau."

"Then what are your instructions?"

"The damned paper must stew in its own juice," he replied. "I am not responsible for its mistakes and muddles. I was opposed to its start from the first. Thank you for your help, but now you had better return to your own **Bystander**. Your predecessor has left us."

Exactly what happened between the General and Harrison I do not know, but the artful old soldier had kept a card up his sleeve, and an agreement was come to that **Illustrated Newspapers** should takeover *Britannia* free of its liabilities and, turn it into a shilling monthly - thus removing a potential dangerous rival out of the road. It was in fact taken over by my old friend Jesse Heitner, one of Fleet Street's most able editors, editor of **The Sphere,** and successor to Clement Shorter. Heitner made it a successful magazine of high-class. Subsequently Heitner also absorbed **Eve**, which Teddy Huskinson had started as a high-class woman's weekly. Finally he incorporated **The Graphic** in **The Sphere**. A man of indefatigable energy, an opportunist, with a very considerable knowledge of printing and production. Heitner's only hobby in peace-time was to drive high-powered cars at breakneck speed up and down the country to find some outlet for his bubbling enthusiasm for action. He is definitely a champion hustler.

My private opinion of Campbell's action in regard to **Britannia** was that he deliberately sabotaged the effort because a weekly able to compete with his shilling journals and only costing sixpence was his constant bugbear. He would break anyone or anything in his path by fair means or foul if it lay in his power, which was exactly what he did to me a few years later. He was quite unscrupulous as to the means so long as he could maintain his monopoly.

Campbell in many respects was a remarkable character. Most of his life had been spent in the Army in the East from which he retired and managed to pick up a job as a canvasser on **The Tatler**. When William Harrison was hunting round to buy up the class papers for his Mills his greatest prize was the acquisition of **The Tatler**, in which he was considerably helped by "Teddy" Huskinson, its editor, who induced its proprietor, the late Sir John Ellerman, the millionaire shipowner, to sell it for a large figure. "Teddy" Huskinson became a director of the

Harrison company and in some respects the most important individual member of the Board, Harrison excepted, and his outward geniality made him generally *persona grata*. He proposed that his friend the Brigadier - always known as "The General" - should become managing director.

The General took hold of things when business was on the uprise in the propitious years which fizzled out so mysteriously. Advertisers tumbled over one another to buy space in his established organs of the moneyed interests. The General himself, a little elusive, highly aristocratic in appearance and manner, collected round himself an advertising staff of like calibre. An air vice-marshal, another general (a lieut.-general this time), a delightful (and incidentally most efficient) colonel, odd majors and captains, with a *soupçon* of ladies of high degree became in one way or another attached to his staff. Between them all they must have swung the average advertising agent and manager off their feet, being mere plebs in comparison. The General occasionally granted interviews, but every year at Ascot, having collected every pass sent to his editors for the grand-stand and paddock, he ran elegant parties to which he invited big advertisers and did them proud. When the slump set in it was not quite so good.

Apart from this aspect of big business, I formed the impression that the General was really an amateur. His knowledge of printing was certainly not profound. His ability to Judge the merits of the papers under his control was apparently limited to **The Tatler** as his criterion of perfection, although it was almost identically the same week after week, the same old artists, photographs, and contributors. As it held the bulk of the advertising it may have been judicious policy, but it did not make it a wise criterion. He understood very little about publishing and less of publicity and as for finance I gathered that he was wise enough to leave it in the hands of the secretary to the company, Mr. W. C. Nisbett, to-day the managing director, and a most able man in every phase of newspaper production; "Nizzy,"as he is known throughout Fleet Street, an astute person a cheerful cynic, and an excellent *raconteur,* in his spare time ran the social side of the firm including dances and a golf section, his idea being to bring everyone together, high and low.

I must own that I was disappointed at the result of the **Britannia** imbroglio. I should have loved to edit that journal and would gladly have dispensed with all the various coloured lights Gilbert Frankau flashed from his sanctum to indicate the particular persons he wished to interview. It would have seemed so much more sensible if the General had instituted a corner in sixpennies as well as shillings, for then he would have had no cause to fear any frontal or flank attack. However, there it was. . . .

On **The Bystander** second edition of service I gathered round me many useful persons. Vernon Woodhouse rejoined me as assistant editor, and as dramatic critic. The redoubtable and witty Peter (Philip) Page came on the staff writing about London doings other than social, Now on the **Daily Mail**, he was then a principal contributor to the "*Londoner's Diary*" in the **Evening Standard**, in close contact with Max Beaverbrook, and was not uncommonly rung up by that go-getter newspaper magnate about 8 a.m. full of ideas while Peter, who had wooed the midnight (and early morning) hours, was snatching a few hours of sleep.

Peter is, I believe, a lineal descendant of the Bourbons via Louis-Philippe XVIII of France who made a morganatic marriage with a clergyman's daughter while an exile in England. Certainly, Peter bears a near resemblance to portraits of the Bourbons, adores France, French cooking and French wines although he is, alas, to-day a martyr to gout, his inheritance from his royal kinsman. Detesting the noise of cities and such modern amenities as telephones, and perhaps to put intangible space between Beaverbrook, sundry editors, and himself, many years ago he acquired unto himself an ancient Elizabethan Manor, called Colville Hall in Essex, together with a ruined gateway, picturesque barns, outhouses, a fish-pond, and many trees. Everything that could be wired off, such as eaves, to prevent birds from nesting and interfering with his rest, was so done, and for like reason he would have no cows or sheep to disturb him. A very talented pianist and musician, Peter would perform for hours on his Bechstein grand, but nothing of the frivolous. It reminds me that Peter claims to be unique as the only Englishman who has ever shared a bedroom with Hitler when he went to the Bayreuth Festival of Wagner in 1924. What he thought of the Führer, however, is his story.

Hannen Swaller was another contributor to **The Bystander** who wrote on theatrical subjects in his usual nonchalant way. In lighter vein D. B. Wyndham-Lewis jested with airy satire on passing events. Also the tall Charles Graves, formerly London commentator of the **Daily Mail**, penned a weekly character study of some famous personality. In Sylvia Lyon, an American girl in her early twenties, a replica of Queen Victoria in her youthful portraits, I discovered a Paris correspondent who wrote with brilliant wit from behind the scenes and largely prognosticated the political rottenness which brought France to her downfall in 1940. I paid a visit annually to the Riviera to make preparations for our annual Riviera number usually staying at such centres as Cannes, Nice, and Monte Carlo, either taking my own car or hiring one to drive myself, as I was all over the place. This Riviera number, which I had originally established, brought in a large revenue, and I always enjoyed my trip. Geraldine Phillips Oppenheim, daughter of the doughty novelist, was our Riviera correspondent and Phillips himself, who then owned his delightful villa overlooking the Cannes golf-course, was an occasional racy contributor.

Our social correspondent, whose knowledge of social movements and whose treatment of them had to be super, was the energetic Barbara Cartland, novelist, dramatist, biographer, society organiser, columnist, and young Mayfair hostess, pretty, gay, and a very loyal friend, who had the entrée every-where and wrote up Society's foibles in a way that titivated our readers. She had first trained on the **Daily Express** largely under the aegis of Max Beaver-brook himself, whose house parties at Leatherhead she often adorned. She was the sister of Ronald Cartland, the first young M.P. to be killed in the present war, whose biography she wrote not long ago for which Winston Churchill wrote the foreword. So by and large **The Bystander** was well to the fore and featured social movements, personalities, sport, jokes, caricatures and short stories. It increased in popularity rapidly.

220

For a time all went well between the General and me but gradually I found a certain coldness creeping into our relations. Also a note of querulous criticism, very vague and intangible but definitely discouraging. It crossed my mind more than once that the inspiration came from some other source. On one occasion he asked me not to feature rugby football. "You are trespassing on Teddy Huskinson's preserves," he complained, "He suggests that if you will leave rugger to him he will give you a free field in hockey."

"The public for hockey is infinitesimal as against that for rugger, General!" I protested, "May I remind you that **The Bystander** has featured rugger and lawn tennis from the beginning whereas **The Tatler** has devoted itself more to hunting and racing. It would be a pity to ask me to sacrifice a feature the paper has always run."

The General gave the game away.

"Don't you appreciate the fact that **The Tatler** is the firm's big money-maker?" asked Campbell testily. "It practically keeps us all and I am not going to let you affect it adversely. If Husky wants to feature rugger exclusively you must give way."

A interesting phase of newspaper business was developing. At the time **The Bystander** was improving its circulation while **The Tatler**, which never varied, was more or less static although it enjoyed more than double the circulation. At the same time some big advertising firms were observing that **The Bystander** was being talked about and were giving it more business, in some cases cutting down the appropriation accordingly in **The Tatler**. The question of circulation was of indifference to the General for we lost on circulation but advertising revenue was another parcel of goods. When I therefore argued that my own paper's advertising pages reflected its increasing popularity he nearly bit my head off.

"Advertising space in **The Bystander** is considerably cheaper than in **The Tatler**," he snorted, "The class advertising market is a limited one and **The Tatler** must stand first of all at all times."

In plain English, it was a notice to keep off the grass. In Campbell's eyes **The Tatler** was the star property and if I made my own paper anything of a rival, it was an offence. It was difficult to know what to do because in the circumstances the more successful I was in adding to circulation the more unpopular I was bound to become; The publisher admitted to me more than once that our circulation was quite satisfactory but I also discovered from a certain source that the wily Campbell had deliberately cut down the printing order and would-be purchasers were told that it was sold out but the bookstall manager or whatnot had a **Tatler**.

Barred in this direction and that, it seemed to me that to be as different from Huskinson's money-earner as possible I should revise our outlook and turn more to affairs. I played second fiddle to him in the "socialite" world, leaving him a clear field in the country house and sporting world but featuring gaiety in the capital, which Barbara carried out admirably, and began to treat public affairs satirically, for these were now looming up prominently. Satire was the only weapon permitted me - but satire can have a sharp edge! I suppose I was always a rebel to smug convention.

At this time the country had suffered from five years of Mr. Montagu Norman's Spartan finance; of endeavouring to balance trade on the Gold Standard which was reimposed by Mr. Baldwin in 1925. In 1930 the great slump as a result reared its hydra head. Trade, national and international; was declining rapidly when suddenly the United States markets crashed and vast fortunes were lost overnight. World credit ran out like sand through an hour-glass and the repercussions in Europe caused such financial sensations as the Hatry collapse and the suicide of Kreuger, the Swedish match king. The Socialist Government of Ramsay MacDonald, which had done nothing tangible to nurse British trade but had squandered public money like water, proved quite incapable of coping with events; Many who saw where the country was drifting became alarmed and Baldwin's critics brought matters to such a head that on October 30 the Tory Party met at Caxton Hall on a motion to depose him from the leadership, when much straight talk was indulged in. The rebels were defeated by 462 votes to 116 but Mr. Baldwin was most indignant, especially when, the following day Vice-Admiral Taylor, who had stood as an independent-Empire Crusade candidate in the Paddington by-election against a strong Baldwinite, was comfortably elected. It was a straw which showed how the wind was blowing but once a political leader acquires control it is more difficult to unseat him than cause a monarch to abdicate. The rank and file never did get rid of Baldwin.

Gradually Nemesis descended upon the Labour Government which had bowed to the autocrat of the Bank of England to place a premium on gold and create wide unemployment. In July 1931, Messrs. Ramsay MacDonald, Lloyd George, and Stanley Baldwin were the star orators at a monster Albert Hall demonstration to advocate world disarmament and, gazing at the blue vault of Heaven above and averting their eyes from the small but growing cloud gathering in Germany, passed a unanimous resolution welcoming Ramsay's coming Disarmament Conference. Meantime, in Munich a man named Adolf Hitler whose Nazi Party in 1919 had six adherents and by now numbered over six millions, was building up an army of Brown Shirts and shock troops, and preaching militarism in frenzied accents, addressing excited mass meetings in all parts. Nobody took much notice. Hitler was then not even front page news.

Parliament adjourned, for the long vacation, Ramsay to Chequers and Baldwin to Aix-les-Bains. But not for long. The Budget crisis suddenly arose. The May Committee announced that there would be a deficit of 120 millions. A gasp of dismay arose and fifty millions were immediately withdrawn from the Bank of England in gold by foreign depositors. England - the word went round - was racing into bankruptcy. It would appear fantastic that such a state of national emergency could have arisen unforeseen by the Treasury and Mr. Montagu Norman, and without their having warned the Prime Minister. And what of Philip Snowden (later Lord Snowden); the Chancellor of the Exchequer himself? Had he no suspicion of this yawning abyss? It apparently took all of them by surprise!

Then perceive Mr. Baldwin bustling back from Alix-les-Bains in the middle of his cure, Neville Chamberlain reluctantly packing up his fishing-rod and returning from Perthshire leaving behind baskets of uncaught salmon, and others, of your political wiseacres from mountain, glen, and forest, re-assembling in dusty London. Crowds thronged Whitehall with mixed feelings, to view the outward and visible signs of the crisis the while Mr. Baldwin was mysteriously closeted with Mr. Ramsay MacDonald at No. 10 Downing Street. On August 23, Kings George V, travelling hurriedly overnight from Balmoral Castle, appeared unexpectedly at Buckingham Palace, and on the following day the Labour Government resigned, but Prime Minister Ramsay was entrusted by the King with the task of forming a "National" Government to weather the financial crisis, and a few hours later, having conferred with the Tory Leader on a pre-arranged plan, he returned to the King jubilantly presenting, his new and phoney Cabinet.

If Messrs. Ramsay MacDonald and Stanley Baldwin had possessed a sense of sardonic humour they must have laughed until their sides ached at the hoax they had perpetrated on the electors who are supposed by some fiction to have a say in the governance of the country. It was out of the frying-pan into the fire! For Ramsay, who as Prime Minister was responsible for the failure of his Ministry, was triumphantly re-appointed to the like office, and Snowden, who as Chancellor was responsible to Parliament and the nation for the country's finances, was reappointed to his same office. Jim Thomas, another Labour Minister, who wise-cracked with royalty, took over the Colonies, and Lord Sankey, also a Labourite, retained the Woolsack. Liberals, who for two years by an unholy pact had retained the minority Labour Party in office, grabbed their share of the spoils, such as Sir Herbert Samuel (now Lord), Lords Reading and Crewe, and last but not least, Sir John Simon, the present Lord Chancellor. The Tories had to wait for the loaves and fishes until later, for only two important portfolios went to them, namely Sir Austen Chamberlain to the Admiralty, and that stalwart "yes" man Sir Samuel Hoare to the India Office.

Honest Stanley Baldwin modestly became Lord President of the Council and Vice Prime Minister, but pulled the strings.

It was quite a happy family party you might say. There had been a slip-up in the national finances to be sure and business looked pretty grim but Mr. Baldwin had placed the whole of the Tory Parliamentary machine at the disposal of the very delinquents who had brought the nation to so sorry a pass. The millions who had voted Tory and "agin" the Labour-Socialists never had a say at all. The obedient Tory Press supported the racket and the people in this so-called democratic land were merely side-stepped. Meantime another 200 millions were hastily withdrawn from the Bank in gold by foreign depositors, indicating their opinion of the deal.

When all this was settled to the satisfaction of Britain's leading statesmen a General Election was held. Posters on every hoarding stressed such subjects as "Safety First," "More Employment," "Back to the Plough," "Better Trade," "No More Foreign Dumping," and so forth as the rewards for supporting the "National Government." one pathetic poster depicted an aged woman counting her mite which would not be disturbed. The continuance of the Gold Standard was loudly upheld. Sir John Simon indulged in bitter forebodings of utter ruin unless the nation supported the Government he now adorned. "Money," he declaimed, "is only worth what it will buy and a collapse of the pound means the worthlessness of shillings and pence. . . The British pound might have followed that course if instant action had not been taken to check it." How it had been checked by re-instating the two men mainly responsible he did not seek to explain; Philip Snowden flatly declared that the Labour Party proposed to seize Post-Office savings to meet the national deficit, a charge hotly denied, but calculated to influence many votes.

The electorate generally speaking was perplexed and nervous. It seemed whatever happened that they were for the high jump. They grasped that the Labour Government had made a sorry mess of things and all they could hope for was a better government when its spending proclivities were nipped in the bud. The result was a veritable landslide for the Labour-Socialists. The Tories romped away with 471 seats National Liberals, 35, the Mac-Donaldites - showing the opinion the electors held of these worthies - but 13; The Opposition of Socialists and Free Liberals could only muster 56 seats among them, and it was the considered opinion that the Tories could have captured all the National Liberal and MacDonaldite seats as well, had they fought them. The rank and file of Conservatives, and those not of the Party but wanting a strong government, heartily disliking the coalition with the MacDonald faction, all were powerless, for Mr. Baldwin, a clever electioneer whatever else he might be, had dished them. Four years later he bamboozled them again and so cleverly that many - but not all - regarded him as the acme of political honesty.

Such is Democracy triumphant!

The new Government, be it said, did affect to practise economy. Its first act was to dock a shilling a week off the pay of the lower deck in the Royal Navy; At Invergordon it led to a strike and the men of the Fleet refused to put out to sea. It was hushed up and the Government capitulated. It raised the income tax by sixpence. It also came off the Gold Standard which before the General Election it was said would mean the nation's downfall, and despite the awful prognostications of Sir John Simon. All the time most of the Press threw dust in the public's eyes.

So, with this and that there were plenty of openings for ribald remarks and quips in which **The Bystander** voice pretty accurately the conclusions of the educated public. The General hauled me over the coals and I defended myself by saying that the journal must be allowed to have some outlook, and as I must take a different line from **The Tatler** what was wrong about it? He argued that the journal's readers would not take our remarks seriously and if one could not treat politics lightly - which after all were the business of all of us - and could only talk round generalities what inducement was there to buy a paper named **The Bystander** which was intended to reflect the views of the man in the street? I might have saved my breath. The General was determined to find some pretext, and so one fine day he wrote me a letter giving me notice.

This time I was determined not to take the situation lying down. I placed all the facts before Mr. Harrison, the Chairman, who promptly countermanded the notice. He told me the General had slandered me. An extra-ordinary man was the General, he hated Harrison like poison, and Harrison in turn had no very high opinion of the General. Anyway, I remained at my post and continued to edit **The Bystander** without let or hindrance for so long as the chairman remained, which, however, was not for very long.

Harrison was at this time in constant close touch with that great lawyer "F.E.", Lord Birkenhead, and one day he suggested that I might give a trial to Birkenhead's talented daughter, Lady Eleanor Smith, as my film critic, who was a great film fan, to-day known widely as a clever novelist who has made the Gipsies her especial subject. I was ready to agree but hinted that if she had ideas on payment at anything like the scale of her father, the cost would be prohibitive.

"How much can you go to?" Harrison asked.

"Not more than five guineas."

"H'm. Not very much is it?"

"Not bad for a thousand words a week in addition to which she would have the *entrée* with a friend to any and every cinema theatre, and you say she is a fan. Think what a lot she would save instead of purchasing seats! However," I added with at laugh, "you are my chairman and can authorise any amount you wish."

"I'll think it over," he said.

A few days later he rang me up and asked me to call for him at the Savoy, where a dinner was being given to him by his staff to celebrate the anniversary of his control of the **Daily Chronicle** (now the **News-Chronicle**). I arrived in time to hear him make a little speech in reply to the toast in his honour accompanied by the usual musical honours.

I believe that by this time Mr. Harrison had formed a good opinion of my discretion, and he certainly confided to me many interesting sidelights on his own experiences, one being his negotiations with the late Lord Reading, a former Viceroy of India, earlier of course the famous advocate and politician, Rufus Isaacs, which resulted in Harrison's purchase of the **Daily Chronicle**, now amalgamated with the **Daily News** as the **News-Chronicle**. **The Chronicle** was then controlled by Mr. Lloyd George, who had purchased the control in or about 1918, and who sold it at an enormous profit in 1927 to the **Daily Chronicle** Investment Corporation, of which his great friend Reading became chairman. The bulk of this purchase price was put up by Messrs; Yule and Catto, the Anglo-Indian millionaires. Yet, by retaining a large block of Ordinary and Deferred shares in the investment Corporation, "L.G." continued to possess voting control, and in 1928, L.G." sold this block to Harrison for about £1,110,000, but few people have ever, heard how near failure was this deal, according to the version; given to me by Harrison himself at the time.

He had agreed to purchase the Lloyd George block of shares in the Chronicle Investment Corporation and had been content in his negotiations to rely on a certificate from Lord Reading which stated that the profits of United Newspapers Ltd; (owning the *Daily Chronicle*), were some £280,000 for the year 1927. The contract for sale had been signed in the summer of that year and it was, officially announced that Mr. Harrison would take over the paper in October a few days before this happened, however, the prospective new proprietor became disturbed to think that he had not followed his usual cautious practice and called in his auditors to check the noble lord's certificate of profits and he insisted on his right to do so. This was eventually agreed upon but on investigation his auditors found that in Reading's certificate profits were overstated by about £70,000 for the year in question. Harrison's intention was to forthwith cancel the contract, and he attended a meeting one Sunday afternoon at Whitehall Place, the residence of Lord St. David's, when half the Lloyd George group, including "L.G.", were present, his object being to state his decision and demand the return of his deposit. In the end he was persuaded to proceed at the contract price and thus avert what, in his own words, would have created a public scandal. Within a year the "L.G." Party group had got Harrison out of the business and without any cost to themselves became in control of the whole Inveresk group. I believe they still control this large group although this is not publicly known. Harrison emerged having lost a huge personal fortune said to exceed seven figures. The loss to the Inveresk Company directly and indirectly over this transaction must have amounted to an enormous sum, which has never been and will probably never be disclosed. The unsolved mystery to this day is: Who now actually controls *United Newspapers Ltd.*, and the great *Provincial Newspaper* group formerly also controlled by Harrison? "L.G." again?

To return to my first meeting-with Lady Eleanor Smith and her father, Lord Birkenhead.

Harrison and I duly reached the Birkenhead mansion, a gaunt corner house in Grosvenor Gardens, where his Lordship was expecting us. As the footman was leading us upstairs to the library Harrison whispered in my ear, "I think you might offer Lady Eleanor ten guineas," an instruction I suspected might happen. We were ushered into a long room lined by book-shelves and standing at the far end before a fire stood the eminent jurist, leaning against the mantelpiece. He wore at brown velvet dinner jacket and had half a cigar in his mouth which had gone out, but had deposited ash on his waistcoat. Seated on a large and comfortable settee facing the hearth was Lady Eleanor Smith.

The appearance of Birkenhead was disillusioning. I had seen him; on a few previous occasions momentarily in the law courts, once or twice in restaurants, and on one occasion in all the majesty of his Lord Chancellor's robes in the House of Lords. He had seemed to me to represent the epitome of a distinguished if arrogant Englishman, tall, well-built, well-dressed, with a long handsome face albeit with a somewhat disdainful expression, which in his case well became him, and sleek, dark hair. That night he seemed to have gone to seed. He lounged; his erstwhile features had become bloated; he was untidy;

his manners were execrable; and in fine he appeared to be a poor replica of the greatest Lord Chancellor of which England could boast for many centuries. It is fair to add that he was then in failing health and died later that same year.

Harrison had scarcely crossed the threshold when Birkenhead started a tirade about some matter or other, without waiting for any introduction or in turn introducing his own daughter, and only paused when the butler appeared in answer to his ring and whom he assailed for not having brought a decanter of spirits and glasses sooner. When these appeared he helped himself to a stiff brandy without offering the slightest hospitality to his visitors. It was rather backward, but finally the great man was appeased, and I was duly presented. Lady Eleanor and I exchanged smiles; "F.E." favoured me with a curt nod which almost seemed to indicate that such a caitiff should realise fully what an honour it was for him to employ this daughter.

"I understand you want my daughter to write film articles for your paper?" he said.

"That is the idea, Lord Birkenhead," I replied.

"It comes to a question of terms, of course. What fee do you propose to offer?"

It must have been awkward for Lady Eleanor, to whom I threw a glance. Her smile seemed encouraging. At the back of my mind loomed the enormous fee of nearly two hundred guineas a week which Britannia had paid her father, the same salary, indeed, as he received when Lord Chancellor. Anyway, I spoke to my brief.

"The fee I can offer Lady Eleanor is ten guineas an article of about a thousand words a week."

"What!" He favoured me with a scathing look. "Did you say ten guineas?"

"Yes - and I may add that it is considerably in excess of what I have previously paid for film critiques."

He frowned:

"Ten guineas you say; Are you aware that the *Sunday Dispatch* have been paying Eleanor fifty guineas a week for articles? Harrison, do you approve of your editor's proposal?"

"I am sure that Lady Eleanor is worth fifty guineas, Lord Birkenhead," I cut in hurriedly to avoid embarrassing Harrison, "but my paper cannot afford a higher figure than I have mentioned. I would have you realise that I am not offering her ten guineas for a series, but a regular post on our contributing staff, which is a very different matter."

"Beaumont is quite right, Birkenhead," put in Harrison. "He cannot enlarge his schedule of expenses."

"Perhaps he does not recognise," said "F.E." with a flash of his old wit, "that Eleanor has been a film addict from birth!"

I laughed at this sally, as did Eleanor herself. Birkenhead, mollified, and sensing that I was not likely to raise the price, asked her if she were agreeable to accept the offer. She agreed.

"All right," said her father, "but on the distinct understanding that it is a permanent post. You must give her a three years' agreement at least." Glancing at me he added, "There is a table over there with a pen and ink. You may as well write out the contract at once."

It didn't work. I glanced at Harrison and he came to the rescue.

"There isn't the slightest need to be in such a hurry, Birkenhead," he said. "I will confirm the arrangement myself."

Whether Harrison sent the letter I never knew. I was under the impression that the next morning he was sailing for the United States and was seen off at Waterloo by the General. I remember that Campbell was in a state of exasperation, for in taking leave of his chairman, who was accompanied by the effervescent Irishman T.P. O'Connor - "Tay Pay" - as his guest, he was told by Harrison that he had purchased "T.P.'s" memoirs for serial publication for a considerable sum in one or other of the Great Eight publications. I also remember that Campbell was highly indignant at my report of the meeting with Birkenhead and the arrangement come to. He told me that I should have walked out of the room sooner than be browbeaten into such an agreement. I can but add that so far as Lady Eleanor was concerned she was reproachless, joined the staff of **The Bystander** and her articles were models of unbiased judicious criticism.

I had been curious to meet Birkenhead in private life, for I had admired him very considerably for many years, both as a politician and lawyer, although the two rarely blend. Born of working-class. parents, with no advantage other than his own personal gifts he made his way to Oxford by scholarships, became President of the Union, impressed Joseph Chamberlain by a public speech, became an M.P. at thirty-four, and with a brilliant maiden speech delivered from the broken Tory Opposition Bench, by its mockery covered the Liberal Government with ridicule and made him famous in a single night. His armoury of biting satire, of flouts and jeers, and his insolent disdain, left his opponents writhing in impotent fury and acclaimed him as a new Disraeli in our midst. He seemed to be the darling of the gods. His law practice rose by leaps and bounds, for he was not only the great lawyer, but a consummate cross-examiner and pleader. His income became very large and in 1908, when only thirty-six, he took silk.

After the retirement of Joseph Chamberlain, "F.E." became. the popular exponent of Conservatism who boldly attacked the parochialism of the Liberal Party in Parliament and on the platform. Lloyd George had to reckon with him and he could draw a crowd equal to L. G. himself. His speeches were reported verbatim. In 1911 when Asquith brought in his Parliament Bill to Whittle away the power of the House of Lords, he moved its rejection and led the opposition to it. He was made a Privy Councillor in 1911 and a member of the Tory Shadow Cabinet. When he threw in his lot with Sir Edward Carson in opposing the Home Rule Bill which proposed to hand over Ulster to the South his popularity with the rank and file grew to its height. This tall and handsome young barrister was expected to become the leader of the Tories and the future Prime Minister. Just as Ulster was preparing to fight rather than be dragooned into acceptance of Home Rule and "F.E." as Carson's chief lieutenant, was ready to join in the fray, the start of the first Great war threw the imbroglio into the melting-pot. Incidentally, I had been briefed to write a series of articles presenting Ulster's case which were intended to be advertised in big display in all the principal national dailies. They did not appear for the same reason.

"F.E." gained prestige by his attitude. In 1915, recalled from France, he became Solicitor General and the following year succeeded Carson as Attorney-General, and was knighted. In 1918, Lloyd George, reconstructing his Ministry, offered him the Lord Chancellorship, which, to his many admirers' dismay, he accepted. It automatically ruled him out of the running as Conservative leader for as Viscount Birkenhead, a peer of the realm, he was no longer in the Commons. It was a great and respected office, but it placed him on the shelf. It seemed, on the face of things, the greatest mistake of his career. In 1922 he made another serious error when he opposed the Tory Party, which wished to regain its independence and was sick of Lloyd George's leadership.

As a result, first Bonar Law and subsequently Baldwin left him out of their Governments, and he was tossed an Earldom as a sop. His prestige had further suffered when he gave his support to the formation of a *Sinn Fein* government in Eire under De Valera, after the rebellion in 1921, the latter's attitude throughout having been to set up a republican government. It was regarded as a desertion of the cause of Ulster, the loyal province, and knuckling down to the worst form of political graft on the part of men deaf to realities. Birkenhead, like every lawyer, was, I suppose, prepared to compromise with principle for the sake of expediency, and is the reason why the legal mind can never rise to majestic heights. Political chickens like this come home to roost sooner or later and we have seen in the present war the result of the tolerance shown to De Valera, which he, of alien origin, ascribed to weakness, whereby Eire, a member of the British Empire, proclaimed her neutrality not from principle but from fear, and has been the indirect means whereby many a fine ship and hundreds of finer characters than De Valera have laid down their lives on the ocean. The American people bear a heavy responsibility for this since they have for too long allowed the Irish-Americans to use them for their primeval vendetta. The day will come when the Irish of the south and west will have to be told that the British Isles must stand as one together and failing acceptance be defeated and extinguished. Otherwise where stands Democracy?

Why Birkenhead accepted the Lord Chancellorship remains a mystery to this day. He cast aside a huge income at the Bar for ten thousand a year on the Woolsack, and, more, his chance to become Prime Minister. Apart from politics he was the outstanding legal mind of our time and a great judge. His eclipse, was a considerable loss to the nation, a personal one felt by very many. There were so many we could have spared so much more easily and to think that he had to augment his income by trade directorships and by journalistic Work was almost a tragedy. I am glad to think I met him "off the record," so to speak, even though it happened to be a side-issue.

Another contributor to **The Bystander** was my niece Daphne du Maurier, to-day a novelist whose stories make her best-seller on both sides of the Atlantic. I believe I happened to be the first editor to publish any of her short stories before she wrote novels. It came about very simply.

My sister - Daphne's mother, known to everyone as "Mo" - mentioned one day that Daphne had written some short stories after returning from studying in Paris with a governess, and that Gerald considered them as far too cynical and unsophisticated for a young girl, although in point of fact it is then that most of us tend to such directions and later grow out of them. He had offered her a generous sum if she would destroy them, but Daphne refused. I offered to read them. Some were inclined to cynicism, but I accepted one, subject to permission to cut it to the length we needed for our short stories. Daphne agreed to this. I cut the MS. myself with some care.

In due course as a proof was sent to Daphne in the usual way, with the suggested deletions, Daphne grumbled, as any author is justified in doing when a story has to be cut down. At the moment when she was probably cursing me Gerald entered the breakfast-room and pricked up his ears.

"What's this?" he demanded. "What has your uncle done?"

"Nothing really, Daddy," replied Daphne. Yielding to pressure I suppose she said that the cuts I proposed would spoil her story. At all events Gerald waxed very indignant .

"The devil he has!" he exclaimed. "I'll soon put a stop to his game!"

Hence I was astonished to receive a long and peremptory wire which forbade me to delete a word or even a comma in the story, and as I failed to obtain any explanation of this extraordinary ukase I duly returned the MS. and said that in view of her father's attitude I was sorry to have to cancel acceptance.

Some time later Daphne called unexpectedly on me. She had brought back the offending script.

"If you care to use my story," she said, "here it is. You can do just what you like with it."

I took it from her and laughed, "Have you daddy's permission this time?" I asked.

She was, let me say, an extremely pretty and dainty blonde, having rather the appearance of a Tudor page. She looked at me with calm blue eyes and with never the flicker of an eyelid.

"Daddy won't interfere again," she said quietly.

I don't know what had transpired between them but certainly Daphne was very definite. The short story with this history duly appeared and indirectly as a result Miss Pearn, the literary agent, then with Curtis Brown, took Daphne under her strong wing, nursed her carefully, and helped largely to make her fame. Each novel has topped the one before and I believe that for the film rights of her latest so far, **Frenchman's Creek**, she was paid over £20,000. Yet she takes singularly little interest in money.

Gerald Du Maurier could be a most delightful and witty companion but like most famous actors was a person of moods. He was extremely generous and not only did he distribute largess with an open hand to his employees but he systematically helped less fortunate actors for he hated to refuse a plea even when he scarcely knew a man - and many took advantage of him. I have sat in his dressing-room when he was changing after a performance, especially on a Friday night, when there would be a succession of faint taps on the door, his dresser would open it cautiously, there would be a whispered conversation, then his dresser would mutter a name to Gerald and Treasury notes were passed out. Others more famous touched him for bigger cheques.

His sympathy for the underdog sometimes led to curious acts. On one occasion he caught a burglar red-handed at his home in Hampstead, Cannon Hall, who plugged him with such a tale of misery that he not only refused to give him in charge when the police appeared but gave him money for his needs. It worried him to think that so many had so great a share of this world's goods while millions lived on the borderline of want, and he sometimes seemed inclined to leftish views.

He was constantly imposed upon by hangers-on and when he died nine years ago as the result of a relapse after a severe operation he was owed large sums he had lent without any expectation of their return.

To an audience in the theatre he appeared as the most natural actor on the stage and his ease and nonchalance set theatrical fashion which still prevails, the absolute opposite to the ham actor of former days. Yet every seemingly casual move, even the flicker of a finger, was the result of careful study of the part. He appeared completely composed and self-collected whereas he admitted to me that he was at all times nervous. First nights were an agony to him but he never showed it.

"I loathe acting," he confided to me. "This mumming business is demoralising and degrading. It would be far more honest an occupation to sweep a crossing!"

He was certainly no admirer of the Press. He said roundly that newspapers were dishonest, that journalists were ignorant, and that so far as the stage was concerned they made their worst and most inefficient reporters their critics. In that view he was not alone. Arthur Bourchier for awhile refused to admit **The Times** critic to his productions and Gerald did the same because he thought the critique exceeded the bounds of fairness.

"Damn **The Times**!" he exclaimed. "I don't care two hoots for their patronage. I can fill my theatre without them. I see no reason to give them two seats on my first night to be sneered at by A.B. Walkley."

As a matter of fact Gerald was very well served by the critics and he obtained more publicity than any other actor of the day. He always kept up an amusing vendetta with the Press and had a tiresome habit of ringing me up and pouring torrential abuse of any newspaper critic who dared treat his production with derision. Only one editor held his regard but that one was thorough. He adored deep-voiced Tom Marlowe of the **Daily Mail**, of whom he used to see much at the Garrick Club, where Tom sat silent with occasional wise-cracks looking rather like an eastern *cadi*.

"There is a man for you!" said Gerald. "Tom Marlowe. Magnificent. Now if you were an editor like him. . ."

He had many eccentricities. One was to collect walking-sticks of which my sister has retained a big collection to this day, of all sorts and conditions, mostly expensive. A friend of mine entered a well-known shop in Piccadilly which specialised in expensive and novel walking-sticks in the days when no gentleman would dream of going out without one. Examining the wares this friend perceived an elaborate stick which, when one pressed a button opened up into a perfect small-bore gun. Admiring the workmanship and craft he asked the price, and was staggered when he heard the figure.

"Surely you won't find any mug ready to pay that for it?" he quizzed.

"You think so, eh?" grinned the manager. He took the mechanism to pieces before my friend's eye; "A perfect little gun in every way, and yet a complete walking-stick. You can go for a walk through your estate and suddenly a covey of partridges rise or perhaps a pheasant near by. You just do this, see? aim, pop, and there you are. I have a customer who will purchase it directly he sets eyes on it and not care about the price either."

"Really?"

"Yes, sir. He often drops in and looks around. 'Got anything new?' he asks, and when he takes a fancy to it he says, ' Send it round to me.' When he is busy he sometimes sends his secretary to report what I have new."

"I suppose you are alluding to Lord Lonsdale?"

"No, sir. To the actor Gerald du Maurier."

That particular walking stick had an amusing sequel. Gerald was playing at the St. James's and one night King George V, Queen Mary, and the Prince of Wales were in the royal box. After the performance

238

the King sent for Gerald, who was popular with the Royal family, to congratulate him. Whether Gerald had really hurt a leg or whether it were a bit of play-acting he had limped through the performance and leant on a walking-stick and in this guise entered the royal box. When questioned he told His Majesty that he had hurt himself only slightly. It was nothing. Then as if by an afterthought he remarked:

"By the by, sir, this stick might interest Your Majesty. It is rather a novelty. Permit me to show you."

With a flourish, lo and behold! the malacca cane became a delightful small-bore, single-barrel shot-gun. The King was vastly intrigued and examined it closely as did likewise the Prince. He said to Gerald:

"A lovely little weapon, du Maurier. I should like to obtain one like it. Where does it come from?"

"I am afraid, sir," replied Gerald, "that this is the only one of its type in existence. I believe it was manufactured in Vienna. But if Your Majesty would condescend to accept it I shall be honoured to send it round to the palace to-morrow."

King George did accept it and I was told that he occasionally used it at Sandringham. My friend who told me the story - which I subsequently confirmed - said that it was how Gerald obtained his knighthood. The answer to that is simple. He was already knighted.

CHAPTER XII

SUCCESSFUL SABOTAGE

"You will never save the soul of England until you destroy the party machine."

CAPT. RONALD CARTLAND M.P.

I REMEMBER READING that Joseph Conrad, the famous novelist who was staying at his birthplace Cracow just before World War No. 1, at the time Austria had hurled her ultimatum at the Serbs; was anxiously asked by the Poles, "Do you think England will go to war too?" He replied; "I do not know if she will go to war but if she does you may be certain that once she takes up arms she will never lay down the sword until she has defeated her enemies."

In a terse sentence he hit off the sterling character of the British people. The less favourable side is the apathy shown by the masses during the years of nominal peace, especially noteworthy since the beginning of the century. They didn't want to be bothered with the squabbles of the European powers and objected to be wasting, as they considered it huge sums in armaments, fleets and armies. The same indifference, and with less excuse, was shown to the strong maintenance of the Empire, yet to every thinker it is the bulwark of our national existence and the true guardian of our freedom. It is really a vital need to our prosperity. Political leaders, with few exceptions, failed to give a lead in these great questions.

These small islands; mere dots on the map of the world, with one tenth of their population implacably hostile and backward, can never maintain their position indefinitely as a great world power without the Empire lands and peoples. The Dominions and Colonies form the outer bulwarks of our power and prosperity as we soon realised when Japan grabbed all of our rubber and much of our oil. I cannot blame the uninstructed public, shockingly neglected as their education has been in such matters, but it can be laid on the cold aloofness of Whitehall which has usually shown a disposition to be more than half ashamed of the Empire, and India in particular, instead of publicising it and popularising it by every means in its power.

War, however, is a great educator. Our service men grilling in the African deserts sweltering in the Middle East in India and Burma, freezing almost to death in the Arctic regions, and battling with U-boats in all the Seven Seas, have gained practical lessons in the true meaning of the British Empire, and I should feel it to be a safe bet that when they return home they will hold very different ideas of the Empire from Hong Kong to Jamaica. Maybe, too, they will see to it that there is in future a complete clear-up of our robot politicians whose job it was to watch these matters.

I was discussing the way people were fooled by our politicians at the time of the 1935 General Election with that remarkable woman Lady Houston. She was declaring that the people were deceived by promises which the politicians had never intended to fulfil.

"How can we blame them?" she asked. "If they could travel more and see what England stands for in they world beyond our shores, and what other countries stand for they couldn't possibly tolerate the leadership of men like Stanley Baldwin and that dour prig Ramsay MacDonald.

"Travel," she went on, "opens the eyes of the dullest among us. I was a poor girl and had to work for my living, and in those days I knew very little. When the opportunity to travel came my way I saw what England meant in the world. Later I came to realise that our country seemed willing to surrender its pride of place and to let upstarts jostle us from our rightful position. So I decided to do everything in my power to rouse our national pride and though I am only a woman - and getting old at that I intend to do what I can while I live."

This conversation took place on her magnificent yacht *Liberty* moored at the time up the estuary of the Seine a few miles below Rouen. Our contact began when she sent me a long telegram of congratulation at something I had written about Mr. Baldwin in **The Bystander**. It led to correspondence and suggestions on her part. Why don't you say so-and-so, or expose this or that scandal, she would ask me, and so one fine day I told her frankly that I was hampered by my directors who objected to my embarking on any political questions and especially resented any criticism of Ramsay MacDonald and Stanley Baldwin. Her response to this was to ask me why I did not start my own paper, to which I replied that I should like nothing better but unfortunately was not a capitalist. I duly received a telegram from Rouen inviting me to visit her on her yacht, suggesting the train, and saying that I would be met at the *Quai de la Bourse*. I accepted the invitation and was duly met by an officer in a spruce white uniform, two semi-bluejackets and a smart white and gold motor-boat.

Downstream we proceeded at high speed along the serpentine Seine until, rounding a bend, there sat *Liberty*, looking like a miniature two-funnelled liner, painted white and gold, sitting in solitary grandeur in a wide stretch of the river. Climbing the companion steps I was received by the captain, my dressing-case was taken by a steward, and the captain led me to a cabin whose various *apéritifs* were inviting. Shortly after a woman secretary explained that her Ladyship had had a bad night and would not be ready to receive me for some little time, but if, I would like to rest she would conduct me to my state-room. It was almost semi-regal on this plutocratic yacht and I began to wonder what I should be expected to do when I was led into the Presence.

Eventually the steward conducted me to a large saloon at whose further end, embowered in hothouse blossoms, and shaded by subdued lights, sat my hostess. She bestowed a friendly smile as I approached and when she laughed the corners of her mouth turned up impishly. I dare say Dame Fanny Lucy Houston - one of the first five Dame Commanders of the last war, awarded her for nursing - was verging on seventy but she looked many years younger. A blue silk bandeau was tied round her head and from its sides peeped little golden curls. Her eyes twinkled with amusement or flashed indignation according to the circumstances. She was affable, understanding, direct, and despite her plutocratic surroundings, definitely homely. The general public believed she was crazy. I found her extremely level-headed if decidedly unconventional.

"I am pleased you could find time to come and see me," she said, as I took her hand, "and hope it may prove worth your while." She added with a laugh: "And mine too."

"It would be well worth my while, Lady Houston," I returned, "if only to have the pleasure of meeting one of the most remarkable women of the time."

"Oh!" she quizzed. "Why do you think I am remarkable?" .

"Am I to tell? You are the nation's fairy godmother on a lavish scale and in unexpected ways. You have a great grip on public affairs. Your enterprises are such that reporters always keep their eyes on you for at any moment you may give them a first-class human story. You intrigue the world."

"I only know that reporters never cease pestering me and it is why I have to seek refuge in out-of-the-way spots like this, I had one of them after me yesterday for an interview."

"At any rate your selection of moorings for your beautiful yacht seems to be cleverly chosen."

"Why do you say that?"

"You are within a few hours' steaming of England and within even easier distance from Paris. And isn't there your residence in Jersey just across the way so to speak? It calls to mind how you escaped from Jersey after your husband Sir Robert Houston died. It was rumoured that your trustees attempted to place you under restraint and insisted that you were - er - "

244

"Crazy. Mad," she interrupted. "Don't mince matters! Lots of people think I am as mad as a March hare. I know these things."

"Anyhow, did you not escape in a small boat to England at night?"

!Certainly. I landed at the bottom of the garden of my house at Sandgate," she laughed. "That spiked their guns. No one has ever held me against my will and never shall."

"Anyway, it was remarkable," I said, laughing too. "Then, of course, there is the famous story of your controversy with Winston Churchill, when Chancellor of the Exchequer, after you had claimed that, with your domicile in Jersey you were not liable for English death duties on Sir Robert Houston's estate."

"Nor was I. But what is your version?"

"That you called on him at the Treasury and told him although he had no legal claim you were prepared to make an *ex gratia* offer of a million and a half and handed him your cheque on the spot. Churchill was almost speechless and you said 'Don't you think I deserve a kiss for this?' whereupon he rang the bell and had you shown out."

"Very garbled!" she laughed. "I arranged to call and hand him my cheque and when I called I found Sir Austen Chamberlain was also present. I said, 'I should prefer to see you alone, Mr. Churchill,' and he replied, 'This is only Austen Chamberlain. I hope you have no actual personal objection to meeting him.' 'I have no personal objection,' I said, 'but does it take two of you men to face one woman?' They laughed and that was the end of it."

Presently her maid entered and she terminated the conversation saying that she was an invalid and was afraid she would not be able to entertain me personally at luncheon for she never took it, but the captain would look after me. She dismissed me with a gracious smile adding that we would confer together later. Thus far our talk had been on generalities.

At tea-time, again ensconced in the corner of her embowered saloon, pouring out tea from an enormous silver pot, she suddenly broached the newspaper project.

"What sort of a paper have you in mind to start?" she asked.

"A sixpenny weekly, not an illustrated but carrying pictures bearing on subjects. It must be an outspoken, independent critic of affairs."

"But why a sixpenny? A twopenny would get you far bigger circulation and hence influence. What is the good of attempting to convert the upper classes? They are either converted already or are dilettantes who are useless anyhow. The upper classes will never stir a little finger for efforts to improve things. They are only concerned lest further privileges should be stripped from them."

"My idea is to work the leaven with the middle classes," I replied, "and if we can influence them as I hope we may we can think about the working classes later. I have brought you a rough scheme or 'dummy' of the sort of journal I have in mind."

She examined the scheme attentively and then remarked:

"I can see that it might be a success. What sort of circulation have you in mind?"

"Assuming it gets a big set-off with clever preliminary publicity. and advertising we ought to establish a sale of at least 100,000. At the same time, without being too optimistic, I don't see why we could not aim at double that figure. Obviously we should pay big prices for big names when the writers have something worth while to say. I should like to run a crusade where necessary - India, for example. I think the truth should be told about that great dependency where we are trying to hand over power to the Brahmins, who are the greatest enemies of India itself."

"Katherine Mayo proved that in her book **Mother India**, didn't she?" observed Lady Houston. "It was a most distressing book."

"I agree," I said, "but the general public don't read such books. Presented attractively they will read a paper and then questions get asked in Parliament and anything may happen."

She thought silently for a few moments and sipped her tea. Then she observed, "I still think a twopenny would be the better. The working man is no fool but he knows so little, and it is his class we need to educate in these matters, don't we?"

"Please bear in mind, Lady Houston," I replied, "that the working man is really the most conservative-minded of all among us. He confines his reading to the papers which pretend to champion him as the under-dog, and while airing grievances they really tend to worsen his positions than improve it, for their methods tend to level things downward. For instance, I have never found any Socialist paper yet advocate profit-sharing as a policy, yet it would give every employee a chance to save for the future and remove the haunting dread of the workhouse in their old age. Their Press is pacifist, dislikes, the Empire, and would gladly surrender the sovereignty of Great Britain to the League of Nations, which would dictate our foreign policy and make war or peace. It will take long to remove these mountains of crass ignorance and prejudice!"

"But someone should do it, my friend," she returned.

"Let us walk before we run. A twopenny would require a great sum and might prove a heavy loss. There is the revenue side to consider, for, let me add, a paper to acquire influence must be a financial success. My sixpenny would be the safest venture for the first move. It would have no competitors except the shilling Weeklies and I believe that when we blow the trumpet their walls of Jericho will collapse."

"Ah! **Trumpet**?" she echoed. "A very good name for the paper, I had thought of a name myself, but **Trumpet**, or, better still, **The Trumpet Call** would answer. My name," she added, with her Puckish grin, "was '**The Pepper Pot.**' What do you think of it?"

I gasped inwardly. "'**Pepper Pot**'. Frankly," I ventured, "it suggests a comic or a cookery paper."

"It suggests hot stuff, too, my friend! Let's agree, however, on the name of '**The Trumpet Call**'. How much money will you need to make this paper all you expect of it?"

"Now we are coming towards bed-rock, my lady!" I exclaimed, as we both laughed at the suddenness of her question. "It will entail a good deal. It would be dangerous to reckon on less than fifty thousand pounds."

Without at moments hesitation she replied, "I am prepared to put up double that amount."

"What!" I gasped. "A hundred thousand!" I stared at her in dazed amazement. Here she was tossing me, as it were, this very considerable sum as though it were a flea-bite. "Well, Lady Houston!"

She faced me with a big smile. "Well?" she queried, "you seem surprised?"

"I am, indeed," I said. "It is an extraordinarily generous and in fact almost overwhelming offer. I do not know how to begin to thank you. After all - you have only just met me - "

"Why did you think I invited you to come here to discuss the scheme?"

"Naturally, I hoped that you might go some way to enable such a paper to be started - but, such a great sum! I shall, of course, leave no stone unturned to make it a huge success, but I must warn you that there are many slips betwixt the cup and the lip, in the newspaper world - "

"Together we shall triumph!" she interrupted. "I always succeed when I set my mind to a task, and I shall play a big part in it. How soon can you start? There's no time to waste with Ramsay MacDonald and Baldwin on the rampage!"

"As soon as possible, Lady Houston," I replied, "but there are many matters which will require careful preliminary consideration - such as business arrangements, collecting a staff, leaving my present post and so on."

"Well get on with it. I am impatient when I make up my mind. Let me know frequently how you progress."

Thus ended this interview. To say I was exhilarated is to put it mildly. At the offset it seemed that my long-hoped-for ambition was about to be consummated. But on the boat crossing to Southampton certain doubts arose. A further conversation had brought it forcibly before me that to satisfy Lucy Houston the new journal would need to be brutally frank and outspoken and that a more subtle approach to our goal would not be at all her idea. She wanted to call as spade a spade every time, especially where the Prime Minister was concerned. She considered him a traitor and she wanted him called it, too. I foresaw many difficulties, although the very opposite to those I had previously encountered, the danger of going too far and of being labelled as extremist right. I also resolved that before I burnt my boats it would be very necessary to arrange matters so that the decision as to policy was left in my hands as well as to ensure my financial position and what interest I should possess in the new journal.

I should mention here that in my firm a new Pharaoh had arisen, for Harrison's difficulties with the **Daily Chronicle** had led to his retirement from the board of Illustrated Newspapers, and the vice-chairman, William Graham, had succeeded. Mr. Graham, an eminent City solicitor was particularly interesting to me at this time, because among his clients, who included such outstanding millionaires as Sir John Ellerman, Lords Rothermere and Camrose, was Lady Houston herself. An astute lawyer himself reputedly of great wealth, with handsome features crowned by a mass of snowy-white hair, he made a striking figure. He always displayed considerable friendliness to me, although on a few occasions I was rebuked for political comment which seemed to him to go too far in adverse criticism. All these capitalists, needless to remark were immense believers in Mr. Baldwin who could do not wrong in their eyes.

Lady Houston meantime kept in close touch and showed some impatience because I had as yet taken no tangible steps, although I was preparing plans which wanted much consideration. One day Teddy Huskinson, whom I had long regarded as the nigger in the woodpile as making me unpopular with the General, walked into my room and greeted me in his usual urbane manner.

"I say, Comyns," he exclaimed, "I have just had a shock. There is a rumour about that you are thinking of leaving us to start a rival sixpenny weekly."

"Why should it give you a shock?" I questioned.

"We can't let you leave us and start up against us. Is there any truth in it?"

"I don't know that I very much want to tell you,"

"Why not?"

"For one thing you are a director and for another I may not have finally decided whether to accept the offer made to me."

"Oh! Then you have had an offer?" he asked brightly.

"I don't mind telling you that it is so. In fact, the offer comes from Lady Houston and since Graham is her solicitor he may know something about it."

"I have heard," said Huskinson, "that she is very difficult. You should be careful, Comyns, before you decide?"

"I doubt if she can be as difficult as your Board and especially the General have proved themselves to be so far as I am concerned," I said with a laugh; "I find her very tolerant and generous. Also we hold the same views."

"I think we should talk this business over," said he eagerly. "I assure you that the directors do not want you to leave us. What do you say to a little dinner with Graham and me?"

"Very kind of you, Teddy," I returned, "but where is it likely to take us? Considering the attitude of the Board indirectly and the General in particular I should have thought you would welcome the prospect of my leaving you."

He ignored the gibe. "Listen," he said, "I know that you have long wanted to start a sixpenny and discuss politics in it. Suppose, instead of leaving us, we grant you the facilities to start such a paper ourselves? You would have the capital behind you and all the service for circulation and advertising. That is the idea Graham and I would like to discuss with you."

Concealing my surprise I asked him point-blank what the reaction of the General would be to his proposal. He shrugged his shoulders.

"He isn't in the picture. Graham decides this business."

"But he will be in it and it is tolerably certain that he will oppose it in every way. He has a horror of any sixpenny undermining the monopoly of the shilling papers."

"Perhaps - but if a sixpenny must go on the market far better ours than a rival firm?"

"I have argued the same thing often. It is a pity you did not think of this aspect before. Campbell - "

"Campbell is merely a servant of the Board. Graham is chairman and what he and I recommend will be approved by it."

The long and short of it was that a few nights later I was invited to dine with Graham at his club, the Junior Carlton, hotbed of orthodox Toryism, Huskinson making the third. My host was both affable and conciliatory, and when, we got down to brass tacks a most attractive offer was forthcoming. I was to start at new sixpenny weekly, would have a free hand to treat on political issues granted that the paper was not scurrilous, my salary was doubled with a three-year contract, and a hint was dropped that I should fill the next vacancy on the Board. Huskinson, for his part, warned me that if I turned down the offer I should have to reckon with all the heavy batteries of the firm which would be brought into action against me - not that the threat influenced me in the slightest.

It all seemed fair and above-board. One is inclined to prefer the devil that one knows instead of the one unknown. Lady Houston offered great possibilities, but on the other hand she was rather eccentric and as yet I had nothing definite in writing. At any moment she might change her mind. I finally decided to accept Graham's offer and wrote to Lady Houston giving her all the facts and begging her to forgive me for withdrawing. She told me that she had instructed her banks, Coutts', to place £100,000 aside for our venture and she was naturally annoyed; although she bore me no ill-will. For her part she proceeded on her own account and before long purchased *The Saturday Review*, a literary review of great reputation in the past, and her first act was to wire me in the Riviera, where I happened to be, inviting me to write the first political article weekly; which I did thenceforth.

Everything thus seemed set for success; but I have learnt to be wary when I appear to reach the height of my climb. There are always ugly abysses yawning below. In this case it was General Campbell, of course. I might have reflected that my friend of the long legs, craning neck and yard-stick cigarette-holder would be lurking in the shadows awaiting his chance to consume me like the monsters of the Egyptian underworld, who pounced upon the souls on their pilgrimage to *Amenta* and the *Isle of the Blest*. I little suspected, however, the snag actually in store for me.

He handed me a contract for three years in due course with an enigmatic sneer.

"So you have your own way at last, Beaumont, eh?" he said affably, "Able to bring out your sixpenny weekly."

"The offer was made to me spontaneously, General, by Graham and Huskinson?" I replied.

"Quite so. But neither of them were acquainted with certain essentials when they discussed the proposition with you. Since their the directors have been forced to vary the conditions in one slight particular. You are to take over the editorship of *The Graphic* reconstruct it according to your ideas, and at sixpence. Your contract and salary stand, of course, as agreed between you."

"Is this a serious decision?" I demanded. "It makes an enormous difference to our agreement."

"Difference or no it is inevitable. **The Graphic**, as you know, has long been a drain on our resources; We cannot afford to keep it alive and finance your new sixpenny as well. You see my point?"

"It is a point which never arose when I came to terms with Mr. Graham," I said. "He offered me - and Huskinson will bear me out - the opportunity of starting a *new* weekly."

"Just unfortunate, my dear Beaumont. But what great difference does it make? **The Graphic** bears a respected name as you ought to know, for you edited it yourself a good many years ago."

"Excuse me, General, it makes a profound difference. It has been my fate in journalism to attempt to rescue one paper after another when it had gone into a decline. It is almost an impossibility. You brought me here to reconstruct **The Bystander** and you have done little else but criticise adversely what I have done. And now you throw the decrepit **Graphic** at me like a bone to a dog!"

"My dear fellow," said the General. "I will explain the reason which makes this step imperative **The Graphic** stands on our books as an asset of £200,000, which sum your friend Harrison paid for it. We cannot afford to write off that capital sums and speculate on the prospects of your sixpenny weekly. So if you propose to start it I am afraid it means **The Graphic** or nothing."

Parvum parva decent! Campbell's excuse was disingenuous, as I discovered later when **The Graphic** did stop and its name was incorporated as a sub-title of **The Sphere**, as it is to this hour. He was determined to make my path thorny. A protest to Huskinson took me nowhere for all he could say was that neither; Graham nor he had the slightest idea of asking me to take over *The Graphic* when they had arranged terms. The plot obviously originated in the tortuous mind of the General who was determined to defeat me. I was in a dilemma; because I had now withdrawn from Lady Houston's proposals, she had made other arrangements, and I must either accept the *status quo* or repudiate the contract with my firm. I fancy my friends were alive to the facts and had I done so they would not have cared a fig provided I could not compete with them.

"I will help you in every way I am able," said the General genially. "You shall produce a shilling weekly for sixpence, print in photogravure and I will give you some coloured pages. You will never have a finer chance of making a crashing success!"

Ominous word "Crashing"! To transform the old illustrated *Graphic* into a journal of articles with illustrations was as likely as not to lose us the old readers and fail to gain new ones. I had to take over the existing paper and edit it and at the same time make full preparations for the new sixpenny.

Printing in photogravure meant going to press far earlier than the usual method on ordinary presses. I was given the shortest time to arrange for the transfer. This spate of work was further complicated, because at this precise moment I had to pass the proofs of a scientific book I had written.

Another serious drawback was that I was compelled to use the name of **The Graphic**, instead of my intention, **The National**, and had to compromise in the end by naming it **The National Graphic**. I was told that apart from the necessity of preserving the name, to change it would cancel all the standing orders in libraries, clubs, hotels, doctors' and dentists' waiting rooms, etc., a valuable consideration. The General was totally indifferent to my plea that the very essence of success was whether we could create a belief in the minds of the public that a new sixpenny was on sale and not a rehash of a former shilling paper cheapened because it was *démodé.*

A yet worse blow was to fall; our live publisher and his staff had thoroughly canvassed the trade; and he reported that the big wholesale newsagents and booksellers were enthusiastic in praise of the sixpenny of which they were shown "dummies." It was, they said, exactly what the public wanted. The first few issues were big, printing orders exceeding l00,000. The day of publication arrived. I went to one or two main line railway stations to see how **The National Graphic** was selling. *It wasn't.*

Piles lay on the stalls, but the public were simp1y not interested in an illustrated named **Graphic**, with or without the prefix *National.* The publisher had along face. Preliminary reports were not at all encouraging. "The public don't know about it," was the general comment. It had not been advertised.

The preliminary advertising had been restricted to the trade papers who had reciprocated by placing larger orders, but the general public were told little or nothing except for some posters. Such, it gradually emerged, were the General's orders, but I was not informed until later, although I did my best to press the need of advertising. In fact thousands should have been spent to advertise **The National Graphic**; but scarcely anything was done except for lavish displays in the trade papers. The result was inevitable. The trade was cluttered up with unsold copies and the public knew nothing about the paper's new appearance.

We of the editorial staff worked whole-heartedly to pull the paper through this crisis, hoping for the best, but anyone conversant with the intricacies of newspaper production will agree that a false start is fatal in nine cases out of ten and I was saddled with an old paper Which for years had gone to seed.

The only aid I received was the kindly act of Lord Beaverbrook who, entirely on his own account, caused a friendly leader to be written in the **Daily Express**, mentioning me and wishing luck to the enterprise. It takes time before a publisher can ascertain a stabilisation figure, but orders fell steadily and eventually heavy returns of back over-ordered copies drifted back. At length the blow fell. The Board told me that the venture was a failure and they had decided to discontinue its publication.

I protested, pleading that the fault lay in the neglect of proper publicity and advertising at the start. I reminded them that they had sent for me on the publication of the first issue and had complimented me on the production and contents; and so it might be presumed that the situation was caused by the neglect to push the sales, an argument to which there was no reply. I begged them to bear in mind that after ten first issues they were unable to estimate correctly whether the paper was a failure based on a percentage of returns for it was insufficient time to ascertain yet at what basic circulation it would stabilise. I reminded them that at the worst its sales, as far as could be ascertained, were well in excess of the old **Graphic**. In short, I demanded more time instead of so hasty a decision.

I might as well have talked to a blank wall. All they did agree to was to give me another fortnight to see if I could sell the paper as a going concern elsewhere. I tried in various directions without result and so finally it sank into a premature grave. I had fought as much at least for my staff as for myself since it meant unemployment to them. To me it placed a stigma on my reputation and I remembered in those bitter days once again that the vulgar keep no account of your hits, but only of your misses.

It did not make it the less bitter to realise that I had been victimised completely. The artful General had won hands down. He had demonstrated to his Board - few of whom knew much about newspaper management - and, as he no doubt fondly believed, to the publishing world that the sixpenny weekly was a drug on the market. Whether Huskinson were a party to a conspiracy to prevent my producing a sixpenny weekly under the *ægis* of Lady Houston by tempting me with a counter-offer which had the bottom knocked out of it directly I had succumbed to the offer I cannot say, but I should like to believe that Husky was a mere tool, and in no sense conscious of the General's intentions. I had known him for years and liked him always. Huskinson unfortunately was killed not long ago in a railway accident.

The General interviewed me in due Course. He said, with a scarcely-veiled sneer:

"Well, Beaumont, as far as you are concerned you have a contract for three years in your pocket. So you can afford to live as a gentleman of leisure for that period!"

"Thank you, General," I returned. "And in reply, may I congratulate you, on the success of your manoeuvre. Forgive me, however, if I suggest that you may have cut off your nose to spite your face."

He took the yard-stick out of his mouth. His heavy eyebrows narrowed.

"What the devil do you mean?" he questioned.

"I mean that the whole business has a sinister ring about it," and one day I hope to expose it. Before long, too, I fancy your Board will realise that you have cost the firm a pretty penny to try to prove that a sixpenny weekly is a false policy - first with **Britannia**, and now with **The National Graphic**."

Nor was its very long before the Board discovered that they preferred his room to his company. To-day, the General is no longer of this world and any hard thoughts I harboured towards him have long evaporated. I have no doubt but that he acted in the best interests of the firm, as he believed, although a policy of tortuousness never wins in the long run.

The striking aspect of the recital is that here was a firm of newspaper proprietors whose subscribed capital ran into several millions and that its fate lay in the hands of an ex-army officer whose training for such a post was merely, superficial. I am far from asserting that a man trained in one profession may not become outstanding in another. Yet such a man would need to possess a special flair. General Campbell had no such flair. In my opinion he was profoundly ignorant of newspaper management and of the public taste. He ran what have been described as the snobs' journals, as a super-snob, using his military title (he was really only a brigadier) and a remarkable and breezy personality as his stock-in-trade. He was, of course, an alien in Fleet Street, as were almost all his employees, the real Fleet Street which works in its shirt-sleeves, ridicules pretentiousness, and regards the world with a good deal of cynical good nature and complete scepticism.

The newspaper proprietors I have worked under in these many years have naturally varied. James Gordon Bennett was, of course, a great journalist and opportunist, with a very shrewd knowledge of human nature. He knew his world completely. So did Northcliffe, to whom the same words can apply, who was rather a sort of Autolycus, a master of the art of emphasising unconsidered trifles and making them of interest, but as the most powerful newspaper proprietor in Europe did not sufficiently stress the greatest matter of all, the looming of the coming war, and the inadequacy of our Foreign Office and our defence preparations. As a master of publicity and an arch-campaigner he could have forced reforms during the years of his prime with his ownership of **The Times**, **Daily Mail**, **Evening News**, and many other organs of public opinion. He was very weak in his understanding of the potentiality of the weekly news-paper. There was F.A. Gwynne, of the **Morning Post,** a man of great perception, Whose knowledge of foreign affairs was profound, but his Toryism was too unbending to enable that great daily to acquire the circulation and influence it deserved, and its make-up and appearance gave it an impression of dullness. There is is an enormous financial stake in journalism, in which appearance, display, type, and setting are all-important. Up-to-date ideas need not be garbed in old-fashioned suits.

Generally speaking my experience of newspaper managements had not proved very inspiring. My feeling has always been that the British Press has lacked independence of outlook, especially in such vital matters as foreign affairs, the Empire, and national defence. It has followed the politicians - otherwise the Government of the day - instead of leading them. Its treatment of international affairs has frequently been too insular. The national dailies have given too much space to trivial affairs and I fear have been too greatly influenced by the long purse of Big Money interests.

As to views, I plump for the right kind of Weeklies after this war. because journals after the style of the American **Life** can ably spread themselves upon a worth-while subject and bring adequate illustrations to strengthen the main points. They can concern themselves with a variety of most important subjects and build up a considerable influence with the public, granted that they are thoroughly financed, produced admirably, and not priced highly. I am not thinking in a high-brow manner in the least, for all sorts of subjects are awaiting attention.

Take profit-sharing for example. After the demise of **The National Graphic**, I became a special feature writer for various journals of the group, and among my allotments was to visit certain great manufacturing firms, accompanied by a photographer or artist, and write up a descriptive account of their methods and treatment of their staffs. Two of these - both household names - had a policy of profit-sharing among their employees. I had the privilege of mixing with them and asking any questions I thought fit. In every case there was contentment among the workers. The prosperity of the firm was their own prosperity. They would not tolerate slackers or malcontents. and strikes were an unknown quantity. The firm's productions were of the highest grade and all benefited. I seriously suggest that a national policy of compulsory profit-sharing, giving the investors the first return necessarily, but after a certain ordinary dividend was paid, then a like amount to the employees will go far to restore our prosperity. It is, to my mind, the only solution of unemployment, prevention of strikes and justice to the working classes. It also prevents waste.

Ronald Cortland, the first M.P. to be killed in action in this war, a friend of mine, and who possessed an intuitive insight into these matters, hit the nail on the head in a speech in parliament just before war broke out.

"It is no use talking about markets unless we do something about men," he declared. "In order to solve our unemployment problem we shall have to recognise that the only solution is savings. The old age problem is not one of unemployment and work, but one of savings, and the ability to retire." Profit-sharing would meet that need.

Another task I undertook was for Capt. Bruce Ingram, the doyen or Fleet Street editors, third of the Ingram dynasty, whose grandfather founded over a hundred years ago *The Illustrated London News*. Bruce has travelled a great deal, is extremely erudite, a bit dictatorial as a big editor should be, and an authority on many matters, including works of art, especially Old Masters. He adores poring over maps. He deputed me in 1933 at the time of the great slump and wide unemployment, to visit the depressed areas in advance of the tour of the Prince of Wales, a tour which by no means met with the approval of Ministers of the Crown. Accompanied by the well-known artist, Captain Bryan de Grineau, I visited such centres as Hull, Glasgow, Dundee, and others; and studied local conditions.

At Glasgow we interviewed the Lord Provost, who said half-jokingly, half-desperately, "I wish you could think of some way to induce manufacturers to start factories here. Industrialists are all tending to move south-wards."

"Because strikes are far rarer in the south, Lord Provost," I replied. "Why is it that Glasgow has such frequent strikes?"

"There are several reasons," he said, "but the main one is that the workers are discontented and demand a higher standard of living."

"In that case," I returned; "Why do not employers consider the merits of profit-sharing?"

The Lord Provost raised his eyes at the question.

"If they were to do so," I continued, "there would be no more strikes and no more slacking and waste. The workers would see to that themselves. And the profits would more than cover any share-out they might make."

"Eh, man," retorted the Lord Provost, "'twould be the thin end of the wedge. Next they would be commandeering the business!"

That was nonsense. I fancy the good man thought I was a Bolshevist.

All this time I was writing also for Lady Houston. The ownership of the *Saturday* gave her a new zest in life. From henceforth she spent most of her life at Byron Cottage, set amid rustic surroundings on Hampstead Heath. There she plotted and planned and was for ever on the telephone to her editors, and if she felt she was helping to put another nail into the political coffin of Ramsay MacDonald she was happy.

CHAPTER XIII

THE LULLABY YEARS

"For no less than nine years the Chief Whip has in two Parliaments driven huge majorities to support policies which have culminated in this catastrophe."

CAPT. VYVYAN ADAMS, M.P.

I CANNOT SAY how much Lady Houston lavished on the **Saturday Review** but it ran into hundreds a week, howbeit a drop in the ocean to a multi-millionaire. Still absorbed with the idea that she could draw in a big public if she made the price within the means of most, she soon brought down the price of that formerly austere and highbrow journal from sixpence to twopence. In so doing she added little if any more circulation and caused shudders to its previous readers who promptly dropped it.

Nevertheless "Lucy," as her familiars and editorial staff spoke of her, was sublimely indifferent to such minor matters. From her citadel she proceeded to fire her heaviest guns at the Government especially in regard to its foreign defence policy. Her special *bête noir*, as I have said, was the Prime Minister, Mr. Ramsay MacDonald, and with him the instrument he so lovingly helped to erect, the *League of Nations*. Her scorn for both was consummate. As she voiced the opinions of a great many, persons The **Saturday** might have carried more weight had she refrained from using her own pen, for her literary ability was not equal to her enthusiasm. Sometimes she wrote a manifesto, and now and again indulged in satirical verse which was rather awful doggerel She insisted on printing week after week her remedy for colds which included a heavy dose of castor oil and gulps of Vaseline. She also caused her editor, Warner Allen, formerly foreign editor of the **Morning Post**, traveller, novelist, and a leading authority on vintage wines, most exquisite suffering by occasionally accepting for publications a series of articles quite unsuited to the journal's requirements. Yet, thanks to the skill and patience of its editor, numbers did read it and it attracted attention in high political circles.

As for Ramsay MacDonald she was relentless in every effort to expose his policy, her passionate dislike being inspired purely by her conviction that he was a dangerous defeatist. This view apparently had fomented in her mind from the time he had refused to allow any public funds to be employed to enable the Royal Air Force to compete for the Schneider Trophy which we had won from Italy in 1927. It was then she stooped to conquer. Those who have witnessed the film *The First of the Few* will recollect that Lady Houston spontaneously donated £100,000 to enable Britain to retain the Trophy in 1931, and at the third consecutive win to win it outright, much to the disgust of the Italians, who had made lavish preparations, descended to many dirty tricks, and hoped to crow over us as the world's premier airmen. In her own characteristic method she sent her cheque for this large sum by a somewhat shabby and shy messenger addressed to the "rude young man," R. J. Mitchell, the genius who designed the ancestor of the modern Spitfire.

I was fortunate enough to be invited to witness the race on September 13th, 1931, on her yacht *Liberty*, and found myself in a gay and enthusiastic party which celebrated the victory of Flight-Lieutenant Boothman who completed the course round the Solent at 340 m.p.h. completely routing the Italian airmen. On that same occasion Flight Lieutenant Stainforth created a record for one course of over 400 m.p.h., an almost incredible speed at the time.

Liberty lay at her moorings on the Solent, but not Admiralty moorings, whereby hangs a tale of Mr. Ramsay MacDonald. As a gesture of thanks for Lady Houston's public-spirited and generous act in financing the British team, whereby Mitchell's *Supermarine S6* won the Trophy outright, the Lords of the Admiralty had offered her Naval moorings conveniently situated between Portsmouth and Cowes. In that short crossing of the ferry-boats passengers had stared at the majestic big white and gold yacht, the third largest steam yacht in Europe. They found something to divert their attention beyond her lines and the fact that she belonged to one of the wealthiest women in the world and one whose public spirit and generosity had endeared her to millions.

Stretching from end to end of her masts was a colossal canvas sign on which was painted in bold letters, "*Wake up England! Down with the Traitor Ramsay MacDonald!*" It attracted wide attention. It reached the ears of the Prime Minister himself whose sense of humour was never his strong point.

Accordingly one fine day the Port Admiral at Portsmouth, acting on Admiralty instructions, made a formal call on *Liberty*, to request the immediate withdrawal of the offending poster. He was received by Lady Houston and the ensuing conversation, so far as I could gather, was something like this:

"I regret to have a somewhat unpleasant duty to perform, Lady Houston," said the Admiral, after making a formal bow, "My Lords of the Admiralty have to take serious exception to the sign you are flying on your yacht."

"Surely, Admiral," replied Lucy, with one of her disarming smiles; "what I choose to do on my own yacht is my business?"

"Ordinarily, yes," admitted the Admiral, "but the sign constitutes a violent attack upon the Prime Minister and my Lords cannot blind their eyes to it. I have therefore to request that you will issue orders to have it removed without delay."

Sir Austen Chamberlain was First Lord of the Admiralty for whom Lady Houston had no great admiration. She asked if he were responsible for the ultimatum. The Admiral was guarded.

"Of that I possess no knowledge," he returned. "My duty is to give your Ladyship the message as received and to obtain your consent to remove the sign."

"Well, Admiral, my reply to the Lords of the Admiralty," said my Lady blandly, "is that I will see them damned first!"

The Admiral was taken aback by this unexpected rebuff and probably not a little shocked to boot. Whether he secretly sympathised with her attitude history does not relate and certainly the Royal Navy had little cause to thank the champion of British disarmament and the steady weakening of our sea power. However, he had his task to fulfil.

"I must remind you," he said, "that your yacht has been privileged to use an Admiralty mooring and in such case the offending signal is liable to be interpreted in a sense we cannot permit. Therefore I shall have to ask your Ladyship to remove Liberty from her present moorings."

"Why should I?" retorted Lady Houston. "I was invited to use it and I don't propose to shift for Mr. Ramsay MacDonald or anybody."

The Admiral was again nonplussed. Afters a pause, he said, "In such an event I am afraid that we shall have to remove *Liberty* off her present mooring forcibly if necessary."

"Thank you, Admiral," was the reply. "It seems to be the only way, doesn't it?"

It was precisely what the Admiralty had to do. The yacht was moved to another mooring but the flamboyant sign was flaunted defiantly in the busy Solent for so long as her redoubtable owner thought fit.

I used to see her frequently at Byron Cottage. Her health was poor and she had her eccentricities. A poor sleeper - she said she scarcely ever slept soundly and never after four a.m. - it was not an uncommon habit of hers to arouse her private secretary and make her accompany her for a jaunt over the heath.

"Sometimes it was bitterly cold," her young secretary confided to me, "but her Ladyship didn't seem to care a jot. 'You don't want to put on stockings,' she would say, '*I* don't.' She walked me along deserted paths in the darkness and was often scared out of my life."

I found this particular secretary for her, a smart girl who had been a reporter on the **Hull Daily Mail**, a fact which weighed much in her favour because she came from that city. Sometime earlier the tram-men employed by the Corporation had gone on strike, who in Lady Houston's view were justified, but they were refused strike pay, their families suffered greatly, and she sent them a generous contribution to enable them to hold out - and she a Tory of Tories! Anyhow the secretary from Hull found life too strenuous with her, resigned, and came to explain the reasons to me.

Her impatience was marked. On one occasion when I called she asked me to accompany her to visit her old friend Sir Thomas Lipton, who would be delighted to show me this wonderful collection of cups won with his various *Shamrocks*. A big open Buick was waiting, driven by her under-chauffeur. She entered the Buick clutching an enormous shabby leather portmanteau which her maid brought her, and seeing that I eyed it curiously, she vouchsafed a Puck grin.

"Can you guess what I have in here?"

"Evidently something precious."

"Jewels, stupid. I never let them out of my sight. There are heaps of thieves lurking about the heath and jewel thieves are cunning rascals."

"But what of your servants?"

"I would never entrust my jewels to the servants. Only a fool would!"

She clutched the worn portmanteau with one arm and held a walking-stick in her right hand. Before long I realised its true purpose. Sir Thomas Lipton lived in Highgate, not far distant, and the chauffeur seemed to me to be driving fairly fast, but it was not fast enough for Lucy. She began prodding him with her stick. "Drive faster, Slowcoach!" she cried impatiently. "Get a move on!"

The result was that her young driver became embarrassed and as ill-luck would have it he drove on the wrong side of a roundabout where it chanced a police constable was on duty, who signalled him to stop. He approached us, fumbled in his hip pocket for his note-book.

"Driving the wrong side of the roundabout," he said laconically to the chauffeur. "Let's see yer licence, mate."

Immediately her Ladyship intervened.

"Only an oversight, officer. I distracted his attention. No harm has been done. Drive on, Turner."

"Here, here, not so fast, Madam. My business is with the driver - " began the constable. She waved him aside.

"And my business is with Sir Thomas Lipton, also we are late and you are wasting my time. I am Lady Houston, of Byron Cottage, Hampstead Heath, and if you wish to summon my chauffeur I will pay the fine. Drive on, Turner."

Drive on he did, leaving the constable speechless with indignation and surprise at this treatment of the Force. Lady Houston glanced at me and chuckled "My chauffeur is a damned fool, Kim," she observed calmly. She called me "Kim," the *nom de plume* I adopted for my articles in her paper.

About 1935 her health became worse, most of her time being spent in bed at Byron Cottage, refusing to go to sea for a voyage, or to one or other residences including at castle in Scotland. She could not tear herself away from her paper and political affairs. The only thing of which she was afraid was a common or garden cold, for which, as I have said, she advertised her somewhat, drastic cure. On one occasion, sitting propped up in bed in her long bedroom, I interrupted her exposition on the political situation with a fit of coughing. She stopped short.

"You have a bad cold, Kim. I refuse to admit anyone to my bedroom with a cold. You are spreading millions of bacilli!"

"It is not a cold," I said. "Only a slight catarrh."

A few minutes later, endeavouring to suppress a tickling in the throat, I had another paroxysm.

"If you took my cure you would never have a cold," she said reprovingly. "It serves you right."

"Sorry," I said, "but the cure sounds worse than the disease. Strong doses of castor oil and spoonfuls of Vaseline! It's a pretty drastic remedy to impose on anyone."

"It is a cure recommended by leading physicians," she countered. "You prefer to go on choking and distributing germs wherever you go?"

We resumed our conversation but as ill-luck would have it the thought that I might cough again created a tingling in my throat and another paroxysm. She rang for her maid who returned with an enormous pot of yellow Vaseline and a table spoon. My hostess dipped the spoon into the Vaseline and it emerged overflowing with the thick viscid remedy, a horrible spectacle. She offered me the spoon.

"Swallow it quickly!" she ordered.

I demurred, protested, refused, and said that the sight of it made me feel sick and if I attempted to swallow it I should undoubtedly vomit.

"Well," she said calmly, "there are three windows and you may have your pick of them if you are sick. Come, swallow it! All you men are cowards in these matters!"

269

She shamed me into taking the mess. I gulped it down, under protest. She, regarded me with interest and some amusement. And it did check my coughing.

It came as a severe shock to all those who knew Lucy Houston well when she died two days before the end of 1936 after a short attack of bronchitis. In many ways, it is a just tribute to pay to her memory, her death was a loss to they nation for there were in those years only too few persons sufficiently jealous of Britain's fair name and her destiny who were in a position to give freely to the cause and at the same time were indifferent to any lure to bow to those in the seats of the mighty. The Duke of Windsor, when Prince of Wales, was greatly beloved by her because he, too, in her eyes, sought the good of the nation and like her was opposed to snobbery which in his case aroused such an outcry. The Prince sometimes visited her at Byron Cottage, and she gladly subscribed large sums to the charities in which he was interested.

Again, when Lord Clydesdale (now the Duke of Hamilton) went to her for aid about his proposed Mount Everest Expedition, a greatly adventurous and dangerous project, he had scarcely to ask her for financial support, for she anticipated the request and donated the handsome sum of £100,000, thus enabling it to be undertaken because she admired the intrepidity of youth and here was an instance of the bold adventurous spirit redounding to the credit of Britain which she loved. She asked nothing in return although she was highly indignant later when **The Times**, having acquired the solo photographic rights at a modest outlay tried to suppress, as she alleged to Col. Astor, her name in relation to the enterprise. Later on she also financed the production of the film of the Expedition inspired solely by national reasons.

As regards the **Saturday Review** she lavished money ungrudgingly to advance the cause of a strong Britain, rearmed and leading the world, in place of the denationalising and halting policy which stigmatised the so-called "National" Government from 1931 onwards. If she exposed consistently the rise of Hitler and stressed its growing threat - as to which she was a true prophetess it was because she hoped to arouse her fellow-countrymen to the realisation of the result of indifference. Similarly if she ridiculed the *League of Nations*, and especially the work of Ramsay MacDonald and Sir John Simon, it was not because there were not certain worthy ideals constituting it but because its potentialities were only existing on paper and yet it was made the excuse to whittle down our national defences. To her mind England was drowsing under an enervating soporific. Was she wrong? History has spoken!

Douglas Reed, in his book **A Prophet at Home** observes that the most enlightened people he met when returning home after living several years abroad were the workings classes, who instinctively (he says) were most sensitive of Britain's honour. Dame Fanny Lucy Houston, to give her her full name, was such a one. She came from working-class parents, a cockney-born girl, which accounted for her shrewd common sense, her humour, and her scorn for Shams. I believe that early in life she became a barmaid at a fashionable Mayfair bar, patronised at the period by scions of nobility and wealthy young men. In their company she picked up a certain amount of education and a considerable knowledge of the world.

She reminded me in some ways of Nell Gwynn, for both women were Cockney-born, and both loved their native land with devotion. If Lucy did not possess a ruling monarch as her protector she had the immensely wealthy Duke of Bedford who settled a considerable sum upon her. Another admirer who followed was the big brewer, Mr. John Gretton, father of the present Col. John (now Lord) Gretton, of *Bass* fame. She first married a baronet, Sir Theodore Brinkman, whom she divorced, and in 1901 Lord Byron, bearing an honoured name. Left a widow, she married for the third time Sir Robert Houston, M.P. and multi-millionaire shipowner, who left her his entire fortune including the Houston Line. He was a black-bearded, shy, some said uncouth man, who had few friends, and adored her, but she showed little desire to accept his advances until in 1924, she nursed him through a severe illness on board his yacht *Liberty* and eventually married him. He died in 1926.

She could never have been beautiful in a classic sense but in her young days she possessed charm, fascination, wit, and liveliness, far more attractive than mere beauty, and it is easy to believe that in her youth she was the toast among the young men-about-town. In disposition, large-minded and free-speaking, she was unaffected, supremely human, and never pretended to be a saint. She was a good friend to me. She told me more than once that she had remembered me in her will and even went out of her way to say that she had fully provided for her family during her lifetime. From a certain source I received a hint that she had left me a bequest of £5,000, and the same amount was left to two or three others who had worked with her.

Unfortunately for me no will was ever found, although knowing her it is extraordinary to believe that she did not leave it somewhere in safe-keeping. Still, as the saying goes, - 'It's an ill-wind that blows nobody any good!'

In those years from 1931 onwards, when Lady Houston was campaigning and I was writing the main talking-point articles on affairs, the locusts were again beginning to swarm, dating back indirectly to that memorable year of 1931 when the Tories were returned to power by an overwhelming majority after the Socialist debacle already referred to, and Mr. Baldwin with a magnificent gesture served as a chief lieutenant to Mr. Ramsay MacDonald in the "National" Government.

Outstanding in this period was the pathetic faith in the League of Nations, a political *Maginot Line* behind which the Powers sheltered in the firm belief that they controlled a machine able to rule out future wars. In due course the various attitudes of Germany, Italy and Japan sent a cold blast down the spines of members. It may have been a grandiose conception on the part of its originator, President Woodrow Wilson, but unhappily it ignored the basic fact that human nature by a decree of the Almighty differs profoundly, so that this world contains rapacious, cruel, and pitiless nations like Germany and Japan with their primitive instincts of "blood and soil" as well as peaceful peoples. The League was a most fruitful cause of the second

World War, because the Axis Powers weighed it and found it wanting.

In England the arch-priest of the League was that æsthetic enthusiast for lost causes, Lord Robert (now Viscount) Cecil, a sort of modern Savonarola, in whose wake followed the archbishops, bishops and clergy of the Established Church, Nonconformist divines, Liberals and Socialists generally, although the politicians' motives were by no means identical with the clergy. Among Ministers next to Ramsay MacDonald himself, the leading figure was that astonishing political phenomenon Sir John (now Lord) Simon, who with few gaps has been in the Ministerial saddled in one capacity or another since 1910. In 1931 he was appointed Secretary of State for Foreign Affairs, although his eligibility for such a specialised post was hard, indeed, to come by. An eminent, counsel, he had travelled little, and his outlook had leaned towards Pacifism. I can only imagine that as the Foreign Secretaryship was a most important Cabinet post, and as he had rendered yeoman service in the General Election by fulminating against the country coming off the gold standard he had a pull for anything he fancied.

Sir John was scarcely installed in Downing Street before Mr. Hitler raised his unwelcome head, for the Nazis, fully parading their militaristic qualities, won 107 seats in the *Reichstag*. If he had wanted information on the menace he had Sir Robert Vansittart at his elbow to guide him. Then came Japan. In September, 1931, the Japs marched into Mukden and in three months occupied the whole of Manchuria. China protested to the League, and Sir John's apologia on behalf of Japan's act of aggression was so eloquent that the crafty Matsuoka warmly congratulated him. It was not a very hopeful start. The following year, which saw Ramsay MacDonald President of the League, also opened to the discordant overture of the Japanese bombardment of Shanghai behind which lay the determined undermining of British and American trade with China and the desire to seize the Customs revenue. British subjects were insulted, maltreated, and in many cases killed. Our own Ambassador was badly wounded by a Japanese plane which deliberately bombed him and his staff. What did our Foreign Minister do about it either in London or Geneva? Nothing! Douglas Jerrold in his *Britain and Europe* says of this Shanghai event; "Though few realised it the world war had begun," but Sir John was far too busy chasing the chimera of disarmament to give a thought meantime to the protection of British interests and British subjects. Also the Press gave no lead. It was flabby as usual.

Two months later another warning ripple appeared upon the surface. The Nazis now controlled Prussia, the militant heart of Germany. Not long ago, Sir Warren Fisher, who as head of the Civil Service and Permanent Secretary of the Treasury until 1939, had as great a knowledge as any man of what went on behind the scenes said, in a letter to **The Times**, "From 1933 onwards Lord Chatfield (former First Sea-Lord), with two or three others of us, never ceased warning consecutive governments of the dangerous implications of Hitler's accession to power and urging the vital necessity of rearmament."

The Government continued for most of the time apathetic if not incredulous, and the public remained uninformed and indifferent. What a charge from such a source! And why did not Sir Warren and Lord Chatfield and the others resign and proclaim their reasons publicly? It might have had an immense influence on national policy.

By February, 1933, the position was that British interests in the Far East were severely threatened by Japan, and in Germany Hitler was becoming a force which it was perilous to ignore. These clouds on the horizon had one good effect. The disarmament bubble burst, although the Democracies were still pursuing the suicidal course of disarmament. Shortly after this, Germany, which had been admitted to the League as a supposedly reformed character, walked contemptuously out of it under Hitler's dictation. He followed this up in March by repudiating the Treaty of Versailles' disarmament clauses and introduced conscription amid the hysterical plaudits of the German nation. The discredited League went into a huddle but took no steps mainly owing to Sir John's apathy.

In March, 1934, Stanley Baldwin, in view of growing concern of Nazi intentions, said robustly that he would not allow Britain to be inferior in air power to "any country within reach of its shores," but when, in November, Winston Churchill asserted in the House that the German Air Force was nearly as strong as ours, Mr. Baldwin flatly contradicted him and declared that it was not half so strong as ours in Europe alone. In the following May, Hitler, in an impassioned speech, claimed that his air strength already exceeded ours throughout the Empire, which later proved to be no more than the bare truth. When Mr. Baldwin was invited to explain the discrepancy between the two statements he rode off with the remark that no British Government could live a day that was content to have its air force in any inferiority to any country within reach of its shores. "We will not suffer a power within striking distance to be superior to ourselves," he declared. Now we know that what Baldwin said was untrue, but what we have never learnt is the source of his information. Was he himself deceived as he deceived the nation or was he trying to stave off an unpleasant situation if the truth had emerged?

Mr. Baldwin contrived to maintain himself in power, for in the autumn of 1935, having transferred positions with Ramsay MacDonald, who became Lord President, while he became Prime Minister, he was again returned to office, his ticket being to "punish aggression," the reference being to Mussolini's designs on Abyssinia, not to Hitler. To avoid, as he said afterwards, losing votes, he piped down on the subject of rearmament, engaging that there would be "no big armaments." A short time later, when the menace of Hitler was even disturbing Big Business and our complacent Ministerial Press, he admitted that "if I had told the country Germany was rearming and we must rearm it would have made the loss of the Election certain from my point of view." What a shocking confession! To retain power he had played down to crass ignorance on the part of the electorate. Nor was that all. He had cruelly misread the character of the British people who always show their sterling qualities when they have their backs to the wall. If he had said frankly to the nation, "I have unwittingly deceived you. Germany - and behind Germany, Italy - are giving every indication of preparing for a war of imperialism, and we are largely unprepared and unarmed. It is my one intention to rearm our native country and assist our Dominions to that end so that we shall not be caught unprepared by land, sea, or air, although I warn you it will mean heavy extra taxation for several years," the whole nation would have risen as a man to support him. He hadn't the calibre of the great British leaders, such as Churchill or Chamberlain or Disraeli before him, and he failed dismally. It is intolerable to think that the man who let us down was honoured with an Earldom and the K.G.!

In 1936 his Government took dilatory steps to rearm our fighting services. And what steps! Sir Thomas Inskip, a worthy and godly-minded lawyer, was made Minister of Defence, with the task of organising the supply of arms, equipment, and so forth. Why was a lawyer appointed to a task which needed; the greatest arms expert in the country? He declared publicly in October, 1938, when we were supposed to be in the middle of the third year of rearmament, "There is a stream which might fairly be called a flood of those armaments, and equipment which we need to complete our defence."

Complete our defence! Dunkirk provided the answer to these claims. His failure was so pronounced that he was promoted to the post of Lord Chief Justice and elevated to the peerage as Lord Caldecote. Perhaps - one day - a more robust Press will raise objections to the outrageous manner in which Prime Ministers bestow honours and emoluments on political failures. Inskip was succeeded - amazing as it may seem to those who were not students of the Baldwin and Chamberlain technique - by another lawyer, a mere solicitor this time, Mr Leslie Burgin, an appointment received by Neville Chamberlain's. supporters in stony silence. However, to keep up the illusion that all was well, one of our elder statesmen, who always contrives to be *persona grata* with the Premier of the day, Sir Samuel Hoare, declared that, "our preparations have already progressed to a favourable point," a statement he made in March, 1939. Sir Samuel's political record is a list of failures and surrenders, but he is still holding high office - and emoluments!

The sequel to all these magnificent preparations, for which added taxation was gladly accepted, was revealed in the tragedy of Dunkirk. Nine months after the war had begun Lord Gort's army consisted of only five divisions, compared with a hundred of the French. It possessed 23 tanks of small size. It was minus a single armoured division and possessed no anti-tank-guns or shells. Its field guns were useless against the German tanks, as they had not the piercing power. It had scarcely any air support to confront the might of the Luftwaffe. Sir Nevile Henderson, our late Ambassador to Germany, blurted out the fact that we did not possess in France or Belgium a single Spitfire, and practically no anti-aircraft guns. Had it not been for the courageous and resolute leadership of Mr Churchill, who boldly filled the gap and led the nation to Herculean efforts, we should have been sunk. As it is, thousands of homes are empty and wives, sweethearts, and mothers mourn their dead. Why were not those guilty of this terrible crime against the nation impeached? Why at the very least, are those politicians responsible for such criminal neglect, able to hold on to high office? The people have not chosen their representatives cleverly. They are too often victims of the Party machine and the Press has not fought against the vested interests. That is why.

But I am forgetting Sir John Simon, now Viscount, who in the critical years from 1931 to 1935 was in control of our national interests abroad. I have mentioned how extraordinarily complacent he showed himself to the growing and dangerous imperialism of both Germany and Japan. However, in 1935, shortly after Hitler had revealed his hand by the introduction of conscription, in the company or Ramsay MacDonald and their then "buddy" Laval, he hastened to keep a mysterious date with Mussolini at Stresa. The British Cabinet at long last were becoming thoroughly alarmed by the growing truculence of Hitler with his eye on the annexation of Austria, with Czechoslovakia and Hungary beyond. It has since been asserted that the real objective of Simon was to come to terms with Mussolini and on the basis of a *quid pro quo* induce him to place an army on the Brenner Pass so that Hitler's designs on Austria might at least, receive some check.

What Simon did not know - nor scarcely anyone else - was that behind the brag and bluster of the swollen frog of the Pontine Marshes, the military qualities of his armies, navy and air force were little more than *opera bouffe*. It has taken this war to reveal again the mettle of the warrior races and they certainly do not include Italy. As for Mussolini, he had built up a hearty contempt for the democratic Powers which he honestly believed would crumble before the might of a resurgent Germany and his Italy. He already feared Hitler. Meantime he wanted to swagger before the world as the founder of his African Empire and was preparing the campaign against the unlucky and barbaric Abyssinians. It suited his book if France and we would connive at Italy's invasion of Haile Selassie's territories. Laval he could understand. Simon, with his amiable countenance, gave the impression that he was willing to treat, and Musso was willing for that, too, so long as he could wring the assent of Britain to his campaign and not be committed in return.

It has been suggested since that Sir John Simon and Ramsay MacDonald were even prepared to shut their eyes to a war against Abyssinia if Mussolini would definitely throw in his lot with Britain and France and unite with them to oppose Hitler's further adventures in Europe. Certainly *Il Duce* had called all his colonial experts to Stresa so that Abyssinia was definitely on the table. It was a phoney meeting in every sense.

Mussolini was probably justified in believing that Britain's attitude in support of Abyssinia was sheer hypocrisy. Politicians and Press in England at various-times had denounced the alleged atrocities of Haile Selassie's Government in no unmeasured terms, more, indeed, than the Italians had done themselves, who, as we have excellent reason to know, are no tyros where cruelty and atrocity are concerned, So Mussolini's experts produced the gruesome and grim records of the British Anti-Slavery Society, and played an ace card. It was very awkward, to say the least of it, that Lady Simon, Sir John Simon's wife, should have written a book strongly denouncing the slave traffic in Abyssinia and demanding its stoppage. What could Sir John say about that?

Little wonder that the Stresa meeting proved abortive and that as a result British relations with Italy deteriorated still further.

Not even his greatest enemy would deny that Sir John was a trier. If one horse unseats him he mounts another. A little later, accompanied by Anthony Eden, he visited Hitler at Berlin, for by this time it had dimly entered the skulls of our political leaders that a devil's broth was brewing in the Nazi cauldron. The Foreign Office, subject to the Prime Minister, of course, as usual practised appeasement. It tried to buy off Hitler with *dane-geld*. He was offered a loan, but to his credit he rejected it, and mean-time the British Government, of which Sir John was so great an ornament, pursued its policy of disarmament. Baldwin, however, forming his new Government in 1935, perhaps realised that the realm of foreign affairs was unsuited to Sir John's versatile genius and transferred him to the Home Office, where his outstanding accomplishment was to smash the British Fascists, who at that time were scrapping with the alien East-end Jews, a perfectly shocking offence, of course.

To tell the truth, 1935 was a pretty critical year in our country's history, for it was in that halcyon period of our enemy's preparations that Mr. Baldwin repudiated any idea of rearmament and stood four-square with the Peace Ballot, which all well-meaning parsons boosted inside and outside their churches. In that same year he uttered a statement which for sheer bathos has never been equalled by any public orator: "If we fail Democracy," he said, "that would indeed be blaspheming against the Holy Ghost!" Did he blaspheme or didn't he? Anyway, he is now a belted Earl, has never stood before the nation in sack-cloth and ashes, and occasionally yet obtains an audience of the King.

In this same year Winston Churchill was a sad thorn in the side of Baldwin. He riddled the Government policy of "wait and see" with exposure and also he put up a splendid fight against Sir Samuel Hoare's India Bill, which surrender to extremists has undermined our position ever since in that immense dependency on whose future our continued existence as an Empire may be said to rest. How many

279

millions, directly, and indirectly, this wretched measure has cost and will cost the taxpayers in the long run it is too early to determine. I wished fervently in those years that Mr. Churchill would stump the country and expose all these betrayals on public platforms, but he didn't. One amazing thing he did was to go out of his way and eulogise Mr. Baldwin, the Prime Minister, at the Conservative Party Conference, in which he said:

"In the Prime Minister we have a statesman who has gathered to himself a greater volume of confidence and good-will than any other man I can recollect in my long public career."

The words may have been true, for Stanley Baldwin, thought to be a sort of John Bull, appealed to the masses as a "safe statesman" who would not let them down, even although his foreign policy was bungled worse and worse, and with his air or serenity, Wisdom, and candour, with his evil smelling pipe and his addiction to Lord's cricket ground, was thoroughly trusted by the *hoi polloi*. But, coming from Winston, who should have known better than any man what the P.M.'s true weight was - well, I give it up. All I can say is great is the Tory caucus! I have often asked myself, Is there any politician in whose sincerity one can absolutely depend? I am afraid that the answer is a lemon. If he were above deception he would not be a politician.

Let use recognise frankly that party interests by no means coincide with national needs. The nation's rights are commonly put up to auction for the benefit of the party in office. Much of our nation's eclipse since. the beginning of this century must be attributed to Asquith's corrupt payment of members on the usual pretext that it was "democratic," but really made Members of Parliament dependent on their party and in effect gradually little more than paid delegates.

The natural result has been that it has placed Ministers in a powerful position because if they are defeated some of their followers may lose their seats and so the income they derive. It was and is purely a piece of legislation for the benefit of a political caucus and to the detriment of the electors, because M.P.s act with their eyes on their Party first and last, and although paid (unlike in the Dominions, where Members are paid only on attendances) our British Members receive their salaries whether they attend to their duties or not. At present we have the scandal of at least two M.P.s - Sir Samuel Hoare and Mr. Malcolm MacDonald - both drawing their salaries as Ministers while Members of the House of Commons, and doing another job of work, so that their constituencies are unrepresented. It is, of course, the antithesis of Democracy.

Altogether it has come about that the Party caucus are all-powerful. The leaders of the Party - whether Tory or Labour - control their own caucus, and the Party leaders who obtain the majority in a Parliamentary election then acquire power and at once cement it by the adroit use of patronage, handing out jobs to their supporters who have a pull. If the programmes put before the public were simple and honest there would be something to be said for this, but they never are. I cannot recall one single straight issue since the last war at any rate. The Tories, for instance, have always promised to maintain national defence, but they transpired to be liars. Both Parties - and the Liberal Party, too, although they are practically defunct - conspire to dupe and mislead the public and gain votes by vain promises and prejudicing their opponents by untrue assertions.

These debilitating caucuses remind me of an Aztec legend. It was in a time of dire despair, their land threatened by a fierce enemy, their king and leaders utterly decadent and useless, while an awful pestilence stalked abroad and mowed down thousands among them. Near their capital the mass of the people while gathered together in despairing mood suddenly perceived on a height the figure of a god-like being, sparkling in the sunshine and radiating a strange and beautiful light, which appeared to their eyes to be a deity come to rescue them from their evils. In serried masses they charged up to the height, but when they came near they saw to their horror that the god-like figure dissolved into a dreadful heap of corruption whose rotting carcase emitted a stench which poisoned all those who had approached it.

Government patronage has grown by leaps and bounds since the days when our legislators entered Parliament in the bulk at least for motives other than material gain. During this war it has attained stupendous height means that they have sold any independence they may have possessed. Mr. Churchill in 1941 passed a Bill to remove all restriction in distributing posts of profit to M.P.s and to-day over two hundred among them are enjoying such patronage. Naturally there is great contest for every vacant seat - but not necessarily to serve the public! Lord Winterton declared that in certain London constituencies Tory candidates were required to pay £800 a year as a condition of adoption. Such are the greased wheels of the caucus. I mention this since you will search in vain for any information on such subjects in the public Press. Press and politicians stand together. Obedient membership of the Commons yields many plums, and the more inflated grows the bureaucracy the more they increase. Apart from paid jobs, legal posts of profit, and company directorships, there are the baubles such us Privy Councillorships, knighthoods, baronetcies, and peerages, although the last, I am pleased to observe, are rather growing out of fashion. In a better world political honours would become extinct and be only accorded to the fighting Services.

Most of these years - to return to my own small part - I was writing on politics, largely for Lady Houston until her death, and did my best to make my generation realise the dangers looming nearer and nearer, but like every-one else who tried to tell the truth I was laughed at, jeered at, called an alarmist, militarist, a jitter-bug, ,and other flattering names. The Press with scarcely an exception soothed the public mind with dope, distracted it with trivial side-issues, and shouted *ad nauseam,* in leading article journalese, *"There ain't goin' to be no War!"*

These are matters which those who have fought and those who have lost their sons and daughters and loved ones should bear always in their memory. Don't let us be fooled again. *When the war is over, 'ware a snap election!*

CHAPTER XIV

OUR TO-MORROWS?

"Democracy depends for its success on everyone doing their duty from the top to the bottom."

(MR.STANLEY (NOW EARL) BALDWIN)

LORD BALDWIN'S precept cited above is impeccable. no fault can be found with it. but, applying it to the years when he was prime minister of Great Britain, did he do this duty by democracy? Did his followers in parliament do theirs? Did the press of this country regard democracy as a sacred charge which must be protected and defended from neglect on the part of those on the top, who held the reins of power, or did it play into the hands of those venal persons who prated of democracy but really used it merely as a convenient slogan? Is our democracy a living truth or is it a sham and delusion?

I find many persons saying, "forget the past - look to the future," but it is when judging of our to-morrows that we must examine into the past. Looking back is the only way of judging forward, paradoxical as it may sound, for governments and their coadjutors are human institutions, subject to the same general laws as individuals of which they are composed. If you are asked to entrust your home and future to some person, you would be a fool not to make close inquiries into his record. Can I trust him? you would ask. It is those who have something to conceal who are naturally most anxious to let bygones be bygones. I hope that when the last shell has been fired, and the nation has once more a voice in the selection of a government, it will not be bluffed by politicians or Press into this "bygones" business, or the public will be dished again.

Unfortunately retribution did not follow when the old gang, the Baldwins and Neville Chamberlains, were on the shelf. Too many of them are on our backs to-day. When Mr. Churchill, in April, 1940, was hailed as the British hero, a modern King Arthur, who was to rescue us from the slough of despond into which our political leaders had led us, most everyone hoped and believed that he would make a clean sweep of the guilty ones. He did not. He riveted the fetters more strongly round our necks probably because he realised only to well the strength of the caucuses, but it was an unkindly cut to throw us to those particular Socialists, men like Herbert Morrison and Bevin, for whom the electors had shown only too definitely that they had no use. Most of the persons in office now supported the pre-war Government in its neglect of our defences, while they rest of the nation is shouted at to toil with blood, and sweat, and tears in order to make up the leeway. It is a point to remember.

To be absolutely frank, I cannot trust the present Government. I wish devoutly I could, but inefficiency allied with extraordinary complacency seems to rule in high places. I dislike even more the hints which have gone out, and more than hints, of our world to be after the war, as so far pictured. Especially do those Eight Points in the joint proclamations by President Roosevelt and our Mr. Churchill stick in my throat, a proclamation which declared that after the war the victors will let bygones be bygones and that all the European nations, victor and vanquished alike, will share in the reconstruction of Europe, will have their independence restored, and will be given free access to trade and raw materials. Is that to be the reward for all our toil, and sweat, and tears? Are we, who have bankrupted ourselves in leading the fight for freedom, to gaze upon the ruins of our Empire and see the vanquished recovering their strength at our expense? It is a doctrine which appears to emanate from the United States, a doctrine which may or may not profit them, but at least they start with a most one-sided advantage, because for fifteen months we were fighting Germany and her allies, single-handed while the U.S.A. would only sell us vital munitions on a basis of "cash and carry."

Today they hold all our overseas wealth gathered in during those fifteen months, just as they feathered their nest in the last war in the first three years, and have taken no steps to adjust these gross inequalities. You may say that we have the benefits of Lease-Lend, but I regard them with natural suspicion.

This sloppy sentiment of *let bygones be bygones* creeps up in various directions which arouse one's suspicions. Our Government's attitude towards Italy after her defeat has been a half-hearted affair and affords little credit to our political astuteness. Our soldiers, sailors, and airmen with great skill and courage defeat the enemy, and our political direction proceeds to whittle down victory by appeasement. The U.S. and British Governments - and we appear again to have largely surrendered the direction of both political and military decisions to America, which is not likely to aid any future much-spoken-of alliance, for we have never yet in our history and never will give way to any foreign powers - are evidently more interested in restoring the defeated enemy than in assisting their own nationals who are suffering a good deal more than is admitted.

Recently, as I write, a minor matter was reported which shows how the wind blows. The British Government paid the sum of £10,000 to the Madagascar authorities for damage done when we landed troops on that island and rescued it from Vichy and the Japs. In these operations we incurred certain casualties. Some homes mourn their dead - and we compensate the Madagascans! Could crass stupidity go much farther? Where will it end? Every taxpayer in Britain ought to rise in indignation against such betrayal of our interests, whose burdens, God knows, are heavy enough, and who cannot get compensation for his own war losses. How can one trust a Government outlook which permits such an imbecility?

Thus our politicians not of yesterday but of to-day. To my mind the public will be fooled and fooled again unless the Press does its job. We do not want a subservient Press which acts as a Greek chorus to rulers who treat their own people with a studied indifference and go around chasing vain chimeras. We badly need newspapers, daily and weekly, which are sternly critical of the Government, for it is only by a ruthless criticism of its shortcomings that any remedy is forthcoming.

If newspaper proprietors and editors are got at by the Government, silenced by big ministerial appointments - such as Northcliffe sternly refused at the hands of Lloyd George at the end of the last war - or titles, or other squeezes, then the public should know about it and so judge the value of their utterances.

During the last forty years, the public Press of Britain has become far more chatty and "popular" but considerably less critical, informative, and public-spirited. Newspapers used to be directed by men of independence and integrity, and advertising revenue was not a corrupting influence, but to-day boards of directors who are in the newspaper business as they might be in sugar, or meat, or fish, or any other trade, are far less inspired by public spirit than in netting big profits. Owing to my service with several big firms, I speak with some knowledge.

The greatest exponent of foreign affairs in the past forty years was Leo Maxse, the brilliant editor and proprietor of **The National Review**, an organ of immense influence in his day, and at whose feet I had the honour of sitting on various occasions. Maxse's sincerity was apparent, his exposition of national affairs crystal-clear, his exposure of graft relentless. He gave the Foreign Office chiefs many a headache. He could not be bought or influenced and he did not write down to his public.[2] They did not need such writing down as we get in our two-million-odd-circulation sheets.

I claim that in my experience of life the average man and woman, whose classical or historical education may be elementary, has a far more intelligent approximation of affairs than many editors appear to imagine. Deeply rooted in their being is a national consciousness of their country and what it means to them. Perhaps more sub-conscious than based on knowledge. They dislike cordially being constantly lectured by some whipper-snapper of a leaders writer of our days as to their duty to the nation, just as they resent lectures from Ministers whose political past is seamy.

---

2 Mr. Maxse exposed the machinations of Lucien Wolf, to whom I have referred earlier, soon after the last war started. I had not ever mentioned his name to Maxse but he had him annotated.

The Prime-Minister in one of his oratorical flights asked, "What sort of a people do they think we are?! I sometimes wonder if he has got to the bottom of it himself. They are a people who want justice and freedom and, apart from archbishops *et dans cette galère*, they believe firmly that charity begins at home. They possess a steadfastness because of some inherent quality which cannot be explained by any biological formula and they expect to find it in others they trust.

This national feeling is not one of vainglory or self-satisfaction, and is totally at variance with that egotistical and perverted pride of the German who finds sadistic pleasure in enslaving, humiliating, and beating other peoples to do his will. It is actually the Englishman's - I include Scotsman's and Welshman's and properly Irishman's - conception of living which he inherited from his ancestors usually unknown. It is impossible for him to tolerate a world dominated by Hitler, even supposing that he were permitted to live on unmolested as Mr. Rudolf Hess so kindly proposed. He is, indeed, the unconscious heir of Simon de Montfort and Hampden, and the great eternal truths for which these men and many others gladly gave their lives.

Admittedly, few ever look upon it in this light. Probably few among the masses thought very much about England before the war, and there was no very good reason then why they should have regarded it as a human paradise. They only became dimly conscious of it, when in 1940 that tie was threatened with extinction, just as their forebears had felt when Philip of Spain sent his great Armada to enslave us in 1588. Then it suddenly became by far the most important fact in their lives, so important that men unhesitatingly chose to sacrifice their homes, their jobs, their worldly goods, their lives. Their wives equally understood and never faltered. It was not as the well-known publicist Arthur Bryant has said, that the Englishman saw his country as a radiant vision or that the land of Britain personified a form of earthly existence so exquisite and comfortable that he preferred to part with life itself rather than exist without it. The life of the average Briton in fact in most cases was drab. No: he was urged onwards by an instinctive purpose and he was roused to full realisation when he heard Churchill's husky but immortal inspiration on the wireless. So, in 1940, as many a time in England's history, the national consciousness of the British people saved the world. Don't take my prejudiced word for it. Here is an unsolicited testimonial from a Swiss source, and anyone who knows the Swiss will agree that they are not a sentimental people. It is from **La Sentinelle** of August 6th 1943:

"It is Britain who is responsible for the tremendous reversal now apparent in the world situation. She has stood fast against all logical hopes, facing the most formidable armed coalition the world has ever seen and taking terrible blows without ever giving in. Only this fierce, proud resistance made it possible for American and Russian factors to make themselves felt.

"If Britain had capitulated in 1940 Switzerland to-day would be little more than a geographical expression; It would be unjust and ungrateful to forget this."

Let us be grateful to Winston Churchill too; He roused the dormant consciousness of the British nation in what had been regarded previously as a "phoney" war. He gave them the courage and cohesion to endure the worst that Hitler could do and the cold resolve to make every sacrifice to enable them to thrash his bullying legions and restore decency to the world. It inspired all the aged and young because it is a spiritual force, a corporate ideal, not necessarily or in any sense religious. It will see the war through to the bitter end but I warn those who are our present rulers that, from this empyrean height, eyes look sternly on those who waver and who apparently lack the iron which should have entered into their souls. Whitehall's un-Spartan-like life of luxury, resplendent repasts and majestic cars, big paid jobs, the retention of Ministers found guilty of utter inefficiency, the lack of any spirit of self-sacrifice among their leaders while thousands die in terrible circumstances - these matters are not forgotten.

What is so vital in the British character is its capacity for furthering the cause of human progress, an ancient trait. It ensures that the

British people, including their brothers in the Dominions and Colonies, and, let me add, those of like breed in the United States, will invariably combine to prevent tyrannous nations from enslaving and devastating their neighbours. Oppressed people never cry to us for aid unheard.

Inherited qualities, yes. How ancient, who will say? In A.D. 70, when the Roman legions were enslaving and slaughtering the people, and ruthlessly massacring the Druids who led them, this sect held a *Diet* or *Eisteddfod*, according to Tacitus, and prophesied boldly the future empire of the Britons and their domination over the world, and this at a moment when they had plumbed the depths of utter despair. At any rate it pointed to some consummate faith in the future destiny of the British race which time proved to be correct.

I might make it clear that I do not claim necessarily intellectual superiority for the entire English race, but I do say that they are blest with certain outstanding qualities which have made them the outstanding nation in reality of Europe since the Conquest, and it might be said of that, how the Normans were close kindred with the English, both being of Norse origin.

The English are far from stupid, but they are slow and easily fooled and inclined to lethargy. They have their full share of the envious, of exploiters, of money-grabbers, of snobs, of hypocrites and bigots. Our educational methods are deplorable apart from seats of learning but our ratio of intelligence was found in the last war to be higher than that of any European people. Professor Lothrop Stoddart, the American biologist, in his **Revolt Against Civilization**, gives the classified figures of intelligence tests instituted by the U.S. Army for non-American recruits; They were surprising. England was easily first in the superiority class, with a figure of 19.7; Scotland next with 13; Germany was fifth with 8.3; and Norway and Ireland were bracketed with 4.1. In inferiority England again led with only 8.7; Scotland was fourth with 13.6; and Italy disclosed 63.4. Such tests are not without significance.

Among British characteristics from time immemorial is their maritime genius, shared certainly with the Norwegians and Danes, both of the same original stock, for the English are Scandinavian in origin and not Germanian. Again, in the history of exploration and colonisation the English have been outstanding from early times, being always an adventurous people. They have carried their lives in their hands through uncharted seas and suffered gladly untold privations to seeks unknown lands, driven by some innate instinct which impelled them onwards. It is the English, more than all others combined, who have opened up and developed the great continents and islands in which others have benefited equally with themselves. They sailed and discovered as individualists, and these advances in world knowledge owed nothing to state regimentation or even assistance.

Most of these discoveries were made certainly in the search for trade, such as our first settlements in India, China, the West Indies and elsewhere. Other nations did likewise though mainly in search of loot and treasure, like the Spaniards who seized and exploited regions and ruled with cruelty over the enslaved population, a charge which can never be laid against us. For many centuries our nation has been the principal transport agency of British and foreign goods, and the reputation we gathered for fair trade and honesty gave the name of Britain a glittering reputation in the seven seas. If our sailors were rough they were neither bullies nor cheats. Nor did we seek to dominate the natives and destroy their independence and freedom unless circumstances, as in India compelled such steps.

What British enterprise and genius has created throughout the world, the majesty of its conceptions has really been the cultural influence throughout the World during the last few hundred years and brought backward races to civilisation. Hong Kong is a spot of the Empire in question. A hundred years ago it was merely la rock with a few poor fishermen living on it. Dr. Sun Yat-Sen, the famous Chinese revolutionary leader, gazing upon that great and prosperous port, full of shipping, large areas reclaimed from the sea, streets of wealthy shops and luxurious palaces on its heights, said, "I began to wonder how foreigners, Englishmen, could do such things as they had done with the barren rock of Hong Kong, within 70 or 80 years, while in 4,000 years China had no place like Hong Kong." Said the great prophet of the Empire, Cecil Rhodes, who appreciated the world, "We are the first race in the world, and the more of the world we inherit the better it is for the human race."

The reason for these matters is not obscure. It is because the English race is passionately addicted to freedom, justice, and equity, although we do not always obtain what we should get from our own administrators, and then we have to fight for it. Many of our laws are ill-digested, or archaic, or just stupid, but that is not the point. They are observed because the people realise the striving to administer justice impartially, even though at times it halts. We are the most law-abiding nation in the world.

Our passion for freedom, not merely for ourselves but for all oppressed peoples needs no stressing by me. It has been carried to such lengths as have seemed incomprehensible to alien nations who think us mad, or fools. and frequently hypocrites. Hecatombs of our lives and millions of pounds have been gladly sacrificed for the cause of freedom - such as putting down slavery in the last century - and doubtless will again if need be. The national conscience is smitten by something inherently evil and action must follow. It happened in the case of Italy's war of savage oppression against Abyssinia, to our minds a modern instance of Ahab and Naboth's vineyard. Yet who - I ask it dispassionately - after fighting a critical campaign at a most difficult moment, at the cost of heavy casualties and vast treasure, would have handed back Abyssinia to its king, lock, stock, and barrel, with no stipulations whatsoever and have presented him with three million pounds of the taxpayers' money to give him a fair start? Would the United States? We shall be better able to judge at the end of this war. I would add that no single voice of protest arose at this proof of magnanimity so modestly performed as though we were ashamed to let our left hand know what our right hand doeth. All the same, we give away far too much of our substance to foreign nations, which rarely show the least gratitude in return.

I expect to be abused for venturing to mentions such matters. So great is our reticence to appear boastful, and so wedded are we to understatement of our own achievements that to tell the truth about such matters is considered bad form. We know well enough in our hearts that what I state is true but we prefer it to come from others. Sometimes they generously admit these matters, more often they sneer and gibe. That acute observer and traveller, Henry R. Luce, the editor and proprietor of America's leading publicist weeklies, *Time*, *Life*, and *Fortune*, came over here at a critical juncture of our own fortunes and remarked, "The British are of course peculiar. One simple truth emerges, that the British are terrific fighters and cannot be beaten. In time of difficulty faith falters or rises to victory. The British don't falter. There is something happening right now in Britain. We might call it the search for war aims. That is part of it but it is both less and more; less definite but infinitely more profound; One Cabinet Minister said to me: 'I believe England wants a crusade.' There is really only one war aim in this war for the western world, and that is to re-discover and re-establish the faith by which men live." He ended, "Shall we be alert to the great quest of our times? - the rediscovery of the faith by which men live?" Shall we? Will our politicians and our Press rise to the occasion? I ask, for little has emerged yet to the surface, except that we are being apparently more and more chained to a great soulless bureaucracy, where regimentation takes the place of individuality, and a drab uniformity usurps the place of freedom. It apparently has the support of the Archbishop of York. The Church has a heavy responsibility.

A peculiar people, says Mr. Luce. We are stamped in a queer mould maybe, our character cemented by some impelling force which binds us willy-nilly, and which we prefer to hide from profane eyes. It is an innate conviction that we are in some way the instrument on earth for the will of the Almighty, a sort of pivotal point in the world of human endeavour and so we have to perform tasks in accordance with the will of the Deity. It is a conviction held by high and low alike, accepted, unquestioningly not only by the religious but by the sceptic. It is profound, unfathomable, yet deeply engraved in our being. It is our destiny to inculcate freedom which we appear to hold as synonymous with democracy. It is the principle which inspired the Druids in AD. 70. It is enduring, and nothing will eradicate it from our systems for so long as Britain endures.

All this must explain our extraordinary altruism, so unaccountable to most European and Asiatic nations. Germans, Italians, French, and others, unable to find a solution for this altruism, say we are crazy or hypocrites, or pretend to philanthropy to disguise our imperialistic intentions. The Isolationists of the United States say the same thing because they are mainly of other than British extraction.

It means, let us realise, a very considerable burden, and put at its lowest, in terms of money, it has considerably increased the National Debt. That our overseas Empire has been made a source of profit would be a bold assertion in terms of £ s. d. because we have laid out or loaned more than we have ever had returned, yet the Colonies in the future must become one of the assets on which we must rely. It is to the Empire, its products, raw materials, and trade to which we must turn more than ever before, and develop its close partnership with ourselves in order to bring in an era of prosperity for us all.

The British Empire is the greatest area over which freedom has been instituted since the dawn of civilisation. There are some parts, such as West Africa and Burma, which, owing to their racial backwardness, are not really capable of absolute self-government, and even if they were I hold that Britain is justly entitled to hold a supervisory hand, which applies also to India. Let the world who dares criticise our administration of our Empire reflect that it has incorporated all the religions of the world and accorded each scrupulous respect even if utterly pagan; has given them law and justice on equal terms with the white man; has developed their natural resources for their benefit as well as our own; has fostered native industries and found marts for them; has even earmarked the land in some parts for native ownership only; and assists them in education and culture. Wherever there has been unfair exploitation it has been subjected to stringent laws for the protection of the natives whose lives are as jealously guarded as those who dwell in these Islands. If we are entitled to regard our work with justifiable pride we can look to the British Empire, and our reward was the splendid response down to the smallest colonies when the war burst upon us. All - with the exception of southern Ireland - threw in their lot with us. That they refused reflects upon the bankruptcy of our past statecraft.

We had among us many carping critics of course, for it is the British way. Those with no imagination or who had never visited the Empire places assailed it as an incubus, poured derision upon it, and regarded it with indifference or even active hostility as if it were a reproach instead of a glorious jewel in the Crown. In such circumstances it is scarcely surprising that certain Americans like Mr. Wendell Willkie - whose forebears were Germans and therefore his mentality is understandable - have thrown out broad hints that our empire should be shorn from us. I wonder what they would say if we suggested that the United States owns too much territory! Fortunately Mr. Churchill put a stop to this nonsense when he said in his forthright way, "Hands off!" Some of them still have the impertinence to lecture us on how India should be ruled!

It is unfortunately true that for the last thirty years the Colonies suffered through a steady decline in the British will to govern. Ministers listened to the ignorant critics instead of treating them with the scorn they deserved. There was a growing disposition to hand over the reality of control to hands quite incapable of such responsibility and who mistook magnanimity for weakness. Our always hopeless intelligentsia with their cramped outlook talked in senseless slogans about "Imperialism," "Reaction," and "Militarism," supported by certain organs of the Press. These men were quite incapable of understanding what the Empire signified to the British race or the world. They detested the achievements of the great men who erected this magnificent edifice, and their pet anathema was the great Englishman Cecil Rhodes, whose name was odious to them, because he fervently believed in the greatness of the Empire. The same men pinned their faith in the League of Nations and hated nationalism like the very devil. The League let us down pretty badly. The Empire never has and never will.

When the Japanese struck at the United States and us the rich Empire settlements in the Orient bent under the savage hammer blows levelled at Hong Kong, Burma, Malaya, and Singapore, with the resultant threat to Australia, New Zealand and India. Hong Kong, Malaya, Burma, and Singapore were lost before they were captured by the enemy because the Imperial idea had largely fallen into decay by discouragement, the futile appeasement of our enemies, and an expectation that America would protect our Eastern possessions - an abdication of our sovereignty. Fortunately our people at home, as well as those overseas, have learnt the true significance of the Empire and I believe confidently that any Little Englanders of to-morrow will get short shrift. The millions of Britons who have gone overseas in this war have gained an entirely new conception of what the Empire means.

I am devoting some space to this theme because the Empire is to-day our great national asset and God knows we need all we can get if prosperity is to blossom forth in the future.

It is necessary, therefore, at this point to emphasize that the first necessity of a great and successful empire is firm authority inspired by conviction and it must never leave hold of essentials. I think we should make it clear as crystal to all our colonies that Britain is the ruling power and that we never intend to hand over control to hostile politicians - like the Congress *wallas* of India - or to natives incapable of loyalty. I should like to have it understood that the white-skinned Englishman is entitled to regard himself as the ruling race, according to the dictates of history and science. Our ignorant sentimental Socialists apparently believe that every man under the sun is born equal, like so many peas in a pod, and hence view our colonies as areas which should be governed by democratic institutions as independent sovereign states.

This happens to be false science. Professor Lothrop Stoddart, like other biologists and anthropologists, has said, "Natural equality is one of the most pernicious delusions that has ever affected mankind. It is a figment of the human imagination. Nature knows no equality."

He goes on to say, "The investigations of biology all point to the conclusion that such inequalities are *inborn*; that they are determined by *heredity*, and are not inherently modified by either environment or opportunity." That complicated piece of machinery we term the brain proves by its convolutions the difference between the white races of the north and the brown and negroid races of the east and south that this is the case. So what?

Amiable politicians must bow to the laws of science. We cannot surrender our power, like a weary Titan, to some Emperor Jones whether in Asia or Africa unless we want to see chaos and widespread suffering. It is the last thing the natives themselves would desire. Nor would it be business and business must enter into all this. Unless we set to work to develop to the full our colonies in our own interests as well as in theirs how are the demobilised men and those now working in munition factories and the like to be able to look to prosperity? We can conduct immense trade with our colonies in every commodity, receiving their raw materials or produce and selling them our manufactures in return. We cannot afford to waste or misuse a single square mile of Empire territory if we are to recover after the war.

Of India I could say much, for it is the crux of our will to govern or surrender to hostile elements. India has suffered ever since the day when we began to lose hold of its government and handed over power to elements unfitted to rule with wisdom and discretion. India has been sacrificed on the altar of political prejudice at home, and crass ignorance of her people and problems. The offer conveyed by Sir Stafford Cripps in March, 1942, conceding them "perfect freedom and liberty," and even an assurance that the Indian peoples would be free "to secede from the Commonwealth of Nations if and when they thought it necessary," was fortunately for the Indians themselves refused, but so far as I am aware the surrender offer still stands. Frightful nonsense has been written and said about India by persons who know nothing of that sub-continent with its 400 millions of people of hundreds of varying races and sects. Is it appreciated that something like £2,000,000,000 of British funds is invested in one way or another in that land? Is it realised that if we handed over power, to hostile elements, or even friendly Indians without the ability to control such immense responsibilities it would only be a question of time before we lost everything? What guarantees could we obtain worth the paper they were written on?

India pays us no taxes or tribute of any kind and during the war we have provided her with some forty million pounds worth of war equipment, and have financed her ordnance factories. India, at the end of the war, will be in a favourable financial condition, and for more than twenty years we have allowed her to legislate frequently against our own interests. The Indian is as free as any Englishman. It has become obvious to all who know our great dependency that we are endangering all India and preparing for a holocaust by endeavouring to graft onto an Oriental people our particular form of democracy, which has succeeded nowhere except in the white lands of the Empire.

I will not trust myself to add more about India at this juncture because I hope to return there after the war and see it with my own eyes when I may write a book without prejudice on the subject. I may, however, cite the Oriental diplomatist, Sir Lionel Haworth, in a letter he wrote in the **Sunday Times** (February 2nd, 1943) touching on India and the Empire, as he seems to me to have summarised this vital set of problems with great skill. He said:

"The opinions in England to-day are mainly based upon the 'wind' that has been issued to the public for many years past. We have still flourishing the theoretical intelligentsia who were responsible for the 'wind of Collective Security, the wind of Economic Sanctions.' It is the same people who are still responsible for most of our troubles in the Empire.

"It is on such opinions that we have brought about the problem of India. After many years Lord Linlithgow now states, 'To-day I see with deep regret little to encourage me to hope that the conflicting claims are likely in any degree to be abated." The real substance is

297

that there is no India. It is a British conception, and when we go it must break up. The rest is wind.

"It is the same with the Empire. They live in a mist of 'windy' dreams, and go about the world, especially to America, apologizing for the wrongs we have committed in bringing about the marvel of the British Empire, which has civilised and educated the world, and has, incidentally, produced the United States."

I thank Sir Lionel, who has simplified my task. What I am aiming at in a sentence is a problem in a nutshell, The Empire, always including India, is our national bread and butter. If we are going to weaken or disintegrate our Imperial links we shall all be beggared. Without wishing to be depressing, for I am really a hopeless optimist, the unvarnished truth is that when peace is signed, apart from all the generous help Ministers seem so anxious to accord to our enemies and friends, a horrible bill will confront the nation, and all the castles-in-the-air airily conjured up by politicians, archbishops, and sentimentalists in general will not put one penny in the till.

The Chancellor of the Exchequer will face a mountain of accumulated debts and no way of meeting a tithe of them except by a continuation of our present paralysing taxation, for all the chickens will come home to roost. The National Debt now totals the stupendous sum of twenty thousand million pounds, not to count certain considerable contingent liabilities, and with all our wealth invested in foreign countries gone with the wind. A simple calculation shows that even if the Treasury are able to stabilise the interest on this at a round figure of, say, 2 per cent, which will depend in the long run upon the national credit, it means a deadweight payment of £500,000,000 a year. *This amount more than exceeds half the national Budget in they year before the war,* and then taxation already stood at a stiff figure with income tax at 4s. 6d. in the £, as well as super-tax and E.P.D.

Sooner or later even our politicians have got to descend from the clouds to *terra firma* and explain how this is to be faced, and at the same time reconstruct and carry through all the reforms they talk of so glibly. There is also looming ahead the Beveridge scheme, which is

298

to cost - trusting to memory - some 300-odd millions a year, all in addition to the stupendous upkeep of the swollen bureaucracy. It must be recollected in addition that when war ceases the thousands of war factories will cease their present production, and even those designed to other uses will necessarily close down until new plans are made and the capital found for new ventures, which can only become assets if the markets are ready. New capital will be practically non-existent, for the Government, with its sugar-tax of 19s. 6d. in the £, and its E.P.D. of 100 per cent - even if it releases a certain proportion - has almost completely scotched liquid capital. If, as some economists and certain Ministers maintain, the Government must still exert control over all commerce and enterprise, funds can only be found by taxation, and it is pretty certain that any suggestion of additional taxation will raise a riot, even if it is continued on the present basis. Moreover, Government control of productions during the war, when profit-making has not entered into the question, has sickened most people, and a continuation of interference by the huge, cumbrous, alertless, and generally inefficient bureaucracy, if it attempted to conduct vast and competitive industrial business, would be disastrous.

Let those who imagine that when the last shell has been fired there will be an immediate fall in public expenditure reflect a little further. It is true that the war is costing us about seventeen millions a day and much of this is mounting up the national debt. But the men in the Forces will continue to draw their pay for some considerable time, and large numbers will be retained in the Services. Those released will have to receive their probably meagre gratuities; Workers in Government and other war factories will have also to be paid, for to throw them on the dole is unthinkable. Lease-Lend will presumably come to a finish and we may expect a bill from our friends in America. We are in addition apparently committed to immense sums for the restoration of the occupied countries and the reconstruction of our own overseas possessions. How is any present system of taxation going to meet these staggering requirements when the national revenue starts saddled with a deadweight debt of over five hundred million pounds a year?

Politicians talk blithely of the necessity of finding employment for all, and that, moreover, on a scale of living which will satisfy the demands of the nation. Yet, when we turn our swords into ploughshares, so will our Allies also, remember, our great industrialised Dominions, and, in addition, our erstwhile enemies, Germany, Japan, and Italy, who are promised equal opportunity of materials and markets. As to our former enemies, it looks as though they are likely to start with an enormous advantage over us, especially for we have no raw materials at our door except coal, as have the United States and Russia - if there are to be no war indemnities imposed, for their national debts, even if they are observed, which is extremely unlikely, are trivial in proportion with ours, and as their standards of living are incomparably lower, notably Japan, what is to prevent them from under-selling us in all world markets? In a word, our manufacturers, even with a free hand, will be crippled at the start by excessive overhead charges in direct and indirect taxation, which in turn demands higher wages.

How many of us have pondered on the economic profligacy of the last forty years? The Victorians worked and saved and built up immense investments in foreign lands, the profits of which reached us in the shape of raw materials, finished goods, and foodstuffs. We also possessed a monopoly of the world's shipping trade, but the Americans have built and are building a prodigious mercantile navy, while we have produced Warships, and they will be in a position to control the world's shipping. Such sources of revenue in the past have enabled us to live at the rate of 684 persons to the square mile, as compared with Russia having only 23. In Queen Victoria's day, and in that of Edward VII, the whole business of Government cost under a hundred millions a year, no bureaucrats interfered with our trade, individualism had its fair chance, the tax gatherer was not grasping a huge proportion of our earnings, and we prospered.

To-day our overseas investments are squandered, sold for munitions, and the food we neglected to grow. We are a debtor, not a creditor nation, and that is seen in the manner we have had to suffer many humiliations in this war. The sombre fact remains that now and in the immediate future we cannot receive a joint of beef or mutton from abroad, a piece of rubber, a pint of petrol, a cup of tea, an orange or banana, unless we can pay for them with exports. To adjust these problems will require courage, determination, and long-sightedness.

So far our economists have mainly indulged in at sort of mumbo-jumbo ritual. Lord Simon, like Lord Keynes, seems to think some new order of international currency will perform miracles, and **The Times** suggests some "adjustment" of our banking system, Which I respectfully propose appears to be a pill to cure an earthquake. The Church, in the majestic form of Dr. Garbett, Archbishop of York, has hinted that the road to prosperity must be some form of Totalitarianism, the Russian system of course, for everything Russian is almost sacrosanct in the prelatic eyes. "Nowadays," he confided to Convocation, "all States are totalitarian, and their influence over the individual is all-pervading," but whether its influence is all-pervading it is conducive neither to freedom nor human happiness. We have it with us at this moment and find that one dose is enough, whoever and whatever we are. We did not go to war to rid the world of tyranny and place the yoke of slavedom on our shoulders, with respect to the Archbishop. **The Times**, shrinking from so unpopular a word as "totalitarian," discreetly proposes a Minister of "National Development," but it means the same thing for it intends to curb all individual activity, control our lives from the cradle and exert the dead hand of bureaucracy upon our every action.

Far be for me to step in where angels fear to tread, but I believe British enterprise and British grit will pull through triumphantly if we tackle the intelligentsia and planners with the same determination we have used to defeat our visible enemies. One idea I have is to reduce the interest on Government loans to 2 percent and even 1 per cent, by the simple operation of issuing Premium bonds, carrying big prizes drawn for half-yearly. Being a sporting nation, loving a gamble at all times, such bonds would probably meet with immediate response. All it needs is that the Government should scrap its archaic ideas that gambling is a form of vice and modernise its outlook. Of course church dignitaries and the *unco guid* would squeal, but I say, let them.

Who cares? Needs must when the devil drives. It would reduce public expenditure by a very considerable amount.

Looking to industry and trade I wholeheartedly advocate a new law of compulsory profit-sharing in all possible business undertakings, excepting, of course, the Civil Service and similar sheltered occupations. A national system of profit-sharing would remove the anxiety which gnaws every wage-earner to-day as to how he or she can fill the stocking for their old age. Those far-seeing firms which have adopted a profit-sharing plan, on equitable lines have never had any cause to regret it. If it consumes a portion of the profit it also ensures far greater efficiency and care among the employees who have a direct incentive to work and save waste. Shareholders stand to gain more by such a scheme than they pay away.

I foresee a snag. The trade union movement would almost certainly oppose it, because the greater contentment among workers and the more harmonious the relations between capital and labour the less need for hordes of trade union leaders. I believe that such a system is long overdue, and if it were operative to-day among the coal-miners we should not experience their restlessness and grave dissatisfaction under existing conditions. To my mind they are justified, for they work under onerous conditions live poorly, and are grossly underpaid, give them a share in the profits of the mine and another spirit would be created, should men, who did not create the coal, take all the profits and treat their workers like villeins? Miners should be the best paid of all manual workers, seeing the onerous tasks they undertake and the great dangers they risk. On the other hand if the 'State' should continue to control the mines the position of the mining industry will certainly become more chaotic than ever, and the miners will be simply out of the frying-pan into the fire, while we produce less and less coal. I urge serious consideration of this profit-sharing scheme as one of potential great benefit to capital, labour, and to the nation at large.

Now I venture to advance another plan for the benefit of the agricultural community. The Government keep on saying that after

302

the War farmers shall not be let down as they were at the end of the last war, but as yet any possible scheme for their benefit has not materialised. I have for years harboured a hope that the day would come when every city, town and even village of size should operate its daily produce market - in great cities several markets. To some extent this would need the co-operation of the State because of its wide application.

The plan is this. All market garden produce, meat, hams, bacon, fish, butter, vegetables and fruit, would be collected from the growers by a service of lorries - they should be cheap after the war and taken to their central depots of distribution, whence they would be carried without delay to the markets themselves. These markets would be under local authorities, who in turn would license a requisite number of stall holders in the market-place, where prices would be controlled for the benefit of the consumer. The grower would receive a guaranteed price sufficient to render him a reasonable profit, and the stall-holders would also enjoy the same amenities. Neither would have to take any risk and the supplies would be ensured to the public. Only home and Empire produce would be sold at such markets, and they would be open for a few specified hours every morning thus giving the housewife ample opportunity of purchasing the best fresh English produce at the cheapest price. The scheme would eliminate the middle-man, and judging from the exorbitant profiteering that gentleman has indulged in, his elimination, would not be an unmixed evil. I have in the past studied the Continental produce markets in such places as Paris, Florence, Nice, and elsewhere where fresh produce was brought in and quickly sold out, and believe such a method in England - a regular daily, price-controlled market - would go far to meet the requirements of the farming industry and serve the needs of the public by bringing them fresh home produce.

Our greatest hope of post-war prosperity is to weld even more tightly our ties with the Empire overseas, on a far greater basis than ever before. The aeroplane has brought even the outlying most, distant possessions within comparatively easy range and it is inevitable that freight-carrying planes will become a commonplace, whereby Africa and even the Pacific will be brought within easy range of ourselves. Our ties with the Dominions, including India, might well be cemented by a holy covenant in which all agree to remain an integral part of the British Empire for a hundred years. It would stabilise the future to the detriment of any future Hitler who might want to take a cock-shy at dominating the world, would encourage trade development between all the Dominions and Colonies. It would be essential to create a ruling Council of the Empire to which all its members would nominate their representatives, an annual real Imperial Parliament, where legislation affecting the Empire as a whole, such as questions of defence, commerce, emigration, development, and finance could be initiated. Such a grand Council of the Empire should assemble annually in various capitals, such as London, Ottawa, Canberra, Wellington, Cape Town, and Delhi. States such as Kenya and Palestine would be members, for I assume that as the League mandates are as dead as mutton we shall and must absorb these territories. The West Indies and other important outliers among the Colonies would be included.

That is all I have to say on the subject, except that here are three projects which offer opportunities if our people are sufficiently enterprising to try new ideas.

It only remains to see that we win the peace. So far, in spite of lavish promises, we Britons never get what we expect, what we are told to expect, and have a right to expect. We must observe a watchful and, I would add, a suspicious attitude towards both the Government and the Press. Winston Churchill is a great man, a man who will live in history as one of Britain's greatest statesmen, probably the greatest in our island history. Yet even Homer nods, and perhaps his worst mistake was to accept the leadership of the Tory Party during the war, for he then identified his cause with the men who with their Party in power brought this war upon through their neglect. How much happier should we have felt had he said that during the war he belonged to no party except Britain!

It is possible that after the war a new central Party may arise which will not hesitate to nail the Union Jack to the mast and proclaim their faith in no unmeasured terms. We want a new Party, one free from the sinister influence of the corrupting caucus, whose motto is "Scratch my back and I'll scratch yours." My late friend Ronald Cartland, young in years but old in wisdom, said a little after the war broke out, "It may be too early yet to picture the Party system at the close of the war. But that the unhealthy supremacy of the Whips' Office will be destroyed already seems assured." I trust he was correct. To my mind the caucus will not die placidly and will require savage assault and almighty slaughter before all its hydra-heads are exterminated. It will not occur if the nation once again neglects politics and shows apathy.

Apathy has been our curse. The three o'clock football results. Cricket scores. Damn the politics! A young soldier who died in Africa a few months ago in action left a letter to his father written beforehand. He said this:

"I should like you to know what it is I died for, and for that reason I am going to try to express my feelings and hopes. There is, I feel, both in England and America a tremendous surge of feeling which for want of a better word I shall call 'Goodness.'

"It is not expressed by politicians or the newspapers, for it is too deep for them. It is the heartfelt longing of all the 'middling folk' for something better. A world more worthy of their children, a world more simple in its beliefs, a world nearer to earth and to God."

It is the same idea as Henry Luce expressed when he said that the only real war aim was to re-discover and re-establish the faith by which men live. It is an idea, a longing, felt by very many among us, one which the Churches would do well to foster instead of charging into economics. We have a long way to go to get it, for as yet indifference to ideals has been to the fore at home. For the last two years our moral outlook and conduct has sagged badly at times.

Let us practise altruism by all means, which means generosity and unselfishness, but remember at the same time that unbridled altruism is an untenable ideal in our present plight. We cannot possibly afford to remain the sole altruists of the world, and our tolerance and generosity must be sealed with the recognition that we must win the peace first for ourselves, for our own kith and kin within the Empire. Let us in the words of our Prime Minister, "Hold our own." Let us fight for our rights with the indomitable courage of our fighting services. I close with an excerpt from a prophetic verse written in 1915 by a generous American poetess, Helen Cone, of New York:

"Bind her, grind her, burn her with fire,
Cast her ashes into the sea -
She shall escape, she shall aspire,
She shall arise in a sacred scorn,
Lighting the lives that are yet unborn,
Spirit supernal, splendour eternal,
ENGLAND!"

THE END

INDEX

311